# THE
# POLITICAL
# POPE

# THE
# POLITICAL
# POPE

## HOW FRANCIS IS
## DELIGHTING THE LIBERAL
## LEFT AND ABANDONING
## CONSERVATIVES

# GEORGE NEUMAYR

**CENTER
STREET**

New York   Nashville

Center Street
Hachette Book Group
1290 Avenue of the Americas, New York, NY 10104
centerstreet.com
twitter.com/centerstreet

First Edition: May 2017

Center Street is a division of Hachette Book Group, Inc. The Center Street name and logo are trademarks of Hachette Book Group, Inc.

The publisher is not responsible for websites (or their content) that are not owned by the publisher.

The Hachette Speakers Bureau provides a wide range of authors for speaking events. To find out more, go to www.HachetteSpeakersBureau.com or call (866) 376-6591.

Library of Congress Cataloging-in-Publication Data has been applied for.

LCCN: 2017930369

ISBNs: 978-1-4555-7016-4 (hardcover), 978-1-4555-7014-0 (ebook)

Printed in the United States of America

LSC-C

10  9  8  7  6  5  4  3  2  1

# Contents

# THE
# POLITICAL
# POPE

# CHAPTER ONE

# The Pope They Have Been Waiting For

You must straighten out your position with the Church," Pope John Paul II shouted at a cowering Ernesto Cardenal, a Catholic priest turned Marxist activist. In violation of his religious vows, Cardenal had joined the communist Sandinista government in Nicaragua, and Pope John Paul II was scolding him before the cameras of the entire world. That sensational scene in 1983 on a Managua airport runway provided one of the most startling images of Pope John Paul II's anti-communist pontificate.[1]

So strong were Pope John Paul II's anti-communist credentials and so effective was his anti-Soviet advocacy that Kremlin leaders, according to historians, hired a Turkish gunman to assassinate him.[2] That attempt failed, and Pope John Paul II continued to denounce the Soviets until their empire crumbled in 1991.

Joseph Ratzinger also opposed communism fiercely. After serving as the head of the Congregation for the Doctrine of the Faith, Ratzinger succeeded John Paul II in 2005 and took as his papal name Benedict XVI. In his role as doctrinal guardian of the Church, Ratzinger repeatedly warned the faithful to reject "liberation theology," a Marxist-inspired ideology disguised as concern for the poor that the

Soviet Union's KGB spies had helped smuggle into Latin America's Catholic Church in the 1950s.

"The movement was born in the KGB, and it had a KGB-invented name: liberation theology," according to Ion Mihai Pacepa, who served as a spymaster for Romania's secret police in the 1950s and 1960s.[3]

The Soviets had long eyed the Catholic Church for infiltration. In the 1950s, Bella Dodd, the former head of the Soviet-controlled Communist Party of America, testified before the U.S. Congress that communists occupied some of the "highest places" in the Catholic Church. "We put eleven hundred men into the priesthood in order to destroy the Church from within," she said. "The idea was for these men to be ordained, and then climb the ladder of influence and authority as monsignors and bishops." As an active party member, Dodd said that she knew of "four cardinals within the Vatican who were working for us."[4]

According to Pacepa, the KGB took "secret control of the World Council of Churches (WCC), based in Geneva, Switzerland, and used it as cover for converting liberation theology into a South American revolutionary tool." Seeking to spread atheistic Marxism among the religious peasants of Latin America, Soviet leaders instructed the KGB to send agents into ecclesiastical circles. In 1968, Latin America's bishops loudly endorsed liberation theology at a conference in Medellín, Colombia. The KGB served as a puppet master at the event, reported Pacepa.

"In the 1950s and 1960s, most Latin Americans were poor, religious peasants who had accepted the status quo, and [Soviet premier Nikita] Khrushchev was confident they could be converted to communism through the judicious manipulation of religion," he wrote. "In 1968, the KGB was able to maneuver a group of leftist South American bishops into holding a conference in Medellín, Colombia. At the KGB's request, my [spies] provided logistical assistance to the organizers. The official task of the conference was to help eliminate poverty in Latin America. Its undeclared goal was to legitimize a KGB-created religious movement dubbed 'liberation theology,' the secret task of which was to incite Latin America's poor to rebel against the 'institutionalized violence of poverty' generated by the United States."[5]

Against this historical backdrop, Pope John Paul II and Pope Benedict XVI viewed the spread of liberation theology in Latin America with alarm. They feared that a Marxist-influenced ideology, which progressive theologians within the Catholic Church were harnessing to their own long-percolating socialist politics, would corrupt the Catholic faith. Pope Benedict XVI called liberation theology a "singular heresy."[6] He argued that it deceives the faithful by concealing "Marxist dialectics" within seemingly harmless advocacy for the lower classes. He drew attention to Marxism's philosophical incompatibility with Christianity and disputed the claim of many churchmen that Christianity could purify the Marxist elements of socialist thought.

How shockingly different statements from the Holy See sound today under Pope Francis. The first Latin American pope in Church history, Jorge Mario Bergoglio has generated headlines not for scolding Marxists but for supporting them, not for rebuking liberation theologians but for honoring them.

Under Pope John Paul II and Pope Benedict XVI, the Western media spoke disapprovingly of a "holy war against liberation theology." Now media outlets eagerly run stories about Pope Francis's sympathy for it. "Liberation Theology Rehabilitation Continues at Vatican," ran a characteristic headline on a story from the Associated Press.[7]

In one of his first major interviews, Pope Francis said that liberation theologians have a "high concept of humanity."[8] A few months after he became pope on March 13, 2013, Francis welcomed the founding father of liberation theology, the Peruvian priest Gustavo Gutiérrez, to the Vatican as an honored guest. Gutiérrez had disappeared from high ecclesiastical circles under Pope John Paul II and Pope Benedict XVI after making a Marxist appeal for "effective participation in the struggle which the exploited classes have undertaken against their oppressors."[9] But after the elevation of Francis, Gutiérrez suddenly found himself basking in praise. Vatican officials pronounced him an impeccable thinker, responsible for one of "the most important currents in 20th century Catholic theology." The Vatican's newspaper, *L'Osservatore Romano*, asserted that the election of Pope Francis would bring liberation theology out of the "shadows to which it has been relegated for some years, at least in Europe."[10]

Leonardo Boff, who has long gloried in his status as a renegade liberation theologian from Brazil, also enjoyed a stunning change of fortune after the election of Pope Francis. Owing to his open Marxism, Boff was silenced by Pope John Paul II's Congregation for the Doctrine of the Faith. Boff was also condemned by the Vatican for his threatened hijinks at the 1992 Earth Summit in Rio de Janeiro, activism that eventually led Boff to leave the priesthood. But these days Boff finds himself back in the Church's good graces. Pope Francis recruited him to serve as an adviser for *Laudato Si'*, his 2015 encyclical endorsing the political agenda of climate change activists.[11]

Taking advantage of the new wind blowing from the Vatican, Miguel d'Escoto Brockmann, whose role in Nicaragua's Marxist revolutionary government in the 1970s led to his suspension from the priesthood, sent in 2014 a request to Pope Francis that his priestly faculties be reinstated. Pope Francis granted the request. "The Holy Father has given his benevolent assent that Father Miguel d'Escoto Brockmann be absolved from the canonical censure inflicted upon him, and entrusts him to the superior general of the institute (Maryknoll) for the purpose of accompanying him in the process of reintegration into the ministerial priesthood," announced the Vatican.[12]

D'Escoto, among his other Marxist activities, had served as an official at the aforementioned KGB-controlled World Council of Churches. No sooner had Pope Francis granted d'Escoto's request than the recipient of the Lenin Peace Prize resumed his Marxist polemics, calling capitalism the "most un-Christian doctrine and practice ever devised by man to keep us separate and unequal in a kind of global apartheid." He condemned Pope John Paul II for an "abuse of authority" and rhapsodized about Fidel Castro as an inspired figure whose murderous regime heralded "the reign of God on this earth that is the alternative to the empire."[13] Even now as a priest in good standing under Pope Francis, d'Escoto lobbies for the Libyans, remains a member of the Sandinista National Liberation Front, and continues to serve as an adviser to Daniel Ortega, whom the Soviets planted in the presidency of Nicaragua in the 1980s.

According to Boff, Pope Francis will eventually rehabilitate all of the condemned liberation theologians from Latin America. Boff believes that Pope Francis is waiting until their old critic, Pope Benedict XVI, dies. "I believe that as long as the retired pope lives, he will neither reconcile nor redeem these theologians," according to Boff. "But, when he is by himself, he will rescue the 500 theologians whose heads were severed. I believe this pope is capable of dismantling this machine of punishment and control, and leave it to the local churches."[14]

# A Radical Pontificate

After only four years of his pontificate, Francis has emerged as one of the most political popes in the history of the Church. His left-wing activism is relentless, ranging across causes from the promotion of global warming theory to support for amnesty and open borders to the abolition of lifetime imprisonment. That alone would make this papacy historically significant. But the ambitions of Pope Francis go well beyond an unusually aggressive political dilettantism. As this book will detail, he is not only championing the radical political agenda of the global left but also subverting centuries-old Catholic teaching on faith and morals, evident in his unprecedented support for granting the sacrament of Holy Communion to the divorced and remarried and in his drive to dilute the Church's moral and theological commitments.

At a time of widespread moral relativism and assaults on marriage, his 2014–2015 Synod of Bishops on the Family served not to strengthen the Church's stances but to weaken them. For the first time in the history of the Church, a pope approved of Catholics in a state of adultery. He also authorized his aides to float unprecedented proposals in favor of blessing the "positive aspects" of gay relationships and couples living together outside of marriage.[15]

Amidst this doctrinal confusion, many cardinals are beginning to feel buyer's remorse. "The more he talks, the worse it gets," says a Vatican official, who asked to remain anonymous, in an interview for this book. "Many bishops and cardinals are terrified to speak out, but they are in a state of apoplexy. The atmosphere is so politicized and skewed. The Church is becoming unrecognizable."

"We haven't hit bottom," says an American priest interviewed for this book. He describes his parishioners as "distressed," so much so that he carries around a list of all the popes to remind them that "bad popes don't live forever."

"I have never been so discouraged about the prospects for the Church," an unnamed prelate said to *Traditionalist* magazine in 2015. In an interview with the Spanish Catholic weekly *Vida Nueva*, Cardinal Raymond Burke, the former head of the Vatican's highest court who was removed from that position by Pope Francis in 2013, disclosed that "many have expressed their concerns to me" and that "at this very critical moment, there is a strong sense that the Church is like a ship without a rudder."[16]

These are "dark times," Bishop Athanasius Schneider of Kazakhstan has said. The liberalism of this pontificate, he argues, is exposing the faithful to "spiritual danger" and creating the conditions for the "fast and easy spreading of heterodox doctrines."[17]

"There are evident manifestations of uneasiness," according to the Vatican correspondent Sandro Magister in an interview with *Italia Oggi*.[18] "It's beginning to look as if the cardinals made a terrible mistake when they decided that this particular Catholic should be a pope," wrote the British Catholic journalist Damian Thompson.[19]

"In the Vatican, some people are already sighing: 'Today, he has already again another different idea from yesterday,'" the German philosopher Robert Spaemann has said. "One does not fully get rid of the impression of chaos."[20]

In an interview for this book, Michael Hichborn, president of a Catholic watchdog organization in Virginia called the Lepanto Institute, recounted, "I had a meeting with a bishop who turned to me and said, 'How do you remain loyal to Peter when Peter is not loyal to the Church?' He was genuinely confused and felt stuck."

Such bewilderment leaves Pope Francis untroubled. He even romanticizes his reckless heterodox activism. "I want a mess," he said at the 2013 World Youth Day in Rio de Janeiro. "We knew that in Rio there would be a great disorder, but I want trouble in the dioceses!"[21] Many Catholics found this a puzzling goal to set for the Church. But his pontificate has undeniably lived up to it. "Mission accomplished," quipped Bishop Thomas Tobin of Providence, Rhode Island, in 2014.[22]

Supremely confident in his chaotic course, Pope Francis is shrugging off the mounting concerns and delighting in his reputation as a socialist and modernist maverick. After Pope Francis early in his papacy decried capitalism as "trickle-down economics"—a polemical phrase coined by the left during the Reagan years that Francis frequently borrows—radio talk show host Rush Limbaugh commented, "This is just pure Marxism coming out of the mouth of the Pope." Talk show host Michael Savage called him "Lenin's pope." Pope Francis took such comments as a compliment. "I have met many Marxists in my life who are good people, so I don't feel offended," he told the Italian press.[23]

## His Communist Mentor

Pope Francis grew up in socialist Argentina, an experience that left a deep impression on his thinking. He told the Latin American journalists Javier Cámara and Sebastián Pfaffen that as a young man he "read books of the Communist Party that my boss in the laboratory gave me" and that "there was a period where I would wait anxiously for the newspaper *La Vanguardia*, which was not allowed to be sold with the other newspapers and was brought to us by the socialist militants."[24]

The "boss" to whom Pope Francis referred is Esther Ballestrino de Careaga. He has described her as a "Paraguayan woman" and a "fervent communist." He considers her one of his most important mentors. "I owe a huge amount to that great woman," he has said, saying that she "taught me so much about politics." (He worked for her as an assistant at Hickethier-Bachmann Laboratory in Buenos Aires.)

"She often read Communist Party texts to me and gave them to me to read. So I also got to know that very materialistic conception. I remember that she also gave me the statement from the American Communists in defense of the Rosenbergs, who had been sentenced to death," he has said. Learning about communism, he said, "through a courageous and honest person was helpful. I realized a few things, an aspect of the social, which I then found in the social doctrine of the Church." After entering the priesthood, he took pride in helping her hide the family's Marxist literature from the authorities who were investigating her. According to the author James Carroll, Bergoglio smuggled her communist books, including Marx's *Das Kapital*, into a "Jesuit library."[25]

"Tragically, Ballestrino herself 'disappeared' at the hands of security forces in 1977," reported Vatican correspondent John Allen. "Almost three decades later, when her remains were discovered and identified, Bergoglio gave permission for her to be buried in the garden of a Buenos Aires church called Santa Cruz, the spot where she had been abducted. Her daughter requested that her mother and several other women be buried there because 'it was the last place they had been as free people.' Despite knowing full well that Ballestrino was not a believing Catholic, the future pope readily consented."[26]

These biographical details throw light on the pope's ideological instincts. Yet many commentators have ignored them, breezily casting his leftism as a bit confused but basically harmless.

"I must say that communists have stolen our flag. The flag of the poor is Christian," he said in 2014.[27] Such a comment would have startled his predecessors. They didn't see communism as a benign exaggeration. They saw it as a grave threat to God-given freedom, as it proposes that governments eliminate large swaths of individual freedom, private property, and business in order to produce the "equality" of a society without economic classes.

In the early twentieth century, as Marx's socialism spread across the world, Pope Pius XI declared the theory anathema. "No one can be at the same time a good Catholic and a true socialist," he said. To hear Pope Francis speak today, one might conclude the reverse: that no can be at the same time a good Catholic and an opponent of socialism.

"Inequality is the root of all evil," Pope Francis wrote on his Twitter account in 2014.[28] One can imagine Karl Marx blurting that out, but none of Francis's predecessors would have made such an outrageous claim. According to traditional Catholic theology, the root of all evil came not from inequality but from Satan's refusal to accept inequality. Out of envy of God's superiority, Satan rebelled. He could not bear his lesser status.

He was in effect the first revolutionary, which is why the socialist agitator Saul Alinsky—a mentor to Barack Obama and Hillary

Clinton (who did her senior thesis at Wellesley on his thought)—offered an "acknowledgment" in his book, *Rules for Radicals*, to Satan. Alinsky saw him as the first champion of the "have-nots."[29]

Were the twentieth-century English Catholic satirist Evelyn Waugh alive today, he would find the radical left-wing political flirtations of Pope Francis too bitterly farcical even for fiction. Could a satirist like Waugh have imagined a pope happily receiving from a Latin American despot the "gift" of a crucifix shaped in the form of a Marxist hammer and sickle? That surreal scene happened during Pope Francis's visit to Bolivia in July 2015.

Evo Morales, Bolivia's proudly Marxist president, offered the pontiff that sacrilegious image of Jesus Christ. Morales described the gift as a copy of a crucifix designed by a late priest, Fr. Luís Espinal, who belonged to the Jesuit order (as does Pope Francis) and had committed his life to melding Marxism with religion. Pope Francis had honored Espinal's memory upon his arrival in Bolivia.[30]

Had John Paul II or Pope Benedict XVI seen such a grotesque cross, they might have broken it over their knees. Not Pope Francis. He accepted the hammer-and-sickle cross warmly, telling the press on the plane ride back to Rome that "I understand this work" and that "for me it wasn't an offense." After the visit, Morales gushed, "I feel like now I have a Pope. I didn't feel that before."[31]

Under Francis, the papacy has become a collage of such politicized images: friendly papal meetings with communist thugs like the Castro brothers, a papal Mass conducted under the shadow of the mass murderer Che Guevara's mural in Havana, papal audiences with a steady stream of crude Marxist theoreticians and anticapitalist celebrities such as Leonardo DiCaprio, "selfies" while holding up an anti-fracking T-shirt, a pro-amnesty Mass said on the border between Mexico and America, a succession of sermons, speeches, and writings that rip into capitalism and tout greater government control over private property and business.

By pushing the papacy in such a "progressive" direction, Francis has become a darling of the global left. His program of promoting left-wing politics while downplaying and undermining doctrine on faith and morals has turned him into the ecclesiastical equivalent of Barack Obama. "Pope Francis is a gift from heaven," the radical academic Cornel West said to *Rolling Stone*. "I love who he is, in terms of what he says, and the impact of his words on progressive forces around the world."[32]

Pope Francis, as liberals once said of Barack Obama, is the "one they have been waiting for." The world is witnessing nothing less than a liberal revolution in the Catholic Church—a revolution that is emboldening the Church's enemies and alienating her friends.

# CHAPTER TWO

# "Who Am I to Judge?"

In one of his last speeches before leaving office in 2013, Pope Benedict XVI dissected the destructive liberalism that spread within the Church after the council of Vatican II. The secularism of Western culture and the media elite had seeped into the Church, he lamented.

"[T]here was the council of the Fathers—the true council—but there was also the council of the media. It was almost a council in and of itself, and the world perceived the council through them, through the media. So the council that immediately, effectively, got through to the people was that of the media, not that of the Fathers," said Pope Benedict XVI. "[It] did not, naturally, take place within the world of faith but within the categories of the media of today, that is outside of the faith, with different hermeneutics. It was a hermeneutic of politics."

To this liberal influence, Pope Benedict XVI traced much of the crisis in the Church. The absorption of modern liberalism into Catholicism had produced, he said, "so many problems, so much misery, in reality: seminaries closed, convents closed, the liturgy was trivialized."[1]

Little did Pope Benedict XVI realize that his mysterious resignation would pave the way for the very liberal Church he feared and for a successor who embodies the very "hermeneutic of politics" he decried.

As the cardinals met to decide on a new pope in March 2013, the Western liberal elite began beating the drum for the selection of a "progressive" and "pastoral" churchman, by which editorialists and activists meant a politically liberal and doctrinally lax one. James Salt of Catholics United, a front group Democrats set up in 2005 to infiltrate the Church, seized on the news of Pope Benedict XVI's resignation and demanded that the Church elect a pope from the "global south" who would "radically shift the agenda of the Church," away from "issues of human sexuality" and toward the "imminent threat of global climate change and its effect on the poorest."

Jorge Mario Bergoglio exceeded their expectations. From the first moment of his appearance on the Vatican balcony, left-wing Western journalists, intellectuals, and politicians showered him in praise. Customarily skeptical of the papacy, they suddenly became cheerleaders for it.

Bill Keller, the former executive editor of the *New York Times*, has explained the liberal obsession with the papacy by writing that "the struggle within the church is interesting as part of a larger struggle within the human race, between the forces of tolerance and absolutism."[2] The liberal elite immediately sized up Pope Francis, with his transparent political liberalism and his distaste for doctrine, as falling on the right side of its self-serving understanding of that "struggle."

That he selected Francis as his papal name was the first act to charm liberals, as they opportunistically portray St. Francis of Assisi as the patron saint of socialism, pacifism, and environmentalism. Instead of challenging this liberal caricature, Bergoglio reinforced it. He told reporters that he adopted Francis as his name because Francis of Assisi was a "man of poverty, the man of peace, the man who loves and protects creation."[3] In truth, St. Francis of Assisi was a rigorously orthodox medieval churchman who would have regarded the liberalism of this pope with horror.

Pope Francis explained that the inspiration to name himself

Francis came to him when Cardinal Cláudio Hummes, archbishop emeritus of São Paulo, Brazil, whispered in his ear moments after his election, "Don't forget the poor." His mention of Hummes was music to the ears of the media. Hummes has long been known to reporters as a critic of the free market with friendly ties to socialist organizations in Brazil.[4] (He is also known for saying that he "didn't know" if Jesus Christ would have disapproved of gay marriage.)

The Western media was also charmed by the opening gestures of Bergoglio, which amounted to a carefully choreographed casualness at the expense of Catholic tradition. Bergoglio declined the traditional vestments a new pope wears upon his election—a red velvet cape—and instead wore a white cassock. Before blessing the crowd, he asked the crowd for a blessing and he pointedly referred to himself not as the pope but merely as the "bishop of Rome." As Bergoglio explained later, his use of that reduced title and his modest description of the meaning of his election ("the diocesan community of Rome has its bishop") were intended to make non-Catholics comfortable with his papacy. "Placing emphasis on the number one title, that is, Bishop of Rome, favors ecumenism," he said.[5]

Less than a year before Bergoglio became pope, in a foreshadowing of the liberal direction of his pontificate, he ran into John Quinn, the ultra-progressive former archbishop of San Francisco, at a coffee shop in Rome. Quinn is the author of *The Reform of the Papacy*, a book that explicitly rejects traditional teaching on the papacy, calls for Protestant-style "collegiality," and urges the Church to adopt the politics and morals of the modern Western world. "I've read your book and I'm hoping what it proposes will be implemented," Bergoglio told a pleased Quinn.[6] In retrospect, Pope Francis has largely implemented it and the left-wing American churchmen that Quinn represents—the so-called seamless garment bishops—have enjoyed a return to power.

All of Pope Francis's heterodox opening gestures after his election caused murmuring among Pope Benedict XVI's former aides and confusion among the faithful, but it excited members of the liberal wing of the Church. The former cardinal of Los Angeles and Cesar Chavez acolyte Roger Mahony tweeted to his followers, "So long papal ermine and fancy lace!" and gushed about the left-wing political orientation of the new pope.[7]

Ernesto Cardenal, the Marxist activist whom Pope John Paul II rebuked, was excited by the emergence of Pope Francis. "We are seeing a true revolution in the Vatican," he wrote.[8]

The openly heretical German theologian Hans Küng said he "was overwhelmed by joy" at the news of Bergoglio's election. "There is hope in this man," said Küng, who correctly predicted that Francis would deviate from the "line of the two popes from Poland and Germany." It has since been reported that Pope Francis and Küng have been exchanging friendly letters and that Francis has signaled an openness to hearing Küng's criticism of papal infallibility.[9]

Formerly condemned liberation theologians immediately grasped the significance of Bergoglio's election, too. Leonardo Boff was quoted in the German press as gloating that Francis is "more liberal" than the college of cardinals realized. "I am encouraged by this choice, viewing it as a pledge for a church of simplicity and of ecological ideals," he said.[10]

It didn't take long for Boff's confidence in this pontificate to deepen. After hearing several of Pope Francis's first speeches and homilies, Boff put his finger on one of the most revolutionary tendencies of this pontificate: "[He] has signaled that everything is up for discussion, which not long ago would have been unthinkable for any pope to say."[11]

The notoriously heterodox German theologian Cardinal Walter Kasper was also energized by the news of Bergoglio's election. As one of the most illuminating figures of this pontificate, Kasper deserves special attention. Kasper had occupied the room across from Bergoglio at the Vatican's hotel during the papal conclave. He gave Bergoglio one of his books, a book on mercy that argued for a loosening of Church teaching and discipline. Pope Francis said that he read it happily.[12] The theme of the book fit with the speech that Bergoglio gave at the conclave, which was a mishmash of progressive complaints about a "self-referential" Church unwilling to "come out of herself" and reach out to the "peripheries."[13]

Under previous pontificates, Kasper's fortunes had fallen and his dissents went largely ignored. But Pope Francis, within the first days of his papacy, rehabilitated Kasper's checkered reputation. During his first appearance from the papal window, Pope Francis pronounced Kasper a theologian whom he admires. Not long thereafter, Pope Francis gave Kasper the green light to revive his campaign, blocked under Pope John Paul II and Pope Benedict XVI, to liberalize the Church's sacramental discipline.

According to *Vanity Fair*, "Kasper meets with Francis every few weeks, and their conversations are casual and straight to the point." "It was once a rule that when you went to see the Pope you had to be vested up in your cassock and sash," Kasper told the magazine. "It's more normal now. He picks up the phone and asks, 'Please, can you come over?,' and then he says, 'Please, no cassock—come as a clergyman.' "[14]

After Kasper urged his fellow bishops to open up Communion lines to adulterers, Pope Francis praised his "profound theology." The Catholic left has taken to calling Kasper the "pope's theologian." Kasper has long argued that the Church should democratize her teachings. Pope Francis agrees with his approach, Kasper told the press:

> On the other hand when we discuss marriage and family we have to listen to people who are living this reality. There's a 'sensus fidelium' ('sense of the faithful'). It cannot be decided only from above, from the church hierarchy, and especially you cannot just quote old texts of the last century, you have to look at the situation today, and then you make a discernment of the

spirits and come to concrete results. I think this is the approach of Pope Francis, whereas many others start from doctrine and then use a mere deductive method.[15]

## Liberal Promotions, Conservative Demotions

Many liberal churchmen in the mold of Kasper enjoyed promotions after the election of Pope Francis. But conservative churchmen such as Raymond Burke quickly found themselves marginalized. In his first year, as the outlines of his liberal pontificate became more visible, Pope Francis dropped Burke not only from the top position on the Vatican's highest court but also from his powerful position on the Congregation for Bishops, which vets ecclesiastical picks for the pope. In what many Church observers saw as an unprecedented slight, Burke was reduced to a ceremonial role overseeing the Knights of Malta.

Giving the demotion even more significance, Pope Francis replaced Burke on the Congregation for Bishops with one of Burke's enemies, Donald Wuerl, the liberal cardinal of Washington, DC, who had long criticized Burke's traditional defense of canon law. (Wuerl has become the face of the "humble" Church of Pope Francis, despite living like a vain Borgia prince. Wuerl has had a high school in Pittsburgh named after himself and resides in a palatial penthouse on Embassy Row in Washington, DC.[16]) The *New York Times*, among other publications, purred over this act of in-your-face papal politics, seeing it correctly as a major snub of conservative Catholics and a sign that Pope Francis was determined to liberalize the episcopate.[17]

"The pope's decision to remove Cardinal Raymond L. Burke from the Congregation for Bishops was taken by church experts to be a signal that Francis is willing to disrupt the Vatican establishment in order to be more inclusive," the *New York Times* reported. "'He is saying that you don't need to be a conservative to become a bishop,' said Alberto Melloni, the director of the John XXIII Foundation for Religious Studies in Bologna, Italy, a liberal Catholic research institute."

In an interview for this book, one American priest said that the snubbing of Cardinal Burke had a shattering effect on morale within conservative priestly circles. "From then on we knew that we would have targets on our backs under this pontificate. The pope hates American conservatives," he said.

Liberal European media outlets, for their part, rejoiced at the demotions of conservative prelates such as Cardinal Mauro Piacenza, who lost his key position as prefect of the Congregation for the Clergy. They cheered the promotion of Archbishop Carlos Osoro Sierra, dubbed "Little Francis," to the important post of archbishop of Madrid. The German left was pleased when Pope Francis gave the large archdiocese of Berlin to Heiner Koch, who has criticized the Church's "hurtful" approach to homosexuals and endorsed Communion for adulterers. Pope Francis made a proponent of sacramental laxity, Bishop Nunzio Galantino, secretary general of the Italian bishops' conference. "My wish for the Italian Church is that it is able to listen without any taboo to the arguments in favor of married priests, the Eucharist for the divorced, and homosexuality," Galantino has said, earning him a reputation as the "prototypical" Pope Francis bishop.[18]

The liberal media also noticed that Francis, in keeping with his claim that the Church isn't sufficiently focused on the third world, has given appointments to liberal churchmen from obscure dioceses in developing countries with minuscule Catholic populations. In 2015, he gave, for example, a cardinal's hat to Soane Patita Paini Mafi, an environmentalist and critic of globalization from the tiny island of Tonga near New Zealand.[19] In 2016, he elevated to cardinal John Riat of Papua New Guinea, an advocate for a "low-carbon lifestyle."[20]

The pope's remaking of the episcopate in his own liberal image delighted the left, which understands the adage that "personnel is policy." Shortly before the November 2016 election, to the applause of the liberal media, he gave a red hat to Indianapolis Archbishop Joseph Tobin. Indianapolis, an archdiocese with fewer than 250,000 parishioners, has never had a cardinal. The Associated Press called it a "surprise pick" and said that it sent a "political message" to his colleagues, given Tobin's reputation for political liberalism: "Tobin has openly opposed efforts by Indiana Governor Mike Pence, now Donald Trump's running mate, to bar Syrian refugees from being resettled in the state."[21]

In a 2016 interview with a friendly reporter, Pope Francis acknowledged that he has been getting rid of conservative bishops by taking advantage of canon law's requirement that bishops submit resignation papers at the age of seventy-five. Even though the pope is not canonically required to accept their resignation, Francis has promptly accepted resignations in the case of conservative bishops while letting liberal bishops linger on. With what his interviewer described as a "wide smile" on his face, Pope Francis said, "Nails are removed by applying pressure to the top . . . or, you set them aside to rest when the age of retirement arrives."[22]

In the first year of his pontificate, Pope Francis repeatedly tele-graphed to the left that he intended to reshape the Church according to its modernist expectations. At his first press conference, he delighted reporters by dispensing with the traditional blessing, explaining that he wanted to "respect the consciences" of the non-Catholics in attendance. He generated more enthusiastic headlines by using a foot-washing ceremony at his first Holy Thursday Mass in Rome to demonstrate his pro-Islamic, pro-feminist leanings. In a clear violation of the Church's canon law—which instructs priests that Jesus Christ only washed the feet of men whom he ordained to the priesthood—Francis made a show of cleansing the feet of Muslim women at an Italian prison.[23] (In 2015, he would officially change the rubrics of the Holy Thursday Mass to include the washing of the feet of women and any member of the "people of the God," which he defines, contrary to his predecessors, as including Muslims.)

The secular chattering class was enchanted by the new "progressive" pope's penchant for combining political liberalism with doctrinal and liturgical looseness. His deliberately casual style—appearing in selfies with a clown nose, placing a beach ball on the altar at St. Mary Major, driving around in a Ford Focus, tweeting out his left-wing musings, and so on—became the subject of innumerable articles of praise.

They also took hope from his "collegiality," which they saw in his unusual decision to form a special cabinet of cardinals to advise him. He created an ecclesiastical gang of eight (it is now nine), which liberals interpreted as a sign that he wished to downgrade the papacy.

"Shortly after his election he named a group of eight cardinal advisers from around the world, reversing centuries of precedent that the Pope, as Christ's vicar on earth, acts alone—and creating a model for a more collegial approach to Church governance," observed *Vanity Fair.* "He has likened the 'group of eight' to a working group, and their meetings—several times a year—are held in the guesthouse conference room rather than an august Vatican chamber. The point is clear: those cardinals aren't princes of the Church; they're heads of households—a Kitchen Cabinet."[24]

## The Council of Cardinals

His appointments to the Council of Cardinals were highly revealing. He stacked it with some of the most liberal cardinals, such as Cardinal Reinhard Marx of Germany. An opponent of free-market economics, Marx, in a jokey reference to his name and to his socialist politics, titled one of his books *Das Kapital.* Marx is a supporter of Communion for the divorced-and-remarried and has called on the

Church to relax her moral teachings. Exhausted by Marx's left-wing musings, Archbishop Jan Paweł Lenga of Kazakhstan once said of him, "There was Marx, Karl Marx. And if present Marx says similar things, then there is no real difference." [25]

Marx is an outspoken critic of the Church's teaching on homosexual acts, saying that "the history of homosexuals in our society is very bad because we have done a lot to marginalize [them]." South African Cardinal Wilfrid Fox Napier tweeted in reply, "God help us! Next we'll have to apologize for teaching that adultery is a sin! Political correctness is today's major heresy!"

Protected by Pope Francis, Marx has disregarded such criticism. As one of the most powerful members of the Church, he is using his clout to advance the agenda of gay activists. "We have to respect the decisions of people," he has said. "We as a church cannot be against it."

Pope Francis made an open socialist, the Honduran Cardinal Óscar Rodríguez Maradiaga, the chairman of the Council of Cardinals. The Catholic left applauded his appointment and some liberals, recognizing his power, call him the "vice pope." [26] Rodríguez frequently lashes out at free-market economics, caricaturing critics of climate change activism as greedy capitalists: "The ideology surrounding environmental issues is too tied to a capitalism that doesn't want to stop ruining the environment because they don't want to give up their profits."

"Who caused the recent crisis in the financial market? Certainly not the poor. It is wealthy America and wealthy Europe that caused it. And this crisis was not made up by Liberation Theology or a consequence of the option for the poor. Those who do not criticize capitalism are wrong not to do so," he has said. [27]

Rodríguez is equally liberal on theological matters. Not long after Pope Francis plucked him from obscurity and made him chairman of the Council of Cardinals, he blasted traditional Catholics in a speech in which he promised "no more excommunicating the world, then, or trying to solve the world's problems by returning to authoritarianism, rigidity and moralism."

Rodríguez feels safe enough behind his "vice pope" status to take shots at the head of the Congregation for the Doctrine of the Faith, Cardinal Gerhard Müller, whom Pope Francis inherited from Pope Benedict XVI. Objecting to Müller's opposition to Communion for the divorced-and-remarried, Rodríguez said dismissively, "He is above all a German Theology professor and he only thinks in black-and-white terms."[28]

Müller has been the odd man out at the Vatican, clear from the fact that Pope Francis ignored his conservative counsel during the Synod on the Family. "Don't go telling on me to Cardinal Müller," Pope Francis joked to priests at a 2016 pastoral conference in Rome after he made a heterodox comment about marriage. According to the Vatican correspondent Sandro Magister, Cardinal Müller's advice "isn't worth a thing" in the eyes of Pope Francis. Magister reports that Müller's criticisms of the synod, "in spite of his role as guardian of doctrine," didn't even receive a serious hearing from Francis.[29]

After Pope Francis released *Amoris Laetitia* (The Joy of Love), his apostolic exhortation reflecting on the Synod of the Family, he made a point of asking the liberal Vienna Cardinal Christoph Schönborn, rather than Müller, to present the document at a press conference. Another holdover from the Benedict era, Cardinal Marc Ouellet, who is prefect of the Congregation for Bishops, has also been frozen out by Pope Francis. His recommendations are consistently ignored.[30]

Meanwhile, the power of liberal churchmen grows. After Cardinal Oswald Gracias, the archbishop of Bombay, was added to the Council of Cardinals, he began making statements in defense of gay activism, a rare position for a cleric to take in conservative India. "I believe maybe people have this orientation that God has given them," he holds. In a letter to LGBT groups, he apologized for "judgmental" priests and told his clergy to "tone down" their sermons.[31]

The lone American on the Council of Cardinals is Boston Cardinal Seán O'Malley, who is a political liberal in the mold of Pope Francis. A gun control advocate, O'Malley befuddled conservative Catholics by saying after the terrorist Boston bombings that the "inability of Congress to enact laws that control access to automatic weapons is emblematic of the pathology of our violent culture."[32]

For liberals reading the papal tea leaves, these appointments carried significant meaning. Their excitement continued to build amidst reports from the *New York Times* and other outlets that Pope Francis, during his tenure as archbishop of Buenos Aires, had endorsed legislation in favor of gay civil unions, an unprecedented stance for a Catholic cardinal to take during the Benedict era.

Many Catholic editors politely averted their gaze from this report, but liberals understood its import. Pope Benedict XVI had explicitly told Catholic bishops that support for gay civil unions violated the traditional teaching of the Church. When the press asked Pope Francis about this instruction, he said, "I do not remember that document well."[33] The more plausible explanation was that he simply didn't agree with it.

Indifferent to Benedict's conservatism, Bergoglio would often ignore or relativize documents from the Congregation for the Doctrine of the Faith that conflicted with his vision for the Church. After becoming pope, he urged other religious to adopt the same attitude. In 2013, he shocked the faithful by telling a group of priests and nuns from the Caribbean and Latin America, who were visiting Rome in June of that year, to follow his rebellious example and disregard correction from the Church's doctrinal office.

"Perhaps even a letter of the Congregation for the Doctrine [of the Faith] will arrive for you, telling you that you said such or such thing," he said to them. "But do not worry. Explain whatever you have to explain, but move forward...Open the doors, do something there where life calls for it. I would rather have a Church that makes mistakes for doing something than one that gets sick for being closed up."[34]

# The Celebrity Left's Pope

Long critical of the Church for "narrowness" and "rigidity," the left thrilled to the rhetoric of a pope willing to echo its anti-Catholic invective. The pope's irreverent asides made it clear to liberals that he disliked conservative Catholics for many of the same reasons that they do.

It delighted the left to see the pope confounding conservative Catholics. The more he adopted the rhetoric and causes of the left, the more praise he garnered from anti-Catholic celebrities. In the words of the ribald comedian Chris Rock, Francis was the "Floyd Mayweather of popes." "I might be crazy but I got this weird feeling that the new pope might be the greatest man alive," Rock marveled.[35]

Actress Jane Fonda could not contain her excitement either, tweeting out to her followers: "Gotta love new Pope. He cares about the poor, hates dogma." Actress Salma Hayek, a supporter of abortion rights and gay marriage, asserted, "Pope Francis is the best pope that has ever existed."[36]

Fonda's ex-husband, the late Tom Hayden, spoke for fellow 1960s radicals when he called the election of Pope Francis "the greatest moment in empowering spiritual progressives in decades." "Francis is on the side of liberation theology, working from within, towards his moment," he wrote. "His choice is more miraculous, if you will, than the rise of Barack Obama in 2008."[37]

HBO host Bill Maher, speaking to Rick Santorum, the Catholic former senator and presidential candidate from Pennsylvania, chuckled over the bewilderment Pope Francis was causing. "What I want to ask is, I mean, I'm not a Catholic, I'm an atheist," Maher said. "But I like the pope better than you do. You're saying the pope should stick to what he knows, and I find that ridiculous."[38] When Santorum appeared on CNN, host Chris Cuomo asked him, "Why aren't you more like your pope?"

The trendy literary community saw Francis as a fictional progressive pope come to life. The *Atlantic* noted the uncanny resemblance of Pope Francis to "Francesco," the modernizing pope from the 1979 bestseller *The Vicar of Christ*. In that book, Francesco devotes his pontificate to left-wing political causes, sells off Vatican treasures to fight world hunger, and waters down traditional teaching where it conflicts with the sexual revolution.[39]

*Gawker*, a scurrilous, anti-Catholic (and now defunct) website, fondly began calling the pontiff "Pope Frank." Week after week in the first year of his papacy, "Pope Frank" mollified the Western political and media elite, signaling that under his pontificate the Church would turn away from traditional teaching and toward the promotion of left-wing political causes.

He peppered his first papal exhortation, *Evangelii Gaudium* (The Joy of the Gospel), with familiar left-wing clichés about the need "to change the world" and "to leave this earth somehow better than we found it" while denouncing "trickle-down theories" of economics. He encouraged priests to operate like political activists in order to protect this "magnificent planet," and he cast the Church as a partner to the United Nations. Throughout the document, he argued that a Church unwilling to engage in left-wing politics stands on the "sidelines in the fight for justice."

Of particular interest to the left-wing media is that he took bitter aim at traditionalists within the Church. "Certain customs not directly connected to the heart of the Gospel, even some which have deep historical roots, are no longer properly understood and appreciated. Some of these customs may be beautiful, but they no longer serve as means of communicating the Gospel. We should not be afraid to re-examine them," he said, offering a preview of his anti-traditionalist program as pope.

Another theme popular with liberals, decentralization, figured largely into the document. Decentralization has long been seen by the left as a means of liberalizing the Church. Instead of challenging this view, Pope Francis pandered to it. Making it sound as if Jesus Christ, who founded the Church on St. Peter, favors a revamping of the papacy, he wrote: "I am conscious of the need to promote a sound 'decentralization;...Since I am called to put into practice what I ask of others, I too must think about a conversion of the papacy [to]...help make the exercise of my ministry more faithful to the meaning which Jesus Christ wished to give it and to the present needs of evangelization...We have made little progress in this regard. The papacy and the central structures of the universal Church also need to hear the call to pastoral conversion."

To that end, he said that he was willing to confer power, "including genuine doctrinal authority," upon national conferences of bishops, and he vowed to undo "centralization" that "complicates the Church's life and her missionary outreach." His predecessors had always taught that those national conferences possess no doctrinal authority at all.

Though ostensibly an exhortation to engage in evangelization, the document said nothing about the necessity of belief in Jesus Christ for salvation and spoke of missionaries more like celibate social workers than transmitters of the Catholic faith.

The liberal media grasped the significance of this document, praising its "inclusive" tone and content.[40] But it drew even more hope from his off-the-cuff interviews. In a series of them during the first year of his pontificate, Pope Francis waved a white flag in the culture war.

## "I Have Never Been a Right-Winger"

The Church is too "obsessed' with the issues of abortion, contraception, and gay marriage, he declared in a bombshell interview in the fall of 2013.[41] For liberals who view the Church as the chief impediment to the spread of the sexual revolution, these words were revolutionary. The pope was parroting one of their favorite talking points, that the Church needs to outgrow its "hang-ups" about modern sexual mores.

The interview appeared in the pages of several left-wing Jesuit publications, one of which was *America*, a magazine known in Catholic circles for its opposition to the Church's traditional moral teachings and theology. The interview put to rest the false narrative of Pope Francis as a "conservative Jesuit," which some commentators in the Catholic press had advanced at the beginning of his papacy. Pope Francis assured his fellow liberal Jesuits that he is as liberal as any of them. "I have never been a right-winger," he said.

The interview astonished orthodox Catholics, as the pope used it to ratify the principal criticism of the Church's most persistent critics. "It is not necessary to talk about these issues all the time," he said, referring to the Church's contested moral teachings. "The dogmatic and moral teachings of the church are not all equivalent. The church's pastoral ministry cannot be obsessed with the transmission of a disjointed multitude of doctrines to be imposed insistently." He would later make the random claim that the most important moral issues facing the world today are youth unemployment and the neglect of the elderly.

His aversion to the moral issues that he mentioned explained the notable silences of his otherwise garrulous pontificate. As the *Wall Street Journal* noted, "Six months into his papacy, Pope Francis had not yet made a major statement on abortion, not even during his homily at a special Vatican Mass with antiabortion activists." "I'm a little bit disappointed in Pope Francis that he hasn't . . . said much about unborn children, about abortion," Bishop Thomas Tobin said. "Many people have noticed that."[42]

When Pope Francis did eventually get around to criticizing abortion, he added the false, insulting, and fashionable caveat that the Church has "done little to adequately accompany women in very difficult situations, where abortion appears as a quick solution to their profound anguish, especially when the life developing within them is the result of rape or a situation of extreme poverty."

"Although he has shown no intention of retracting the Church's opposition to abortion, he has alarmed conservatives by taking a less forceful tone than his predecessors," reported Reuters. After Pope Francis announced in 2015 at the beginning of the "year of mercy" that he wanted to make it easier for women to get forgiveness for abortions by not having to seek absolution from bishops, Catholics for Choice rejoiced, "This is a pope who is not stuck in the pelvic zone."

"Pope Francis: Church Too Focused on Gays and Abortion," blared the BBC in a typical headline from the beginning of his pontificate. Besieged by such stories, conservative Catholics expressed confusion. In their experience since Vatican II, the Church, particularly in Western countries, hadn't shown a preoccupation with controversial moral issues but a cowardly avoidance of them.

Cardinal Timothy Dolan of New York City, in a frank interview with the *Wall Street Journal* not long before Pope Francis's election, spoke about this silence of the Church on hot-button moral issues after Vatican II. He conceded that the post–Vatican II Church in America had "gotten gun-shy" on those issues.

Pope Paul VI's encyclical opposing artificial birth control, *Humanae Vitae*, "brought such a tsunami of dissent, departure, disapproval of the Church, that I think most of us—and I'm using the first-person plural intentionally, including myself—kind of subconsciously said, 'Whoa. We'd better never talk about that, because it's just too hot to handle,'" he said. The soft-pedaling started, he continued, "when the whole world seemed to be caving in, and where Catholics in general got the impression that what the Second Vatican Council taught, first and foremost, is that we should be chums with the world, and that the best thing the church can do is become more and more like everybody else."[43]

That is precisely the stance to which the Church has returned under Pope Francis. Disappointing conservative Catholics, Dolan quickly changed his tune after the election of Pope Francis. In an interview with George Stephanopoulos on ABC, he oddly affirmed the propaganda of the Church's critics by saying, "We have to do better to see that our defense of marriage is not reduced to an attack on gay people. I admit, we haven't been too good at that."

Cardinal Müller implicitly challenged Pope Francis's caricature of an obsessed Church. "It's not as if other bishops or Pope Benedict had constantly spoken about abortion, sexual morals or euthanasia," he said to a German newspaper.[44] But the damage was already done by the pope's remark. Liberal politicians quickly adopted it as a rebuttal against socially conservative Catholic opponents.

## The Signature Phrase of Pope Francis

Against an "obsessed" Church, Pope Francis presented himself as a font of understanding. Indeed, nothing pleased liberals more than what has become the signature phrase of his papacy: "Who am I to judge?"

"He did more with those five words than the last five popes," burbled the pop singer Elton John. "He is my hero."[45]

The inane line came in response to a question during a press briefing on Pope Francis's trip back from Brazil in July 2013. Francis had been asked about the presence of gay priests in the Church. He brushed the issue off, saying breezily, "Who am I to judge them if they are seeking the Lord in good faith?"[46]

Ever since then, the press has feted Pope Francis as "gay-friendly," a welcome contrast in its view to Pope Benedict XVI, whom liberal pundits demonized as a "homophobe" for simply upholding the Church's perennial moral teaching and traditional priestly discipline.

For conservative Catholics, the context of the pope's remark made it even more dubious. What had prompted it was a scandal involving a homosexual priest named Monsignor Battista Ricca. Bizarrely, Pope Francis had promoted Ricca to the highest ecclesiastical position at the Vatican bank despite an amazingly sordid past for a priest. "Pope's 'eyes and ears' in Vatican bank 'had string of homosexual affairs,'" ran a headline in the United Kingdom's *Telegraph* in July 2013.[47]

The appointment flabbergasted the veteran Vatican correspondent Sandro Magister, who established beyond any reasonable doubt that Ricca's scandalous past included an affair with a member of the Swiss Guard, a beating he received at a gay bar, and a grimly comic incident involving the discovery by firemen of Ricca trapped in an elevator with a young male prostitute.[48]

Pope Francis disregarded this information and appointed Ricca anyway. Far from hurting Francis's image as a "reformer" in the eyes of the Western media, the Ricca scandal only sealed it. Liberals were pleased to learn that Francis was not only encouraging the very gay priestly candidates whom Pope Benedict had instructed seminaries to stop ordaining but was promoting them to top positions.

While winning him plaudits from the press, the pope's remark demoralized orthodox clergy and laity exhausted by countless gay scandals in the Church. "When the Pope rhetorically asked, 'Who am I to judge a gay person of good will who seeks the Lord?,' he effectively gave the green light for homosexual men to enter the priesthood," complained Fr. Michael Orsi, a research fellow at Ave Maria Law School.[49]

An official at the German branch of Vatican Radio felt so emboldened by the pope's words he decided to run a picture of two lesbians kissing as an accompaniment to an article titled "Moral Theologian: Church's Sexual Morality Is in Motion" on its website. Vatican Radio eventually took the picture down after Catholics complained that it was scandalizing children, but that the picture had appeared at all indicated the change of atmosphere under Pope Francis.[50]

Conservative Catholics had hoped that Pope Francis would

disband the long-discussed gay mafia inside the Church. But the Ricca scandal erased that hope.

"So much is written about the gay lobby. I have yet to find anyone who can give me a Vatican identity card with 'gay' [written on it]. They say they are there," Pope Francis said vaguely in 2013.[51] Such comments suggested that he was more apt to joke about the gay mafia than eliminate it, even as embarrassing confirmations of its existence continued to trickle out. One member of the Swiss Guard was quoted in the European press in 2014 saying that Vatican officials had solicited him for sex more than twenty times. A former commander in the Swiss Guard described the Vatican as a "magnet" for gays.[52] A Polish priest and theologian working at the Congregation for the Doctrine of the Faith came out to an Italian newspaper in 2015 as homosexual and said that he had a gay partner. He resigned, but the "Vatican said [his] dismissal had nothing to do with his comments on his personal situation, which it said 'merit respect,'" reported Reuters.[53]

"The gay mafia is so strong," says a former seminary official interviewed for this book. The plethora of gay-friendly bishops Pope Francis has promoted "tells you where the power is in the Church," he says.

The homosexual magazine the *Advocate*, out of gratitude for his subversion of Church teaching, declared Pope Francis in December 2013 its "Person of the Year." It thanked him for signaling a lack of seriousness about the Church's stance on homosexuality and drew hope from his earlier support for gay civil unions as archbishop of Buenos Aires:

It's actually during Pope Francis's time as cardinal that his difference from Benedict and hard-liners in the church became apparent. As same-sex marriage looked on track to be legalized in Argentina, Bergoglio argued privately that the church should come out for civil unions as the "lesser of two evils."

That's all according to Pope Francis's authorized biographer, Sergio Rubin. Argentine gay activist Marcelo Márquez backed up the story, telling *The New York Times* in March that Bergoglio "listened to my views with a great deal of respect. He told me that homosexuals need to have recognized rights and that he supported civil unions, but not same-sex marriage."[54]

Catholics in the pews were not so wowed. On November 10, 2013, the *New York Times* devoted a front-page story to conservative angst about Pope Francis. Titled "Conservative U.S. Catholics Feel Left Out of the Pope's Embrace," the article noted that members of the "church's conservative wing in the United States say Francis has left them feeling abandoned and deeply unsettled."

By the time of his 2015 visit to the United States, dismay with the pope had grown to the point that the *Wall Street Journal* headlined an article "Conservative Catholics in U.S. Greet Pope Francis with Unease."

"The Catholic Church…faces a growing crisis of moral consistency and credibility," wrote pundit and former presidential candidate Pat Buchanan.[55] "The church of Pius XII and John Paul II taught that the truths of the Ten Commandments brought down from Sinai and the truths of the Sermon on the Mount are eternal. Those popes also taught that a valid marriage is indissoluble, that homosexuality is unnatural and immoral, that abortion is the killing of the innocent unborn, an abomination. Yet one reads regularly of discussions inside the Vatican to alter what is infallible church teaching on these doctrines to make the church more appealing to those who have rejected them."

Conservative Catholic commentators in Latin America, whose voices were drowned out in the din of praise following Bergoglio's election, had warned that his pontificate would prove disastrous. To these observers familiar with his tenure in Buenos Aires, the maddening incoherence and people-pleasing relativism of his pontificate were all too predictable.

"Of all the unthinkable candidates, Jorge Mario Bergoglio is perhaps the worst," wrote Marcelo González. "This election is incomprehensible: he is not a polyglot, he has no Curial experience, he does not shine for his sanctity, he is loose in doctrine and liturgy, he has not fought against abortion and only very weakly against homosexual 'marriage' [approved with practically no opposition from the episcopate], he has no manners to honor the Pontifical Throne. He has never fought for anything else than to remain in positions of power."[56]

Lucrecia Rego de Planas, a Catholic editor in Latin America, knew Francis from his time in Argentina and remembered his holier-than-thou poverty posturing. None of his first acts of ostentatious humility—which included the rejection of the papal apartments for a floor of the Vatican hotel—surprised her.

In a blistering letter that she wrote to Pope Francis, she recalled his habit of showboating at the expense of the Church:

> When I met you during those retreats [in Buenos Aires], while you were still Cardinal Bergoglio, what struck me about you and left me disconcerted was that you never behaved like the other cardinal and bishops. Allow me to mention just a few examples: you were the only one who never genuflected in front of the Tabernacle or during the Consecration. If all the bishops showed up in their priestly frocks, because that was what a particular gathering required, you would show up in your street clothes and priest's collar. If everybody sat in the seats reserved for the bishops and cardinals, you left the seat reserved to Cardinal Bergoglio empty and sat further back, saying "I like it here, this way I feel more at home." If the others arrived in a car that corresponded to the dignity of a bishop, you arrived last, busily and in a hurry, telling all about whom you met on the public transit that you had chosen to get there.
>
> When I witnessed these things—I'm ashamed to say—I would think to myself: "Ugh . . . there he goes again, always

trying to attract attention to himself! For if one truly wanted to be humble and simple, wouldn't it be better to behave like the other bishops, so as to go unnoticed?"[57]

As even his sympathetic biographer Paul Vallely acknowledged, Pope Francis has a weakness for contrived acts of humility. On his first papal trip, for example, he rebuked an aide for putting his briefcase on the plane, thus depriving him of the opportunity to look modest. He instructed the aide to retrieve the briefcase so that he could be seen carrying it, wrote Vallely:

> "Where's my briefcase?" asked Pope Francis. The papal entourage had arrived at Fiumicino Airport in Rome for the pontiff's first trip abroad. Jorge Mario Bergoglio had been pope for just four months and was now bound for Rio de Janeiro, where 3.5 million young people from 178 countries were waiting to greet him at World Youth Day in Brazil. And he could not find his briefcase.
> "It's been taken on board the plane," an aide explained.
> "But I want to carry it on," said the pontiff.
> "No need, it's on already," the assistant replied.
> "You don't understand," said Francis. "Go to the plane. Get the bag. And bring it back here please."[58]

A less gullible and ideologically driven media might have questioned a pope so eager to advertise his humility. Instead, the media breathlessly reported his obviously scripted acts of humility, such as paying his own hotel bill at the Vatican after the conclave or calling to cancel his newspaper subscription. They reported on humble deeds, both real and imaginary, from the free haircuts and tours of the Sistine Chapel he ordered for the homeless to nightly ministrations that never occurred.

"Is Francis Leaving Vatican at Night to Minister to Homeless?" ran a ludicrous headline in the *Huffington Post*.[59] No such ministry happened. But it didn't matter. Journalists covering Francis saw themselves as propagandists first and reporters second. Out of affection for his leftism, they were determined to cast him as the first pope to notice the poor.

## Obama's Pope

Barack Obama, capturing the drift of this hagiography, disguised his appreciation for the pope's left-wing politics in safer praise for his "empathy" and "humility." "I have been hugely impressed with the Pope's pronouncements. He seems like somebody who lives out the teachings of Christ, incredible humility, an incredible sense of empathy to the least of these, the poor," Obama said.[60]

But it was the politically correct third-worldism of the first Latin American pope that Obama found most exciting. When Obama learned that Pope Francis planned to canonize the slain left-wing archbishop Óscar Romero, a movement that had stalled under Pope John Paul II and Pope Benedict XVI, he immediately issued a statement: "I am grateful to Pope Francis for his leadership in reminding us of our obligation to help those most in need, and for his decision to beatify Blessed Oscar Arnulfo Romero."[61]

Obama also appreciated that Pope Francis was giving greater attention to left-wing politics than to theology, thereby making it easier for the left to shape politics and culture without religious resistance. As the New York Times put it, "His de-emphasis of issues like abortion and same-sex marriage and his championing of the poor and vulnerable—articulated in his mission statement, 'The Joy of the Gospel'—have impressed a second-term president who argues that income inequality undermines human dignity."

At the end of 2013, Time magazine crowned Pope Francis its "Person of the Year." The honor reflected the liberal elite's giddy mood about his papacy and the aid it offered to the global left.

"What makes this Pope so important is the speed with which he has captured the imaginations of millions who had given up on hoping for the church at all," the magazine editorialized. "In a matter of months, Francis has elevated the healing mission of the church—the church as servant and comforter of hurting people in an often harsh world—above the doctrinal police work so important to his recent predecessors. John Paul II and Benedict XVI were professors of theology. Francis is a former janitor, nightclub bouncer, chemical technician and literature teacher."

The "healing mission of the church" was *Time*'s euphemism for Pope Francis's identification with global socialism. Beneath all of its patter about his outreach to the poor lay the real reason for the magazine's decision to honor him: he was advancing left-wing politics and liberalizing the Church after his two conservative predecessors. Many other popes had performed corporal works of mercy for the poor. But because they upheld orthodoxy and did not enlist the Church in the causes of the global left, their charity went unpraised by the liberal elite. *Time* had finally found a pope it could champion without reservation. "He is embracing complexity and acknowledging the risk that a church obsessed with its own rights and righteousness could inflict more wounds than it heals," it concluded.[62]

The media insisted on portraying Pope Francis as the "people's pontiff." But to conservative Catholics, these laurels from the media only proved his status as the elite's pontiff. In a moment of ecclesiastical indiscretion in 2013, Philadelphia archbishop Charles Chaput let slip to the *National Catholic Reporter* that orthodox Catholics are "generally not happy with Francis" but that lapsed Catholics and non-Catholics who disdain Church teaching feel enthusiasm for his pontificate.

"[Church-going Catholics] are not actually the ones who really talk to me about the new pope. The ones who do are nonpracticing Catholics or people who aren't Catholic or not even Christian," Chaput said. "They go out of their way to tell me how impressed they are and what a wonderful change he's brought into the church. It's interesting to see that it's the alienated Catholic and the non-Catholic and the non-Christians who have expressed their enthusiasm more than Catholics have."[63]

Summing up the left's manipulative attitude toward the pope perfectly, new-age enthusiast Jennifer Vanderslice said to the *Guardian*, "He is such a worldly and non-judgmental pope and is so dynamic. He will never change me into a Catholic but I do like the way he is spreading peace and talking about helping the poor and the less fortunate...It is refreshing to hear a pope who can strike a chord in so many people, whether they're Catholic or not. You can take what you need and leave the rest."[64]

Timothy Egan, a *New York Times* columnist who describes himself as "lapsed but listening," also summed up Francis's appeal for his secular readers concisely: "He is—gasp—a liberal." At long last, a progressive occupies the chair of St. Peter, exulted Egan: "Pope Francis has shown himself to be a free spirit and a free thinker...He talks to atheists...He calls for the faithful to 'mess up the church.'... Francis has befuddled the guardians of dogma and medieval sexual doctrines who have long kept sunlight out of the Vatican."[65]

Sandro Magister has observed that Pope John Paul II and Pope Benedict XVI "were mostly popular inside the Church, even if they were harshly criticized from strongholds of non-Catholic public opinion, whereas Francis' popularity is more conspicuous outside the Church, even if it isn't eliciting waves of conversions."[66]

"The mass media are trying to create a spirit of Pope Francis, just as they created a spirit of Vatican II," commented Bishop Robert Morlino in the *Wisconsin State Journal*. "Many Catholics fell for that the first time. I hope they won't fall for that again."[67]

If anything, Pope Francis's liberal spin on Catholicism appears to be causing Catholics, both practicing and lapsed, to take Church pronouncements less seriously. According to polling data released by Pew Research in 2016, only one in ten American Catholics said that they rely a "great deal" on Pope Francis's moral direction. Seventy-three percent of Catholics said that they prefer to rely on their own judgments.[68]

Even in his homeland of Argentina, support for him is beginning to wane. In 2016, reported the *New York Post*, "a recent local poll revealed that Francis—the former Jorge Mario Bergoglio, archbishop of Buenos Aires—has tumbled from the first to the ninth most 'trustworthy Argentine' in just two years."[69]

According to *Politico*, in a piece titled "Pope Alienates Base, Sees Numbers Drop," attendance at Vatican events has been steadily declining over his pontificate:

> In 2015, more than 3.2 million pilgrims visited and attended papal events, liturgies or prayer services at the Holy See, the Vatican said at the end of December. That was a sharp drop from the 5.9 million visitors received by Pope Francis in 2014. And it was less than half of the 6.6 million pilgrims who visited the Vatican during the first nine-and-a-half months of his pontificate in 2013.[70]

Pope Francis calls the Church on his watch a "field hospital." But if it is one, many of his patients appear to be dying. Pews in many dioceses remain as empty as ever. As one wan headline put it in 2013, "Pope Francis' Appeal Not Measurable Yet in Church Attendance."[71]

Pope Benedict XVI said that the crisis in the Church deepened after it followed the liberal zeitgeist. But Pope Francis rejects that view, pushing "reforms" rooted in following the liberal zeitgeist even more slavishly.

"We are not living an era of change but a change of era," Pope Francis has said, aligning himself with the Church's critics. "Before the problems of the church it is not useful to search for solutions in conservatism or fundamentalism, in the restoration of obsolete

conduct and forms that no longer have the capacity of being significant culturally . . . Christian doctrine is not a closed system incapable
of generating questions, doubts, interrogatives—but is alive, knows
being unsettled, enlivened."[72]

Pope Francis isn't suppressing what his predecessor called the
"council of the media" but giving new and even louder voice to it.
To liberals, this signifies a "springtime" in the Church. To conservative Catholics, reeling from four years of chaos and confusion, it
feels more like the dead of winter.

"It takes your breath away," says a Church insider interviewed for
this book. "Things are spinning out of control. When you go to the
Vatican, you look up at the papal apartments and the light is out.
That is a metaphor for this pontificate."

CHAPTER THREE

# The Left's Long March
# to the Papacy

The election of Jorge Bergoglio marked the culmination of the left's long march through the Church. For decades, liberals, both inside and outside the Church, had labored for the elevation of a progressive pope who would incorporate the tenets of modern liberalism into Catholicism. That movement has been gathering strength since at least the advent of the modernist heresy in the Church, which Pope Pius X addressed in his 1907 encyclical *Pascendi Dominici Gregis*.

To read that encyclical today, one might think Pope Pius X was writing about the papacy of Francis. Pope Pius X warned that the modernists wish to fashion a faith "suited to the times in which we live," based not on the immutable doctrines of Catholicism but on the subjectivism of "modern philosophy." He foresaw a Church that would chase after elite fads, defer to the spurious claims of modern science, bow down to the secularism of the state, treat all religions as equal, cast Jesus Christ as a mere human political activist, reduce priests to social workers, and Protestantize its worship and doctrine.

Despite Pope Pius X's efforts, modernism continued to spread in the Church throughout the twentieth century, bubbling up most visibly at Vatican II and in its aftermath. "More important than the documents, the council has consecrated a new spirit, destined in the course of time to remake the face of Catholicism," wrote Xavier Rynne, the pseudonym for Fr. Francis X. Murphy, in the pages of the *New Yorker*.[1] The liberalism of Francis's pontificate can be traced to that modernist spirit.

To the delight of the left and the dismay of conservative Catholics, it has come out that leading modernists in the Church had been plotting for years to make Bergoglio pope. One of the architects of Bergoglio's election to the papacy was Belgian Cardinal Godfried Danneels, who has acknowledged this plotting.[2]

Danneels is known for his association with the Church's abuse scandal. The Belgian press once caught Danneels coaching the victim of a molesting bishop into delaying a disclosure.[3] But he is even more famous for his outré liberalism. In 1988, he sparked anger in the Church by leading a delegation of Catholic theologians to hobnob with "Professional Humanists" in Amsterdam. In the 1990s, he advised the king of Belgium to sign an abortion law. In the 2000s, he sent a letter to the Belgium government giving his blessing to gay civil unions. "The [Church] has never opposed the fact that there should exist a sort of 'marriage' between homosexuals," he said falsely.[4]

As he bragged to his authorized biographers, Danneels, along with a veritable who's who of ultra-progressives in the Church, presided over what he called a "mafia" that opposed Pope Benedict XVI and eventually helped elect Pope Francis. Danneels disclosed to his biographers that he and this group of liberal bishops had met for many years in the Swiss town of St. Gallen to promote the election of Bergoglio. They called themselves the St. Gallen group.

"The St. Gallen group is a sort of posh name. But in reality we said of ourselves, and of that group : 'The Mafia,'" Danneels said in September 2015.[5]

The group started meeting in 1996 and numbered among its members Achille Silvestrini (who was long seen as a liberal alternative to Pope John Paul II), Carlo Maria Martini (the former cardinal of Milan who openly espoused socialism and a rejection of the Church's traditional moral theology), Walter Kasper (whom Francis would later tap to liberalize Church teaching on marriage), Basil Hume (the English cardinal known for his support of "democratic" reforms within the Church and his advocacy for liberalizing the Church's moral stances), and Karl Lehmann (the German cardinal who opposes the Church's teachings on marriage and birth control). In 2016, Lehmann advised his fellow liberals in the Church to take advantage of the "freedom that has been granted by the pope."[6]

"The election of Bergoglio was prepared in St. Gallen, without doubt. And the main lines of the program the pope is carrying out are those that Danneels and company were starting to discuss more than ten years ago," Danneels's biographer Karim Schelkens said at a press conference in 2015. Danneels's other biographer, Jürgen Mettepenningen, added, "They wanted Church reform, they wanted to bring the Church closer to the hearts of people; they moved forward by stages. At the beginning of the year 2000, when John Paul II's end was becoming more foreseeable, they thought more strategically about what was going to happen to the Church after John Paul II. When Cardinal Silvestrini joined the group it took on a more tactical and strategic character."[7]

The diocese of St. Gallen has confirmed to the press the existence of the group. Its press office acknowledged that a "private circle met on a regular basis from 1996 until 2006 and that 'the now-deceased Cardinal Carlo Maria Martini and the then-bishop of St. Gallen, Ivo Fürer, initiated these meetings." The press office conceded that the bishops "spoke about the situation in the Church at their yearly gatherings in St. Gallen" and they "also spoke—when the health of Pope John Paul II was continuously declining—about the question as to which qualities a new pope should have."[8]

During the pontificates of John Paul II and Benedict XVI, leaks from unnamed Vatican cardinals to the press, clearly intended to undercut the conservatism of these pontificates, were routine. It is suspected that many of those leaks came from members of the St. Gallen group. Standing on the Vatican balcony near Pope Francis shortly after his election, Danneels can be seen looking jubilant. Danneels has said that the election of Francis constitutes his "personal resurrection." Under any other pontificate, his role in the Church's child abuse scandal would have sent him into a quiet retirement. But under Pope Francis he has received high-profile assignments. To the outrage of orthodox Catholics, he turned up at the 2015 Synod on the Family as a delegate personally chosen by Pope Francis.[9] In 2016, Pope Francis made one of Danneels's protégés, Archbishop Jozef de Kesel of Brussels, a cardinal despite his open heterodoxy, evident in his praise for homosexuals' "way of living their sexuality."[10]

The St. Gallen group had hoped to place Bergoglio in the papacy in 2005, but its effort failed. It has been established that Bergoglio came in second to Ratzinger at the 2005 conclave.[11] According to Danneels's authorized biographers, a frequent question during the meetings of the St. Gallen Group was "How can we avoid Ratzinger as Pope?"

Failing to stop Ratzinger in 2005 had embittered members of the group and explains their frequent sniping at him during his pontificate. Mainstream newspapers would often quote anonymous ecclesiastical sources harrumphing about "chaos" and "crisis" in Pope Benedict XVI's Church. One of those murmurers was Jorge Bergoglio.

This was revealed in 2015 when one of his bumbling media aides blurted out a criticism of Pope Benedict XVI for delivering a speech in Regensburg, Germany, critical of Islam. The Western media had taken great offense to the speech for not adhering to its propagandistic view of Islam as a religion of peace. Amidst the media furor, Bergoglio's aide said, "If the Pope does not recognize the values of Islam and it is left like that, in twenty seconds we will have destroyed everything that has been built over the last twenty years." Bergoglio didn't bother to distance himself from his aide's comment. The Vatican was so outraged by the episode that it confronted Bergoglio, according to the Argentine press. "How is it possible that your spokesman made such declarations and [you] did not feel bound to contradict him and remove him immediately?" an Argentine newspaper quoted a Vatican official as saying to Bergoglio. Later, the papal nuncio in Argentina indirectly criticized Bergoglio for his sniping at Benedict through intermediaries. "The Holy Father," the papal nuncio said, "is the victim of a persecution, he has been abandoned by the opponents of the Truth, but above all by certain priests and religious, not only bishops."[12]

Given this history, it is puzzling that Pope Benedict XVI has said that he didn't anticipate the election of Bergoglio after his resignation. He had some names in mind "but not his," Benedict told an interviewer in 2016.[13]

## The Pact of the Catacombs

The election of Jorge Bergoglio brought the St. Gallen group out of the shadows, but other factions within the Church also emerged, eager to take credit for the presence of a liberal on the chair of St. Peter. Modernists in Germany pointed with pride to his election as a vindication of the Pact of the Catacombs, a secret manifesto signed by socialist bishops around the time of Vatican II which called on the bishops to engage in left-wing political activism, eschew traditional titles, and advertise their poverty loudly. The document received its name from having been signed at a church near the catacombs in Rome.

"His program is to a high degree what the Catacomb Pact was," Cardinal Walter Kasper said to reporter David Gibson.[14] It "was forgotten," said Kasper. "But now he [Francis] brings it back."

"With Pope Francis, you cannot ignore the Catacomb Pact,"

Massimo Faggioli, a professor of church history at the University of St. Thomas in Minnesota, said to Gibson. "It's a key to understanding him, so it's no mystery that it has come back to us today."

Many of the signatories of the secret manifesto came from Latin America, according to Gibson. They were loath at that time to publicize their activism, for fear of triggering backlash from communism's critics, Gibson writes:

> The problem was that the social upheavals of 1968, plus the drama of the Cold War against communism and the rise of liberation theology—which stressed the gospel's priority on the poor, but was seen as too close to Marxism by its conservative foes—made a document such as the Catacombs Pact radioactive. "It had the odor of communism," said Brother Uwe Heisterhoff, a member of the Society of the Divine Word, the missionary community that is in charge of the Domitilla Catacombs.
>
> Even in Latin America the pact wasn't publicized too widely, lest it poison other efforts to promote justice for the poor. Heisterhoff noted that he worked with the indigenous peoples of Bolivia for 15 years but only learned about the Catacombs Pact when he came to Rome to oversee the Domitilla Catacombs four years ago.
>
> "This stuff was a bit dangerous until Francis came along," said Faggioli.[15]

According to the text of the Pact of the Catacombs, the bishops pledged to politicize the Church for the sake of ushering in the "advent of another social order":

> We will do our utmost so that those responsible for our government and for our public services make, and put into practice, laws, structures and social institutions required by justice and

charity, equality and the harmonic and holistic development of all men and women, and by this means bring about the advent of another social order, worthy of the sons and daughters of mankind and of God.

Another passage in the document calls for the redistribution of wealth by international institutions. It said the bishops have a duty "to request jointly, at the level of international organisms, the adoption of economic and cultural structures which, instead of producing poor nations in an ever richer world, make it possible for the poor majorities to free themselves from their wretchedness."

*L'Osservatore Romano* has praised the Pact of the Catacombs:

After almost 50 years, Pope Francis—a man who comes from a continent where many Bishops made tremendous efforts to apply Council Vatican II in the context of poverty—assumed in the program of his pontificate the theme of "a poor Church, a Church for the poor." Those words of the Pope have encouraged diverse groups to celebrate the 50 year anniversary of the Pact of the Catacombs. Thus, since November 2014 special celebrations have taken place at the Catacomb of Domitilla. The Commission of Justice and Peace, the International Union of Superior Generals and the Union of Superior Generals, for example, organized a prayer vigil. The Divine Word Missionaries and the Missionary Sisters Servants of the Holy Spirit held a day of reflection at the Catacomb on January 15, 2015 on the occasion of the feast day of their founder, St. Arnold Janssen. And so the commemorations continued, up to the numerous meetings that have taken place in these last days.

Retired bishop Luigi Bettazzi of Ivrea, Italy, is the last living signatory to the Pact of the Catacombs. "The remembrance of the pact has been revived thanks to the atmosphere Pope Francis has indicated for the whole church to follow," he has said.[16] According to the historian Roberto de Mattei, Bettazzi was known as the "red bishop":

> In July 1976, when it seemed that Communism might take power in Italy, Bettazzi wrote a letter to the then Secretary of the Italian Communist Party, Enrico Berlinguer, in whom he recognised the tendency to realize: 'a unique experience of Communism, different from the Communism of other nations' and asked [him] 'not to be hostile' to the Church but 'to stimulate' rather 'an evolution according to the needs of the times and the expectations of men, above all the poorest, whom you know better how to interpret at the most opportune time.' The leader of the Italian Communist Party replied to the Bishop of Ivrea with a letter—Communists and Catholics: Clarity of Principles and Basis of Agreement, published in 'Rinascita' of October 14th, 1977.[17]

Another "red" bishop who signed the document was Dom Hélder Câmara. A Brazilian archbishop, Câmara wore his socialism on his sleeve—"My socialism is special, it's a socialism that respects the human person and goes back to the Gospels. My socialism it is justice"—and wouldn't even condemn armed Marxists: "And I respect a lot priests with rifles on their shoulders; I never said that to use weapons against an oppressor is immoral or anti-Christian. But that's not my choice, not my road, not my way to apply the Gospels."[18]

Socialists inside the Church are pressing for the canonization of Câmara—a movement that Pope Francis is entertaining. In 2015, the Vatican's Congregation for the Causes of the Saints quickly approved a request that the canonization process for Câmara be opened up—a development *America* magazine called "ground-breaking." Wrote its correspondent Gerard O'Connell: "[Câmara] died on Aug. 27, 1999, but his memory lives on. Pope Francis remembers him; they have much in common. Addressing the Brazilian bishops in Rio de Janeiro in July 2013, Francis recalled 'all those names and faces which have indelibly marked the journey of the church in Brazil' and listed Dom Hélder among them. That was significant."[19]

In 1953, Manning Johnson, a former propaganda director for the Communist Party in America, testified to the U.S. Congress that determined Marxists had infiltrated Catholic seminaries. "In the earliest stages it was determined that with only small forces available it would be necessary to concentrate Communist agents in the seminaries and divinity schools," he said. "The practical conclusion, drawn by the Red leaders was that these institutions would make it possible for a small Communist minority to influence the ideology of future clergymen in the paths most conducive to Communist purposes."[20]

At the time, many scoffed at this testimony. But who doubts the influence of the radical left's long march through the Church now? In 2009, the heretical theologian Hans Küng, a supporter of the Pact of the Catacombs who now corresponds with Pope Francis, dreamed of a pope like Barack Obama: "What would a Pope do who acted in the spirit of Obama? Clearly, like Obama he would...proclaim the vision of hope of a renewed church, a revitalized ecumenism, understanding with the Jews, the Muslims and other world religions and a positive assessment of modern science..." Küng got his wish.

## Pope Francis among the Communists

In 2015, Pope Francis made a speech in Bolivia before a group of communists, socialists, and leftists called the World Meeting of Popular Movements. It was an electric moment for the left, proof that the papacy had fallen into its hands. Sharing the platform with open Marxists such as Evo Morales, Bolivia's president, who donned a jacket emblazoned with a picture of Che Guevara, Pope Francis exhorted the radicals in attendance to continue their social agitation.[21]

"Chavez died and Fidel is sick. Francis has taken up that leadership role and is doing everything right," gushed an organizer of the event, João Pedro Stédile of Brazil's Landless Workers Movement.

Pope Francis told the group exactly what it wanted to hear: that capitalism, not socialism, is the cause of their poverty. "The new colonialism takes on different faces. At times it appears as the anonymous influence of mammon: corporations, loan agencies, certain 'free trade' treaties, and the imposition of measures of 'austerity' which always tighten the belt of workers and the poor," he said.

He decried the "offenses of the Church," referred to capitalism as the "dung of the devil," and urged them to keep "organizing":

You, the lowly, the exploited, the poor and underprivileged, can do, and are doing, a lot. I would even say that the future of humanity is in great measure in your own hands, through your ability to organize and carry out creative alternatives, through your daily efforts to ensure the three "L's" (labor, lodging, land) and through your proactive participation in the great processes of change on the national, regional and global levels. Don't lose heart![22]

Many churchmen on the left's long march to the papacy died on the journey. But they have enjoyed a posthumous victory under Pope Francis. He has made a point of honoring Marxists inside the Church, such as the late Mexican bishop Samuel Ruiz.

During his 2016 visit to Mexico, Pope Francis visited Ruiz's tomb. Ruiz was known for pushing liberation theology, third-world ideologies, and the rights of indigenous peoples and playing fast and loose with the sacraments, which eventually led Pope John Paul II's Vatican to condemn him. Ruiz's close associates were thrilled when they heard that Pope Francis was going to visit his tomb, interpreting it as a moment of vindication for the liberation theologians banned by the Church. "Pope Francis is a Latin American, and his duty now is to pick up the work that men like Ruiz have done in the past," Bishop Raúl Vera said.[23]

"I believe that a key moment in the Pope's journey to Mexico will be his visit to the tomb of Bishop Samuel Ruiz García in Chiapas," said liberation theologian Leonardo Boff. "This is a reparation and a lesson for the Roman Curia, which is aware of having persecuted and impeded the advancement of a truly indigenous pastoral ministry from the indigenous people themselves and from their culture."

During the same visit, Pope Francis rebuked Mexico's bishops for not doing enough to push liberation theology, a lecture that left them so annoyed that an editorial in a publication for the archdiocese of Mexico City asked after the visit, "Does the pope have some reason for scolding Mexican bishops?"[24]

Many of the themes of Pope Francis's pontificate were foreshadowed by movements within liberal church circles in Latin America, Western Europe, and the United States. The press has praised Pope Francis for transforming the "tone" of the Church, but his "Who am I to judge?"-style rhetoric is a reprisal of the "medicine of mercy" rhetoric pervasive on the Catholic left for over two generations. Figures such as Milwaukee's former archbishop Rembert Weakland—who spearheaded the bishops' letter against Reaganomics and endorsed the "genital expression" of homosexuality—can be seen as forerunners of this pontificate.[25]

The winds of liberalism sweeping through the Church for decades pushed Bergoglio into the chair of St. Peter and knocked Joseph Ratzinger off it. One of the mysteries of Ratzinger's pontificate is that it had happened at all. He had always been outnumbered by liberals at the Vatican and didn't even want the papacy in the first place. As head of the Congregation for the Doctrine of the Faith, he had asked Pope John Paul II if he could resign and devote himself to private study. Pope John Paul II rejected his request.[26] The circumstances around his resignation remain murky, but it appears that the reluctance with which he entered the papacy (he has told a biographer his unwanted election left him "incredulous") and the resistance he felt from factions like the St. Gallen group and the gay mafia during it contributed to his resignation.

Across many quarters of the Church—from chanceries to left-wing Catholic colleges and universities to socialist organizations such as the Catholic Campaign for Human Development—modernist Catholics had been eagerly waiting for a chance to replace Ratzinger with a progressive in the style of Bergoglio. The *National Catholic Reporter*, a heterodox newspaper that often serves as a barometer of what liberal bishops are thinking, hinted at this when it reported during Ratzinger's pontificate:

> One need only talk to a sampling of theology departments to know that in many places theologians are lying low. Our seminaries will certainly be playing it safe for the foreseeable future. Moral theology of the sort that might raise substantial questions or handle difficult sexual or other life issues is being left to those who regurgitate the party line. More adventuresome and sophisticated theologians are out there, but they're not going to raise their heads too far above the barricades.[27]

Feeling empowered by the election of Pope Francis, those "sophisticated" theologians now not only lift their heads above the barricades but happily fire upon conservative Catholics. Once critical of "conservative" purges within the Church, they now conduct their own.

They have put pressure on Catholic publications to fire conservative Catholics thought to be out of step with this progressive pontificate. After Adam Shaw of Fox News criticized the liberalism of Francis in 2013, he lost his job at the Catholic News Service.[28] When Ross Douthat, a columnist at the *New York Times*, balked at the liberal drift of the pope's Synod on the Family, a long list of Catholic academics, many of whom had no problem criticizing Pope John

Paul II and Pope Benedict XVI, ganged up on him, writing his bosses, "This is not what we expect of the *New York Times*."[29] After a conservative Canadian blogger criticized one of Pope Francis's media aides, that aide enlisted the help of a law firm in intimidating the blogger. He only called off the law firm after media attention to his heavy-handed petulance caused the Vatican embarrassment.[30]

Charles Curran, one of the most notorious modernist dissenters from the 1970s, understood the significance of Pope Francis's election. He will "leave the door ajar," he said, assuring his fans that Francis's rise to power represented more than just a "change of style."[31] Dissenting sister Jeannine Gramick has written that the renegades from the Vatican II era have reappeared and now tell her, "My hope is in Pope Francis and what he is doing for the entire church."[32]

The liberal media cast the election of Pope Francis as a chance for a hidebound institution to move into the "future." But his election had less to do with the future than the past. It represented the Catholic left's victory in a theological civil war that had been raging for more than a century. As Cardinal Kasper said after Pope Francis's election, speaking for the modernists who had bided their time until his pontificate, "[we] now have the wind at our backs."[33]

# CHAPTER FOUR

# The Liberal Jesuit from Latin America

Jorge Bergoglio is the first pope to come from the Jesuit order. That is one of the keys to understanding his liberal papacy and the cachet that he enjoys in the eyes of global socialists. As a liberal Jesuit from Latin America, he is seen by the left as the quintessential "progressive" priest.

Once a bastion of orthodoxy and discipline, the Jesuits fell under the influence of socialism and modernism in the twentieth century. By the time Bergoglio entered it, the order was rapidly moving to the left, both politically and theologically. "I was very, very undisciplined," Pope Francis has said.[1] In another era, that quality might have disqualified him from the Jesuits. In the 1960s, it made him a natural fit.

Bergoglio was a protégé of Pedro Arrupe, the head of the Jesuits from 1965 to 1983, a period of unprecedented liberal ferment within the order. Arrupe had grown up in Basque Spain, like the founder of the Jesuits, St. Ignatius of Loyola. This led conservatives to joke in the 1970s about Arrupe's liberalism: "One Basque founded the Jesuits, another one is going to destroy them." But to liberals, he was a "refounder of the Society in the light of Vatican II."[2]

"I remember him when he prayed sitting on the ground in the Japanese style. For this he had the right attitude and made the right decisions," Pope Francis recalled.[3] Compared to St. Ignatius of Loyola, a strict disciplinarian, Arrupe was enormously permissive, allowing socialism, loose morals, and liturgical irregularities to spread throughout the order.

By the end of his tenure, the politics of the order had become so embarrassingly left-wing that Pope John Paul II decided to intervene personally in its internal affairs. He rejected Arrupe's chosen successor and sent his own personal delegate to lead the order until a more appropriate replacement for Arrupe was found. Explaining the unprecedented move, a Jesuit spokesman at the time acknowledged that Pope John Paul II "wants the Jesuits to be more religious and not get too involved in politics."[4]

The politically minded Bergoglio was an ideal candidate for the Arrupe-era Jesuits. He had grown up in Argentina, where he was exposed to and inspired by communist and left-wing political influences.

"It's true that I was, as my whole family, a practicing Catholic. But my mind was not only occupied with religious enquiries, for I also had political concerns, even though they didn't go beyond an intellectual level," he said. "I read *Nuestra Palabra y Propósitos* [Our Word and Resolutions] and was enchanted with all of the articles of one of its conspicuous members—a well-known figure of the world of culture—Leónidas Barletta, who helped me in my political formation." The publication to which he refers in this quote was put out by the Communist Party of Argentina, and Barletta was a communist filmmaker. (Bergoglio has also spoken fondly of a communist teacher from high school, who "questioned us about everything.")[5]

Bergoglio was more of a political activist than a Catholic intellectual. He started doctoral studies but didn't finish them. (As pope, he told a fellow Jesuit, "Studying fundamental theology is one of the most boring things on earth.")

Bergoglio became a Jesuit in 1969 and quickly rose to a coveted leadership position in the order under Arrupe. At the mere age of thirty-six, he was made the provincial superior of the Jesuits in Argentina. "That was crazy," Pope Francis has said.[6]

Arrupe had identified Bergoglio as a rising liberal star in the order. Like Arrupe, Bergoglio was imbued with the liberal zeitgeist after Vatican II and followed his lead in opposing armed Marxism but making allowances for its theoretical variants within the Latin American Church. In 1980, Arrupe produced a feeble letter titled "On Marxist Analysis," which blessed a measure of Marxism within the Jesuit order, provided that it made an attempt to shoehorn Christianity into its message.

"It seems to me that in our analysis of society, we can accept a certain number of methodological viewpoints which, to a greater or lesser extent, arise from Marxist analysis, so long as we do not attribute an exclusive character to them," Arrupe wrote. "For instance, an attention to economic factors, to property structures, to economic interests that motivate this or that group; or again, a sensitivity to the exploitation that victimizes entire classes, attention to the role of class struggle in history (at least, of many societies), attention to ideologies that can camouflage for vested interests and even for injustice."

Vatican officials were perplexed by the mixed message of Arrupe's letter and didn't care for his alarmism about anti-communism, which was evident in this passage from it: "Finally, we should also firmly oppose the efforts of anyone who wishes to take advantage of our reservations about Marxist analysis in order to condemn as Marxist or Communist, or at least to minimize esteem for, a commitment to justice and the cause of the poor, the defense of their rights against those who exploit them, the urging of legitimate claims."[7]

## Arrupe's Liberal Enforcer

"The Society has been moving Left ever since Arrupe," says a Jesuit interviewed for this book. "Arrupe liked to promote young liberals to be provincials. The more traditional Jesuits were pushed aside and the progressives were promoted."

In 1975, Arrupe summoned Jesuits worldwide to a meeting in Rome. The purpose of the event was to consolidate the Jesuit order's liberal direction after Vatican II. "At the 1975 General Congregation, a worldwide gathering of Jesuits, Fr. Arrupe managed to refashion the Society's identity so that it was dominated by social justice concerns," according to the *Catholic Herald*.[8]

Conservative Jesuits in Spain, upset by the direction of the order under Arrupe, had petitioned Pope Paul VI for relief from Arrupe's modernist rule. Arrupe needed someone to "quell" this rebellion, according to Pope Francis biographer Austen Ivereigh.[9] Arrupe turned to Bergoglio, who was the superior of one of the group's leaders, to play his liberal enforcer.

"On the eve of the general congregation, [the conservative Jesuits] had created a new network, Jesuitas in Fidelidad ('Jesuits in Fidelity'), which was lobbying against both the [general congregation] and Arrupe," writes Ivereigh. "In the run-up to GC32 the Jesuits in Fidelity were distributing the book in preparation for a planned protest. In the presence of two witnesses, Bergoglio ordered Puyadas [one of the group's leaders] under pain of obedience to leave Rome, which the Spaniard was forced to do in order to remain a Jesuit. Together with his old Maximo colleague and now Chilean provincial, Father Fernando Montes, Bergoglio then headed to Termini rail station, where they successfully persuaded other ultras arriving from Spain to return home."[10]

That Arrupe would enlist Bergoglio's help in marginalizing

conservatives within the order explodes the claim of some Catholic commentators at the beginning of his pontificate that he was an "old-school Jesuit." Bergoglio was very much of Arrupe's new school. As pope, Bergoglio has made a point of emphasizing that he was "never" a conservative and that he didn't care for traditional Jesuits who viewed St. Ignatius of Loyola's *Spiritual Exercises* in a way "that emphasizes asceticism, silence, and penance."[11]

The *New Yorker's* James Carroll quotes a senior Jesuit official, Fr. Joseph Daoust, as saying that the 1975 General Congregation was a watershed moment in Bergoglio's ideological formation:

> If Jorge Mario Bergoglio had a conversion moment, Daoust told me, it was probably at the 1974–75 Jesuit Congregation, the worldwide meeting in Rome of the society's leadership that was summoned by Superior General Pedro Arrupe, of Spain, a controversial liberalizing figure. Arrupe's priesthood had been defined by the experience of being in Hiroshima when the atom bomb fell, and as Superior he set a new course. Given what Bergoglio was facing in Buenos Aires, the gathering must have been tumultuous for him: his own positions were being challenged. The order embraced an unprecedented understanding of itself. "We can no longer pretend that the inequalities and injustices of our world must be borne as part of the inevitable order of things," the Congregation declared. To be a Jesuit today "is to engage, under the standard of the Cross, in the crucial struggle of our time: the struggle for faith and that struggle for justice which it includes." The Jesuits affirmed "belief in a God who is justice because he is love."
>
> Critics regarded the turn as a betrayal of transcendent values in favor of an overemphasis on the secular world.[12]

Bergoglio's tenure as a young provincial general was rocky and ended after only one term. Much has been made by pundits of his "exile" after it. Some have claimed that he fell out of favor, owing to resentment toward his supposed "conservative" objections to the left-wing drift of the order.

That is false, and Pope Francis has himself debunked the claim:

My style of government as a Jesuit at the beginning had many faults. That was a difficult time for the Society: an entire generation of Jesuits had disappeared. Because of this I found myself provincial when I was still very young. I was only 36 years old... I had to deal with difficult situations, and I made my decisions abruptly and by myself. Yes, but I must add one thing: when I entrust something to someone, I totally trust that person. He or she must make a really big mistake before I rebuke that person. But despite this, eventually people get tired of authoritarianism.

My authoritarian and quick manner of making decisions led me to have serious problems and to be accused of being ultra-conservative... But I have never been a right-winger. It was my authoritarian way of making decisions that created problems.[13]

In other words, the bad-mouthing of Bergoglio within the Jesuit order arose from essentially personal, not philosophical, resentments. Certain Jesuits disliked his high-handed manner. "Bergoglio was kind of a jerk," one Jesuit who served under him told the press.[14] Others saw him as an obnoxious busybody. Reuters recounted a telling story of his meddling at a Jesuit residence in Buenos Aires after he had been named auxiliary bishop of Buenos Aires:

He returned to the city, but instead of moving into a house at the archdiocese, went back into a Jesuit residence. There, colleagues from that period say, he began to meddle again. Once, when a friend of the order left them a gift of pastries, Bergoglio grabbed it and carried it to the kitchen, where maids and cooks could share the goodies.

"We didn't need a bishop to teach us how to share," recalls one Jesuit present, who requested anonymity because he does not want to offend the pope.

After a few months, some Jesuits began to ask when Bergoglio would leave. Eventually, says a senior Jesuit at that time, the order formally asked him to move.[15]

In the end, these resentments helped rather than hurt Bergoglio's ambitions, since Jesuits closely tied to their order are rarely promoted to bishop. As David Gibson of the Religion News Service wrote, "Paradoxically, his virtual estrangement from the Jesuits encouraged Cardinal Antonio Quarracino of Buenos Aires to appoint Bergoglio as an assistant bishop in 1992. 'Maybe a bad Jesuit can become a good bishop,' an Argentine Jesuit said at the time… The fact that he had been somewhat rejected, internally, by the Jesuits, if not for that he probably would not have become a bishop,' said Fr. Humberto Miguel Yanez, an Argentine Jesuit like Francis, who heads the moral theology department at the Gregorian University in Rome."[16]

According to Argentine criminal prosecutor Jack Tollers, a longtime observer of Bergoglio, conservative Latin American Jesuits viewed Bergoglio as an opportunist willing to work both sides of the political street when ecclesiastical advancement required it.

"In those days a group of us youngsters were very good friends with a local Jesuit priest very much known for his anti-progressive stance. In those days, most Catholics in this country leaned one way or the other," Tollers has said. "But I remember quite distinctly how this Jesuit told us that this Bergoglio fellow played quite another game, playing the progressive music most of the time, but now and again switching sides to the more conservative band if need be. This was when John Paul II had been recently elected and of course there was quite a lot of 'band switching' going on in those days. But Bergoglio did it in a somehow blatant manner that was the talk of those days, all of it underscored by a surprisingly successful career."[17]

The circumspect quality to Bergoglio's liberalism at the time, motivated by his need to navigate the pressures and opportunities of Church politics, explains his supportive but cautious approach to liberation theology. "As head of the Jesuits in Argentina and then as a bishop, Francis never joined in the attack on liberation theology— but he was never a forceful defender of it either," Harvard Divinity School professor Harvey Cox has written. "As a bishop, he claimed that he favored it, but not in an ideological way. When debates about the movement split both the church and the Jesuits, Francis tried to patch up the divisions. He has subsequently conceded that he often did it with a heavy hand, which he now regrets."[18]

In 2016, with the blessing of Pope Francis, the Jesuits made their general superior a Venezuelan, Fr. Arturo Sosa, whose communist sympathies have long been known. He has written about the "Marxist mediation of the Christian Faith," arguing that the Church should "understand the existence of Christians who simultaneously call themselves Marxists and commit themselves to the transformation of the capitalist society into a socialist society."[19]

## A Champion of the Spirit of Vatican II

Bergoglio is not only the first Jesuit pope in the history of the Church but also the first pope to have been ordained after Vatican II. That combination of influences forms another key to understanding his papacy and the left's warm reception of it. Like many priests educated at that time, Bergoglio viewed the pre–Vatican II Church as hopelessly unenlightened. He has said that his liberal grandmother weaned him off what he saw as the rigidity of the pre–Vatican II Church. During an interview in which he randomly declared that

Buddhists go to heaven, he lampooned the pre–Vatican II Church for its dim view of ecumenism:

> I remember my first experience of ecumenism: I was four or five years old and I was walking along with my grandmother who was holding my hand. On the other pavement there were two women from the Salvation Army wearing that hat which they no longer wear and the bow. 'Are those nuns, granny?' I asked. To which she replied: 'No, they are Protestants, but they are good!' That was the first time I heard someone speaking well of people who belonged to different religions. The Church's respect for other religions has grown a great deal, the Second Vatican Council spoke about respect for their values. There have been dark times in the history of the Church, we must not be ashamed to say so because we are also on a journey, this interreligiosity is a gift.[20]

As pope, Bergoglio's reliance on such caricatures of the pre–Vatican II Church has been constant. He shares none of the sympathy that his two immediate predecessors felt for the pre–Vatican II Church. He is keenly aware of his status as a son of Vatican II, saying, "I am the first Pope who didn't take part in the Council and the first who studied theology after the Council and, at that time, for us the great light was Paul VI." In a characteristic comment, he criticized the pre–Vatican II Church for taking too hard a line on suicide, whereas "I still respect the one who commits suicide; he is a person who could not overcome the contradictions in his life."[21]

He routinely subjects the Church to severe criticism, but exempts from his critical gaze the post–Vatican II Church, which he regards as an era of enlightenment beyond questioning:

> With the Council, the Church entered a new phase of her history. The Council Fathers strongly perceived, as a true breath

of the Holy Spirit, a need to talk about God to men and women of their time in a more accessible way. The walls which for too long had made the Church a kind of fortress were torn down and the time had come to proclaim the Gospel in a new way. It was a new phase of the same evangelization that had existed from the beginning. It was a fresh undertaking for all Christians to bear witness to their faith with greater enthusiasm and conviction. The Church sensed a responsibility to be a living sign of the Father's love in the world.[22]

In his interview with the Vatican-approved Jesuit publication *La Civiltà Cattolica*, Pope Francis made a plea for a politically correct Catholicism inspired by the spirit of Vatican II. Yet he seemed oblivious to the devastation that the embrace of a diluted and politicized Catholicism caused his own religious order. Even the liberal author Garry Wills, famous for his aggressive criticism of the Catholic Church's conservatism, has had to acknowledge that the Jesuit order's liberal experimentation after Vatican II backfired, causing it to spiral into a period of heterodoxy and decadence.

"Entering the Jesuits used to take one into a stable world; but that is far from the experience of recent times," Wills wrote in the *New York Review of Books*. "A thirty-five-year-old still studying theology says: 'My novice master left to marry, my formation director left for a relationship with another man, et cetera. One cannot help but get the sense that we of this generation of Jesuits may be the last of the Shakers.'"[23]

If future historians of this pontificate find themselves in an ironic Gibbonian mood, they will find it a revealing measure of the crisis in the modern Catholic Church that Bergoglio, the first Jesuit pope, emerged at the very moment the Jesuit order was at its most corrupt and chaotic. Flattering the liberalism of the Jesuit editors of *La Civiltà Cattolica*, Pope Francis scolded "small-minded" traditionalists for their "pastoral" incompetence, a laughable claim in light of his own order's disintegration.

"There is no going back," he has said. "Whoever goes back is mistaken."[24] Such confident talk would imply that his own order is moving forward briskly. It isn't. The Jesuits to whom he was speaking preside over pews that are largely empty and seminaries that look like ghost towns. To take just one measure of the Jesuit order's failure, the vast majority of graduates from Jesuit universities in the U.S. Congress vote for gay marriage and abortion rights.[25]

In the book *Passionate Uncertainty*, the sociologists Peter Mc-Donough and Eugene Bianchi, despite approving of the liberal direction of the Jesuit order, still conclude that its "soft-boiled" spirituality and embrace of radical left-wing politics hastened its crack-up. Limiting their study to American Jesuits, they noted that the number of Jesuits who quit the priesthood and abandoned the order after Vatican II outnumbered the ones who stayed. Far from energizing the order, the liberal spirit-of-Vatican-II approach, which Bergoglio as pope has sought to renew, wiped it out.[26]

The same holds true in the archdiocese of Buenos Aires. Under the self-consciously progressive and "pastoral" leadership of Jorge Bergoglio, the vocation rate didn't rise; it plunged. Pews didn't fill up; they emptied out, as many disaffected Catholics joined booming conservative Protestant sects. Shortly after Francis's papal election, Vatican correspondent John Allen, who is sympathetic to the pope's liberalism, traveled to Buenos Aires and reported that "vocations to the priesthood have been falling in Buenos Aires on [Bergoglio's] watch, despite the fact they're up in some other dioceses. Last year the archdiocese ordained just 12 new priests, as opposed to 40–50 per year when Bergoglio took over."[27]

As pope, Bergoglio has doubled down on the very liberalism that crippled his own order and archdiocese. The movements most strongly associated with the modern Jesuits and Latin American

Catholicism have largely defined his pontificate. "Who am I to judge?," the saying for which Francis is most famous, would never have come out of the mouth of a pre–Vatican II pope. But it is not surprising coming from a Jesuit like Francis, who swallowed the liberal interpretation of Vatican II whole, evident in his comment that Vatican II mandated a "re-reading of the Gospel in the perspective of contemporary culture."[28]

## Jesuitical Situation Ethics

The German philosopher Robert Spaemann sees in this pontificate a return to the situation ethics that Pope John Paul II rejected, "an influential movement...which can be found as early as the 17th century among the Jesuits."[29] The popularity of Jesuitical situation ethics diminished under Pope John Paul II and Pope Benedict XVI, as they battled the "culture of death" and the "dictatorship of relativism." But under the pontificate of Francis, it has been revived, even though the magisterium of the Church has repeatedly condemned it.

"Many of the things established in 'situation ethics' are contrary to the dictates of reason, of truth and of that which is reasonable, they display traces of relativism and modernism, and stray enormously from Catholic doctrine transmitted over the centuries," the Congregation for the Doctrine of the Faith declared in 1956. Pope Pius XII condemned situation ethics by name, saying that no "situation" justifies the suspension of moral norms rooted in the natural moral law.[30]

Jesuits educated around the time of Vatican II also fell hard for modern psychology, asking trendy therapists such as Carl Rogers to hold "encounter groups" for them and to teach them about "nondirective therapy."[31] That helps explain the distinctly therapeutic feel to many of the pope's musings. To anxious priests, he has given the advice, "Go to a doctor who will give you a pill for your nerves."[32] That would be unusual advice from most popes, but not this one.

He has never questioned the damaging liberal fashions within the Jesuit order, reserving his scorn instead for "bankrupt" Thomists and other traditionalists whom he deemed insufficiently progressive for failing to "understand how human beings understand themselves today."[33] In 2016, during a meeting with Jesuits in Poland, he encouraged confessors to go easier on penitents. "We need to truly understand this: in life not all is black on white or white on black," he said. "No! The shades of grey prevail in life. We must them teach to discern in this grey area."[34]

With its free-floating concepts of mercy and sin, Pope Francis's 2016 papal exhortation *Amoris Laetitia* reads like something Carl Rogers could have written. More than a few commentators have noted the Jesuitical casuistry of the document, with its slippery appeals to non-judgmentalism and its tributes to the primacy of conscience.

"Situation ethics is back," says Thomas Pauken, author of *The Thirty Years War*, in an interview for this book. "Francis was infected by the virus of 1960s liberalism."

*Amoris Laetitia* is "typical of a Jesuit," said Archbishop Bruno Forte, who helped Pope Francis draft it. Forte recounted how Francis told him that they needed to use ambiguity to loosen up the Church's prohibition on Communion for adulterers. According to Forte, Francis said to him: "If we speak explicitly about Communion for the divorced and remarried, you do not know what a terrible mess we will make. So we won't speak plainly, do it in a way that the premises are there, then I will draw out the conclusions."[35]

Were a conservative pope to operate in this Machiavellian manner, the liberal media would object. But it approves of Pope Francis's Jesuitical methods. The leftist filmmaker Michael Moore has praised him for his devious patience ("he bided his time") and his "long game."[36]

"Francis would like to liberalize church doctrine on marriage, the family, and homosexuality, but he knows that he lacks the support and institutional power to do it. So he's decided on a course of stealth reform that involves sowing seeds of future doctrinal change by undermining the enforcement of doctrine today," writes Damon Linker of the *Week*. "The hope would be that a generation or two from now, the gap between official doctrine and the behavior that's informally accepted in Catholic parishes across the world would grow so vast that a global grassroots movement in favor of liberalizing change would rise up at long last to sweep aside the old, musty, already-ignored rules."[37]

As archbishop of Buenos Aires, Bergoglio was often criticized for his Jesuitical opaqueness at the service of modernist incrementalism. Argentinian journalist Elisabetta Piqué has reported that Vatican officials under Pope John Paul II and Pope Benedict XVI saw Bergoglio as "not being orthodox enough" and didn't trust his recommendations for bishops.

"They would get his lists and drop the names he submitted. Adriano Bernardini, the papal nuncio under Benedict XVI, did 'not like Bergoglio at all,'" she wrote. "Bergoglio [was] accused of not defending doctrine, of making pastoral gestures that are too daring, and of not arguing publicly and with greater determination with the Argentine government of the time."[38]

As archbishop, Bergoglio surrounded himself with liberal advisers, one of whom was Victor Manuel Fernández, a theology professor at the Catholic university in Buenos Aires. Fernández was famous for his flakiness, writing such books as *Heal Me with Your Mouth: The Art of Kissing*. A defender of situation ethics, Fernández criticized Pope John Paul II for his opposition to relativism's denial of intrinsically evil acts. Consequently, according to Vatican correspondent Sandro Magister, "the congregation for Catholic education blocked the candidacy of Fernández as rector of the Universidad Católica Argentina, only to have to give in later, in 2009, to then-archbishop of Buenos Aires Jorge Mario Bergoglio, who fought tooth and nail to clear the way for the promotion of his protege." Fernández now serves Pope Francis as a ghostwriter. Magister has found striking parallels between passages in *Amoris Laetitia* and Fernández's writings.[39]

Fernández's friendship with Pope Francis has contributed to the chaos at the Vatican. Fernández made news by attacking the head of the Congregation of the Doctrine of the Faith, Cardinal Gerhard Müller. Fernández belittled Müller's role as a guardian watchdog, saying, "I've read that some people say the Roman Curia is an essential part of the Church's mission, or that a Vatican prefect is the sure compass that prevents the Church from falling into 'light' thought; or that this prefect ensures the unity of the faith and guarantees a serious theology for the pope." In fact, claimed Fernández, "The Roman Curia is not an essential structure. The pope could even go and live away from Rome, have a dicastery in Rome and another one in Bogot[á], and perhaps link-up by teleconference with liturgical experts that live in Germany."

Angered by this comment, Müller shot back that Fernández had drifted into heresy. Fernández is "fundamentally wrong and even heretical," said Müller. "In this matter, one only has to once read the Dogmatic Constitution *Lumen Gentium* of the Second Vatican Council in order to recognize the ecclesiological absurdity of such thought games. The residence of the pope is the Church of St. Peter in Rome."[40]

## A Lax Archbishop

The same odd silences on controversial moral issues that have characterized his pontificate also defined his tenure as archbishop of Buenos Aires. Pro-family activists complained that Bergoglio wouldn't lift a finger to help them protest the cultural relativism of the Argentinian legislature. In fact, according to Piqué, he would discourage them from holding protests. "Bergoglio shock[ed] Rome on the pastoral level by his intolerance of the obsessive strictures of some clergy on the subject of sexual ethics," she reported. "In 2010, in the midst of the episcopate's battle to stop the passing of the law on same-sex marriage in Argentina, the idea for a prayer vigil is announced. Esteban Pittaro, who works for internal communications at Austral University (of Opus Dei), sends an e-mail to the archbishop of Buenos Aires, informing them of the idea." Bergoglio told Pittaro not to hold it.

Bergoglio preferred to play the prototypical "cool" priest of the post–Vatican II era and the liberal Jesuit order. He didn't like formal titles and musty traditions (he once referred to them as a "dictatorship of the church"), would try to impress the worldly with stories about his past as a "bouncer," and would chuckle at the mischief of others. According to his sister, Bergoglio "taught swear words" to her son, which resulted in the boy swearing during one of his sermons at an "important mass." "After Mass, Jorge came to us and could not stop laughing," she said.[41]

Above all, he sought to cultivate an image of humility. To this day, priests chuckle at the lengths to which he would go to foster that image. For example, he famously didn't own a car, preferring to travel by subway. But one priest interviewed for this book said that Bergoglio would occasionally get rides from people, then ask them to "drop him off a block or two from his home so that he could be seen walking to it." "He is a little bit of schemer," said the priest. "There was an ostentatious quality to his humility."

"Father Jorge," recalled Argentinian Catholics, was also happy to be seen presiding over "tango" and "Pinocchio" masses. He had a decidedly casual approach to Church discipline. "On communion for the divorced and remarried, it is already known how the pope thinks. As archbishop of Buenos Aires, he authorized the 'curas villeros,' the priests sent to the peripheries, to give communion to all, although four fifths of the couples were not even married," reported Sandro Magister.[42]

"He explicitly permitted a homosexual couple to adopt a child. He kept in touch with priests who were expelled from the official church because they had gotten married," said the liberation theologian Leonardo Boff.[43]

Advocates for abused children within the Church saw Bergoglio as similar to other bishops in his laxity and negligence. Bishop Accountability.org has done a study of his record as archbishop of Buenos Aires and found it to be dismal:

> Jorge Mario Bergoglio was archbishop of Buenos Aires from 1998 to 2013 and president of the Argentine bishops' conference from 2005 to 2011. During these years, as church officials in the US and Europe began addressing the catastrophe of child sexual abuse by clergy—and even as Popes John Paul II and Benedict made public statements—Bergoglio stayed silent about the crisis in Argentina.
>
> He released no documents, no names of accused priests, no tallies of accused priests, no policy for handling abuse, not even an apology to victims.
>
> In his many homilies and statements (archived on the Buenos Aires archdiocesan website), he attacked government corruption, wealth inequities, and human sex trafficking, but he said nothing about sexual violence by priests.
>
> In *On Heaven and Earth* (first published in Spanish in 2010), a wide-ranging collection of conversations with Argentine rabbi Abraham Skorka, he suggested in fact that the problem did not exist in his archdiocese: "In my diocese it never happened to me, but a bishop called me once by phone to ask me what to do in a situation like this and I told him to take away the priest's faculties, not to permit him to exercise his priestly ministry again, and to initiate a canonical trial."

Bergoglio's implication, that he handled no abusive priests, is implausible. Buenos Aires is Argentina's largest diocese, and Bergoglio was one of its top executives from 1992 to 2013—a period when tens of thousands of victims worldwide reported their abuse to the Church. Based on data disclosed in dioceses in the US and Europe, we estimate conservatively that from 1950 to 2013, more than 100 Buenos Aires archdiocesan priests offended against children and that dozens of them were known to archdiocesan supervisors, including Bergoglio.[44]

Since assuming the papacy, Bergoglio has made numerous statements about sexual abuse, but he continues to show a blind spot on the issue, as Vatican correspondent John Allen has reported:

Pope Francis' response to the sexual abuse mess in the Church has come under mounting fire. Though the merits of any particular item in the bill of indictment may be debated, the overall effect has been to seed doubt as to whether the fight against child abuse is truly a priority for the pontiff.

To begin with, Francis continues to draw criticism for his 2015 appointment of Bishop Juan de la Cruz Barros Madrid to the diocese of Osorno, Chile, despite his reputation as an apologist for that country's most notorious abuser priest, Fernando Karadima.

The one-year anniversary of Barros' installation was marked on March 21, and one of Karadima's victims, Juan Carlos Cruz, publicly complained that "the Church does not listen to the people" and added that Pope Francis "is a sadness because he doesn't care what has happened in Osorno."

Adding insult to injury, Francis was captured on an iPhone video last year telling a Chilean Catholic that opposition to the Barros was being whipped up by "leftists" guilty of "foolishness."

On another front, one of the two survivors named to the Pontifical Commission for the Protection of Minors, Peter Saunders of the U.K., was recently given an involuntary leave of absence by other commission members because of his outspoken criticism of Pope Francis, including on the Barros dispute.[45]

The only group of Catholics whom Archbishop Bergoglio treated severely were conservative Catholics, whose interest in the traditional Latin Mass he blocked. "He has persecuted every single priest who made an effort to wear a cassock, preach with firmness, or that was simply interested in *Summorum Pontificum* [Pope Benedict's authorization for wider use of the traditional Latin Mass]," Argentine journalist Marcelo González has written.[46] Bergoglio referred to conservative religious orders as "restorationist factions" and decried their "rigid religiosity."

To many observers of Bergoglio's time as both a provincial within the Jesuit order and archbishop of Buenos Aires, his elevation to the papacy was mystifying. Pope Francis biographer Paul Vallely has quoted "senior Jesuits" in *Pope Francis: Untying the Knots* who feared a Bergoglio papacy:

I was really shocked when I began to contact the people I knew in the Jesuits to say, "Who is this man, Bergoglio?" And one of them passed on to me an email, which he'd had a few days before the election, and it was from a very senior priest who was the current leader of the Jesuits in another Latin American country, serving provincial, and he wrote this:

Yes, I know Bergoglio. He's a person who's caused a lot of problems in the society and is highly controversial in his own country. In addition to being accused of having allowed the arrest of the two Jesuits during the time of the dictatorship, as provincial, he generated divided loyalties. Some groups almost worshipped him, while others would have nothing to do with him, and he would hardly speak to them. It was an absurd situation. He's well-trained and very capable, but he's surrounded by this personality cult, which is extremely divisive. It will be a catastrophe for the Church to have someone like him in the Apostolic see. He left the Society of Jesus in Argentina in ruins, with Jesuits divided, institutions destroyed, and financially broken. We have spent two decades trying to fix the chaos this man left us.

"This was an extraordinary thing to read, and it wasn't a lone voice," Vallely said. "Three other very senior Jesuits told me similar things."[47]

But Bergoglio's dubious résumé didn't give others in the liberal media any pause. They overlooked his failures as a provincial and archbishop and looked forward to the "mess" that he promised to create in the Church. Their skepticism gave way to gratitude. They had at long last found a pope to their ideological liking—a liberal Jesuit from Latin America for whom the "spirit" of Vatican II served as his primary compass.

# CHAPTER FIVE

# The Unholy Alliance

The election of a liberal Jesuit to the papacy thrilled Democrats in the United States, whose unholy alliance with the Catholic left goes back many decades. Barack Obama, one of the pope's most prominent supporters, has long been a beneficiary of that alliance. The faculty at Jesuit Georgetown University in Washington, DC, ranked as one of the top donors to his campaign.[1]

In a grim irony, Obama, whose presidency substantially eroded religious freedom in America, rose to power not in spite of the Catholic Church but because of it. The archdiocese of Chicago helped bankroll his radicalism in the 1980s. As he recounts in his memoirs, he began his work as a community organizer in the rectory rooms of Holy Rosary parish on Chicago's South Side. The Alinskyite organization for which he worked—the Developing Communities Project—received tens of thousands of dollars from the Catholic Campaign for Human Development.

Obama was close to the late Chicago cardinal Joseph Bernardin. A proponent of the seamless garment movement within the Catholic Church in the 1980s, a movement that downplayed abortion and emphasized political liberalism, Bernardin was drawn to the socialism and relativism of the liberal elite. He was so gay-friendly that he requested that the Windy City Gay Chorus perform at his funeral.

He embodied Obama's conception of a "good" bishop, and one can see in his admixture of left-wing politics and relativistic nonjudgmental theology a foreshadowing of the rise of Pope Francis.

Cardinal Bernardin put pressure on his priests to work with Obama and even paid for Obama's plane fare out to a 1980 training session in Los Angeles organized by Saul Alinsky's Industrial Areas Foundation.[2] The conference was held at a Catholic college in Southern California, Mount St. Mary's, which has long been associated with Alinsky's group.

This alliance between the Catholic left and the Democratic left explains the honorary degree Obama received from the University of Notre Dame in 2009, even as he plotted to persecute the Church under Obamacare's contraceptive and abortifacient mandate. Notre Dame's former president, Fr. Theodore Hesburgh, who supported honoring Obama, had been close to Monsignor John Egan, the socialist who started the Catholic Campaign for Human Development and sat on Saul Alinsky's Industrial Areas Foundation board.

The unholy alliance also explains how the Democratic Party, despite its support for abortion and gay marriage, won a majority of the Catholic vote in Obama's two presidential elections. At the 2012 Democratic convention in Charlotte, nuns such as Sister Simone Campbell shared the stage with abortion activists from Planned Parenthood. A liberal dean of a Catholic university, Sister Marguerite Kloos, even got caught in an act of voter fraud that year, forging the signature of a deceased nun on a ballot.[3] As Thomas Pauken writes in *The Thirty Years War*, "the radicalization of elements of the Catholic clergy turned out to be one of Saul Alinsky's most significant accomplishments."

The election of Pope Francis was seen by Alinskyite activists as a dream come true. "I think that Pope Francis is quite an inspiring figure," Al Gore said at UC Berkeley in early 2015. The former vice president turned radical environmental activist called Pope Francis a "phenomenon" and laughed at his liberalism: "Is the pope

Catholic?" Gore said that he is so "inspiring to me" that "I could become a Catholic."[4]

Leftists frequently turn up at the Vatican, often invited by one of Pope Francis's closest advisers, the socialist Honduran cardinal Óscar Rodríguez Maradiaga. Before the pope's visit to the United States, a group of left-wing activists and officials from unions and organizations such as the Service Employees International Union (SEIU) and PICO National Network (an Alinskyite group founded by the liberal Jesuit father John Baumann) descended on the Vatican to confer with curial officials about the trip.[5] Around the same time, more than ninety members of the U.S. Congress sent Pope Francis a letter, urging him to focus upon politically liberal themes. The leader of this group was Rosa DeLauro, a Catholic who supports abortion rights.[6]

In 2016, it was revealed through disclosures by WikiLeaks that the billionaire socialist George Soros bankrolled much of this lobbying. He spent hundreds of thousands of dollars in an attempt to shape the pope's visit to the United States. According to the leaked documents, Soros's Open Society Foundations sought to create a "critical mass" of American bishops and lay Catholics supportive of the pope's priorities. The documents made special mention of Rodríguez, a champion of PICO, as a useful ally for ensuring that the pope's speeches in the United States pushed socialism.[7]

The hacked emails exposed the depth of the plotting:

Pope Francis' first visit to the United States in September will include a historic address to Congress, a speech at the United Nations, and a visit to Philadelphia for the "World Meeting of Families." In order to seize this moment, we (Open Society) will support PICO's organizing activities to engage the Pope on economic and racial justice issues, including using the influence of Cardinal Rodriguez, the Pope's senior advisor, and sending a delegation to visit the Vatican in the spring or summer to allow him to hear directly from low-income Catholics in America.

In the emails, the Soros operatives make it explicitly clear that they view Pope Francis as a propagandist for their causes:

At the end of the day, our visit affirmed an overall strategy: Pope Francis, as a leader of global stature, will challenge the "idolatry of the marketplace" in the U.S. and offer a clarion call to change the policies that promote exclusion and indifference to those most marginalized. We believe that this generational moment can launch extraordinary organizing that promotes moral choices and helps establish a moral compass. We believe that the papal visit, and the work we are collectively doing around it, can help many in our country move beyond the stale ideological conflicts that dominate our policy debates and embrace new opportunities to advance the common good.

After the meeting, they rejoiced at its success, informing John Podesta, the chairman of Hillary Clinton's campaign:

Our visits were dialogues. We conveyed our view that the Pope is a World leader of historical significance; that his message of exclusion, alarm over rising inequality and concern about globalized indifference is important for the U.S. to hear and see animated during his visit; and that we intend to amplify his remarks so that we have a more profound moral dialogue about policy choices through the election cycle of 2016. In our meetings with relevant officials, we strongly recommended that the Pope emphasize—in words and deeds—the need to confront racism and racial hierarchy in the US...

Conversations that were originally scheduled for thirty minutes stretched into two hour dialogues. As in our breakfast conversation with Cardinal Rodríguez, senior Vatican officials shared profound insights demonstrating an awareness of the moral, economic and political climate in America. We were encouraged to believe that the Pope will confront race through a moral frame.[8]

Further disclosures from WikiLeaks confirmed the plotting of Democratic officials to infiltrate the Catholic Church in order to "foment revolution" beneficial to their radical causes. In 2012, in the midst of Catholic backlash over Obama's contraceptive mandate, John Podesta received a note from Sandy Newman, president of Voices for Progress.

"There needs to be a Catholic Spring, in which Catholics themselves demand the end of a middle ages dictatorship and the beginning of a little democracy and respect for gender equality in the Catholic church," Newman wrote to Podesta. "I don't qualify to be involved and I have not thought at all about how one would 'plant the seeds of revolution,' or who would plant them." Podesta replied that the Democrats had set up Catholic front groups to plant those seeds: "We created Catholics in Alliance for the Common Good to organize for a moment like this. But I think it lacks the leadership to do so now. Likewise Catholics United. Like most Spring moments, I think this one will have to be bottom up."[9] Podesta was wrong. It would come from the top down, as the following year Francis rose to the papacy and began politicizing the Church in the exact manner that the progressives had envisioned. Indeed, Podesta would later encourage Hillary Clinton to enlist the pope's leftism in her campaign. In one hacked email, he advised that she send out a tweet to "thank him for pointing out that the people at the bottom will get clobbered the most by climate change."[10]

Podesta and his aides also discussed how they could exploit Pope Francis's support for Obama's Iran deal. Podesta was sent a report in which Christopher Hale of Catholics in Alliance for the Common Good proposes getting bishops and cardinals to lean on senators temporizing about the deal.

In another email, which underscores how the media and the Democrats teamed up to enlist Pope Francis in their politics, a liberal columnist, Brent Budowsky, counsels Podesta: "John, HRC should get ahead of the progressive curve before the pope's trip to the U.S. in September, which will be big deal for a week, saturation coverage, heavy progressive populist, impact after he leaves affecting the trajectory of the campaign. Here's my take, written more in news analysis style...Brent" In the attached column, Budowsky writes, "The visit of such a popular pope will almost certainly give a lift in principle to Democrats and liberals who cheer Francis and rededicate themselves to the values and visions he stands for."[11]

## Bernie Sanders Goes to the Vatican

Pope Francis has been influenced by *Pedagogy of the Oppressed*, a book that sought to spread Marxism among the peasants of Latin America. The Alinskyite left in America regards that book as a classic. The author of the book is the late Paulo Freire, and Pope Francis has made a point of visiting with Freire's widow. The meeting was set up by Cardinal Hummes, the Brazilian whom Francis credits with inspiring him to name himself after St. Francis. Pope Francis "considered the meeting with me because of the writings of Paulo, because of the importance of Paulo for the education of oppressed people, poor people, black people, for women, for minorities," Ana Freire said.[12]

The politicians in America most associated with the Alinskyite left, such as New York City's mayor Bill de Blasio, have bragged about the utility of Pope Francis to their causes.

After the Vatican invited him to speak at a conference in 2015 about environmentalism, de Blasio said: "This is a leader such as we haven't seen before, really. He is saying things so clearly and so powerfully all over the world that need to be said. He's moving people on an extraordinary level. And we have few truly international leaders in any sense. What he is doing is, he's creating an international voice of conscience that I can't think of any previous parallel for."[13]

"Maybe I have given the impression of being a little bit to the left," allowed Pope Francis in a 2015 understatement. It is more than just an impression for socialists like Bernie Sanders, Hillary Clinton's opponent in the 2016 Democratic primaries. In an interview with Vatican spokesman Fr. Thomas Rosica, which a Catholic television station in Canada aired in 2015, Sanders spoke about Pope Francis as a fellow socialist.

"Well, what it means to be a socialist, in the sense of what the pope is talking about, what I'm talking about, is to say that we have got to do our best and live our lives in a way that alleviates human suffering, that does not accelerate the disparities of income and wealth," Sanders said. It pleased Sanders to see Pope Francis inveigh against the "idolatry of money, and to say maybe that's not what human life should be about, and that is a very, very radical critique of the hyper-capitalist system, world system, that we're living in today."[14]

In April 2016, at the height of the Democratic primaries, Sanders accepted an invitation from the Holy See to lecture at the Vatican and meet Pope Francis. No other presidential candidate received an invitation. "We invited the candidate who cites the pope the most in his campaign, and that is Senator Bernie Sanders," said Bishop Marcelo Sánchez Sorondo, head of the Pontifical Academy of Social Sciences. The *New York Times* describes Sánchez Sorondo as an "Argentine who is close to the pope" and quotes him as saying that the concerns of Sanders are "very analogous to that of the pope."[15]

In an interview with the leftist Italian newspaper *La Repubblica* during his visit to Rome, Sanders praised the pope's socialist commitments: "Look, I believe that the reason for which I was invited to participate in this conference is that many of the issues which the pope tackles are similar to mine."

While in 2016 Francis's Vatican rolled out the red carpet for a socialist who famously honeymooned in the Soviet Union, it adopted a decidedly frosty tone toward Republicans. Pope Francis denounced the GOP's nominee, Donald Trump, for opposing open borders. Offending large numbers of religious conservatives who support the enforcement of just immigration laws, Pope Francis said that Trump is "not Christian" as he intends to build a "wall" between the United States and Mexico.[16]

George Soros has been pouring money into groups such as the aforementioned Catholics in Alliance for the Common Good to capitalize on the so-called Francis effect in U.S. politics. In 2016, that group, which was founded by an aide to Obama, put out a "Pope Francis Values Reflection Guide" to steer Catholics toward voting for Hillary Clinton. A coalition of Catholic front groups for the left disseminated the document, including the Columban Center for Advocacy and Outreach, Conference of Major Superiors of Men, Faith in Public Life: Catholic Program, Franciscan Action Network, Leadership Conference of Women Religious, National Advocacy Center of the Sisters of the Good Shepherd, Pax Christi USA, Pax Christi International, and Extended Justice Team of the Sisters of Mercy of the Americas.

The material in the guide isn't even remotely Catholic. It is simply a regurgitated version of the Democratic Party platform. In the section titled "Questions to Consider When Reading about or Listening to Candidates," the guide offers this guidance: "How does each candidate challenge anti-immigrant rhetoric?...How does each candidate respond to questions about the wealth gap in this country? What ideas does she or he have for addressing this?... How does each candidate talk about climate change? Does he or she have any policies for addressing this issue... What is each candidate's position on voter identification laws and other restrictions that suppress voting among people of color?... How is each candidate talking about our Muslim neighbors and refugees from the Middle East?"[17]

For such Soros-funded Catholic front groups, the pontificate of Francis has been a shot in the arm. They have used it to jump-start the politicization of Catholicism that had begun to fade under his predecessor's pontificate. Pope Benedict had urged priests to stay out of politics unless it touched upon "non-negotiable" moral positions of the Church. No one could imagine Soros-style liberals putting out a "Pope Benedict XVI Values Reflection Guide."

"As Catholics, we are called by our faith to engage in this election. Pope Francis says that 'a good Catholic meddles in politics, offering the best of one's self so that those who govern can govern well,'" they piously say in their voting guide. Never mind that the good Catholics whom they extol, such as Joe Biden and Nancy Pelosi, support positions diametrically opposed to centuries of Catholic teaching on abortion and the traditional family.

## Pope Francis Democrats

Indeed, it has now become chic for pro-abortion, pro–gay marriage Catholic officeholders to invoke Francis as an inspiration for their left-wing politics, including their cultural liberalism. He is "starting to sound like a nun," Pelosi has said. "He challenged us to rescue our planet from the climate crisis that threatens the future of our children."[18]

Joe Biden has long supported abortion rights and gay marriage in defiance of Church teaching. He has even officiated at gay weddings.

Yet he boasts of his cozy relationship with Pope Francis. He said that he knew Pope Francis "as well as anybody" and that they share a socialist interpretation of Catholicism.

"I was raised in a tradition called Catholic social doctrine," Biden has said. "It is that is legitimate to look out for yourself, but never at the expense of someone else. It is legitimate to do well, but never at the expense of not looking at what's behind you. We need to create a culture which, as Pope Francis reminds us, cannot just be based on the worship of money. We cannot accept a nation in which billionaires compete as to the size of their super-yachts..."[19]

Despite Biden's support for making scientific use of aborted embryos, he has been invited to speak at the Vatican on the subject of medicine.[20] Such invites have undercut the efforts of conservative Catholic bishops who chastise secularized Catholic politicians.

"According to published reports, Vice-President Joseph Biden, a Catholic, has joined Vatican officials in promoting health care for the poor, a noble idea to be sure," commented Rhode Island bishop Thomas Tobin. "But I wonder if the pro-abortion Biden wants to include abortion and contraception in that health care he wants to provide for the poor."[21]

In 2013, the *Chicago Tribune* pointed to the liberalized atmosphere under Pope Francis as one of the factors explaining the passage of gay marriage in Illinois. The relaxed attitude of Pope Francis had emboldened Catholic Democrats to support the legislation, the paper observed:

> Advocates soon received additional help from Pope Francis, who warned that the Catholic Church could lose its way by focusing too much on social stances, including opposition to homosexuality.
>
> "If a person is gay and seeks God and has good will, who am I to judge him?" Francis said in July.

The comments sparked a wave of soul-searching by several Catholic lawmakers who had battled to reconcile their religious beliefs with their sworn duty to represent their constituents who were increasingly supportive of gay rights even as Cardinal Francis George remained opposed.

"As a Catholic follower of Jesus and the pope, Pope Francis, I am clear that our Catholic religious doctrine has at its core love, compassion and justice for all people," said Rep. Linda Chapa LaVia, a Democrat from Aurora who voted for the bill after spending much of the summer undecided.

House Speaker Michael Madigan also cited the pope's comments in explaining his support for the measure.

"For those that just happen to be gay—living in a very harmonious, productive relationship but illegal—who am I to judge that they should be illegal?" the speaker said.[22]

Nancy Pelosi has taken to using Pope Francis as a foil against Republican opponents. Referring to a former GOP presidential candidate's opposition to gay marriage, she said that she didn't "think that Pope Francis would subscribe to what Marco Rubio just said."[23]

Jack Conway, Kentucky's attorney general, who supports gay marriage, hid behind Pope Francis's relativistic remarks too, saying, "Our new pope recently said on an airplane 'Who am I to judge.' The new pope has said a lot of things that Catholics like me really like. I have, as someone who grew up as a Catholic listened to some of the words of the new pope and found them inspirational."[24]

In 2016, Tim Kaine, a Catholic senator from Virginia, cited Pope Francis's support for contraceptive use in cases involving the Zika virus during a debate over the promotion of Planned Parenthood funding. Later that year, Hillary Clinton made Kaine her vice presidential running mate. Kaine is a poster boy for the close ties between the Church and the Democratic Party. Educated by Jesuits, Kaine supports abortion rights and gay marriage while passing off his economic leftism as "Catholic social justice." He calls Pope Francis his "hero."[25]

Like the pope, Kaine was influenced by Latin American liberation theology. Kaine has spoken of his respect for the late Marxist priest Fr. James Carney, to whom Kaine made a special visit in Central America in the 1980s during Carney's time as a chaplain to communist guerillas.[26] Hillary Clinton correctly assumed that the U.S. bishops would offer little criticism of her addition of a heterodox Catholic to her ticket or criticism of her campaign in general. Several of the Francis-friendly bishops even ran interference for her. San Jose's bishop, Patrick McGrath, wrote a letter to his flock in which he said that Donald Trump's complaint of a rigged system "borders on the seditious."[27] Even after it came out that Clinton's aides had engaged in anti-Catholic bigotry (in exposed emails, they called conservative Catholics "severely backwards"), few bishops complained.

Just days before the presidential election, Pope Francis denounced politicians who speak about erecting "walls," prompting *Slate* and other publications to run such headlines as "It Sure Sounds Like Pope Francis Doesn't Think Americans Should Vote for Trump."[28] He made no similarly voluble criticism of Hillary Clinton's policies. Yet in the end the pope's influence proved hollow. The "people's pontiff" looked more like the liberal elite's pontiff as Clinton went down to defeat, with Trump even winning the Catholic vote fifty-two to forty-five. According to the Italian press, many of Pope Francis's aides viewed the election as a "bitter defeat."[29]

## Liberals Suddenly Wrap Themselves in the Papal Flag

When Pope Francis made his visit to the United States in 2015, he made no direct mention of the Obama administration's assault on

Christianity or questioned the legion of pro-abortion Catholic politicians like Tim Kaine who have aided and abetted it.

In 2016, all of the Democratic presidential candidates wrapped themselves in the papal flag. Normally, they argue for the "separation of church and state" and warn against "priests in politics." But they desperately wanted Pope Francis to intervene in their politics. "Democrats certainly love Pope Francis," wrote the *Atlantic*'s Emma Green. On the eve of his 2015 visit to the United States, they lined up to praise him, she noted. Hillary Clinton took to the pages of the *National Catholic Reporter* to say, "I am deeply moved by Pope Francis's recent teachings on climate change." So too did former Maryland governor Martin O'Malley.[30]

(Later, Hillary Clinton, exploiting the confusion Pope Francis has caused in the Church, cited his liberal stances in her remarks at the Al Smith Dinner hosted by the archdiocese of New York City shortly before the election. She placed his politics next to hers, urging Catholics to "embrace his message," which she identified as "calls to reduce [economic] inequality, his warnings about climate change, his appeal that we build bridges, not walls.")

Bernie Sanders was impressed to hear Pope Francis quote the long-time Marxist Dorothy Day during his speech before Congress. "The name Dorothy Day has not been used in the United States Congress terribly often," Sanders said to the *Washington Post*. "She was a valiant fighter for workers, was very strong in her belief for social justice…This would be one of the very, very few times that somebody as radical as Dorothy Day was mentioned."[31]

Under Pope Francis, the movement to canonize Day has picked up speed, despite opposition from conservatives who draw attention to her defense of communist regimes. The *Huffington Post* calls her the perfect saint for the Francis era since she "fused socialist ideas with Catholic social teaching."[32]

The other Catholic figure to whom Pope Francis referred in his speech before the U.S. Congress was the Trappist monk Thomas

Merton, another controversial figure within the Church. In the 1960s, Merton had toyed with leaving the religious life after having an affair with a nurse and grew increasingly more radical in his politics.[33] "Merton was above all a man of prayer, a thinker who challenged the certitudes of his time and opened new horizons for souls and for the church. He was also a man of dialogue, a promoter of peace between peoples and religions," Pope Francis said in the address. In fact, Merton had become so leftist and lapsed from orthodox Catholic norms by the end of his life that the U.S. bishops dropped any mention of him from their 2006 *United States Catholic Catechism for Adults*.[34]

Sister Simone Campbell, whose Soros-funded Nuns on the Bus campaign epitomizes the cozy relationship between the Catholic left and the Democrats, has predicted that Pope Francis will push American politics to the left.

"In this, the first presidential election in the era of Pope Francis, attempts to control the 'Catholic vote' through issues of personal sexuality—often nothing more than a crass political calculation—will no longer work as well, if at all," she has written. "Instead, those who seek to divide our nation will find themselves up against a spiritual leader who has taken the teachings of our faith that have resided for many in the dusty tomes of Catholic scholarship and philosophy and made them breathing realities in our daily lives. In doing so, he has energized Catholics to embody the center of our faith—active concern for the common good and attention to the needs of those around us."[35]

Campbell hit the campaign trail again for Democrats in 2016. Nuns on the Bus, she said, would galvanize "Pope Francis voters" to support progressive candidates.

Under Pope Benedict XVI, Catholic Democrats faced growing criticism from Church officials for their stances in favor of abortion and gay marriage. That pressure has disappeared under Pope

Francis. When Notre Dame conferred an honorary degree upon Obama, almost a hundred bishops condemned that decision. When Notre Dame conferred one on Joe Biden, whose status as a Catholic makes his anti-Catholic stances even more egregious, only a handful of bishops criticized the decision. "The new Francis atmosphere had a lot to do with their silence," says a Church insider interviewed for this book.

Under Pope Benedict XVI, the Vatican told U.S. bishops to withhold Communion from Catholic politicians who defy magisterial teaching. Under Pope Francis, the Vatican now tells them to give it to them. A measure of this changed atmosphere is that the U.S. bishops no longer even debate the matter. "In a way, I like to think it's an issue that served us well in forcing us to do a serious examination of conscience about how we can best teach our people about their political responsibilities," New York City cardinal Timothy Dolan has said. "But by now that inflammatory issue is in the past. I don't hear too many bishops saying it's something that we need to debate nationally, or that we have to decide collegially. I think most bishops have said, 'We trust individual bishops in individual cases.' Most don't think it's something for which we have to go to the mat."[36]

## The Pope's Gift to the Democrats

Pope Francis's address before Congress lived up to the left's expectations. He made no explicit mention of Church teaching. He focused instead on many of the ideological priorities of the left.

As he entered Congress, Pope Francis embraced John Kerry, Obama's Catholic secretary of state, who has made the promotion of gay marriage a "priority" of the State Department. The pope's speech could have been written by Kerry himself. Pope Francis called for open borders, telling Americans not to be "fearful of foreigners." He called for the abolition of the death penalty and the end of the "arms trade." He spoke of governmental wealth redistribution and urged Congress to support climate change activism.

The address delighted the left while leaving the right cold. Progressives noted that the only example he gave of an attack on the sanctity of life was not abortion but the death penalty. After the speech, two leftists from the Institute for Policy Studies, a Marxist organization, gushed: "His clear call to end the death penalty was the only example he gave of protecting the sanctity of life: Even amid a raging congressional debate over Planned Parenthood, he never mentioned abortion."[37]

In a measure of the alienation that Catholic Republicans felt about the pope's visit, Congressman Paul Gosar chose not to attend the speech. "If the Pope stuck to standard Christian theology, I would be the first in line. If the Pope spoke out with moral authority against violent Islam, I would be there cheering him on. If the Pope urged the Western nations to rescue persecuted Christians in the Middle East, I would back him wholeheartedly. But when the Pope chooses to act and talk like a leftist politician, then he can expect to be treated like one," Gosar explained.[38]

Conservatives noticed how little religion figured into his visit. "During his remarks, which were regularly interrupted by rounds of applause from the assembled lawmakers, Pope Francis condemned the death penalty, called for better environmental stewardship, and even talked about the ills of political polarization. He did not, however, mention Jesus Christ, whose life, death, and resurrection form the very foundation of the Christian faith," commented the *Federalist* in an editorial.[39]

In his talk at the White House, he also omitted any mention of Jesus Christ. He did, however, find time to endorse Obama's climate change proposals. Obama invited to that White House event a who's who of dissident Catholics and progressive Protestants, from radical nuns to gay Anglican bishops to transgender activists. This upset conservative Catholics, but not Pope Francis.

One of his press aides, Fr. Thomas Rosica, scolded an unnamed Vatican official, quoted in the *Wall Street Journal*, for criticizing Obama's guest list: "If some Vatican officials unnamed have expressed concern, that's their issue and they should come forward and give their name." Obama's press secretary, Josh Earnest, responded to critics by pointing out that Francis's Vatican didn't care about the guest list: "I would point you to the wide variety of comments we've seen from senior Vatican officials, including from Father Rosica over the weekend."[40]

Pope Francis's speech to the United Nations during the trip to the United States also avoided any mention of unfashionable Church teachings. The speech was a sustained tribute to the political program of the left, presented in platitudinous language and laced with dubious generalizations.

"A selfish and boundless thirst for power and material prosperity leads both to the misuse of available natural resources and to the exclusion of the weak and the disadvantaged," he said. He endorsed the Iranian nuclear deal, touted trendy global-warming claims, pushed the cause of debt forgiveness, denounced weapon manufacturers, and lavished praise upon UN diplomats. That they routinely advance proposals at odds with Church teaching went unmentioned. The speech had no distinctively Catholic content to it at all.

It is clear that Francis's Vatican has few friends to the right and almost no enemies to the left. He has entrusted the Pontifical Academy of Social Sciences to Margaret Archer, a British sociologist who has written that she identifies with the "Marxian left," reports Michael Hichborn of the Lepanto Institute. She was made president in 2014. Hichborn reports that other members of the Pontifical Academy of Social Sciences include Joseph Stiglitz, who is "chairman of

the Socialist International Commission on Global Finance Issues"
and "Partha Sarathi Dasgupta, a major proponent of contraception
and population control."[41]

The chancellor of the Pontifical Academies of Sciences and
Social Sciences, Archbishop Marcelo Sánchez Sorondo, is given
to intemperate attacks on critics of climate change activism. To a
pro-lifer who questioned why his academy has hosted proponents
of abortion and population control, he offered the rawly polemical
reply: "The Tea Party and all those whose income derives from oil
have criticized us, but not my superiors, who instead authorized me,
and several of them participated."[42]

## The Cupich Appointment

Pope Francis's first major appointment in America was Blase
Cupich, whom he sent to the archdiocese of Chicago. The appointment spoke volumes about Pope Francis's desire for a politicized
Church. Cupich is as, or even more, liberal as Joseph Bernardin, the
late cardinal of Chicago, and he has used his status as one of Francis's prized prelates to push political liberalism unapologetically.
"Pope Francis doesn't want cultural warriors," said Cupich, explaining his appointment.[43]

Cupich sounds more like a spokesman for the Democratic Party
than for the Catholic Church. He is notorious for downplaying the
issue of abortion, for prioritizing the wish list of the progressive left,
and for his loud ecumenical gestures, such as holding "Catholic-
Muslim Iftar" dinners. After undercover videos of grisly activities at
Planned Parenthood appeared in 2016, Cupich lectured pro-lifers
on the importance of other "issues": "we should be no less appalled
by the indifference toward the thousands of people who die daily
for lack of decent medical care; who are denied rights by a broken
immigration system and by racism; who suffer in hunger, joblessness

and want; who pay the price of violence in gun-saturated neighbor-hoods; or who are executed by the state in the name of justice."[44]

Cupich frequently bashes the free market, touts extreme environ-mentalism, and soft-pedals the Church's teachings at odds with a relativistic culture. At the Synod on the Family, he told members of the press that he had distributed to every priest of the archdio-cese of Chicago Cardinal Kasper's proposal to grant Communion to adulterers. Defending the logic of situation ethics, Cupich said that conscience is more important to him than Church teaching: "The conscience is inviolable. And we have to respect that when they make decisions and I've always done that."[45] Democrats have also cheered him for his policy of giving Communion to Catholic politicians who support abortion and gay marriage.

While he respects the consciences of the heterodox, he has con-siderably less respect for the consciences of conservative Catholics. He has browbeaten them for not accepting his liberal interpretation of Vatican II, pouting that "eventually" they will have to accept it. The archdiocese of Chicago under his leadership has become an engine of left-wing activism, with church officials serving as advo-cates for amnesty and gun control. A report on CBS called him "America's Pope Francis" and he lived up to the billing by telling the liberal interviewer what she wanted to hear, that homosexuals can be "good parents."[46]

Cupich has teamed up with Illinois senator Dick Durbin, a pro-abortion Catholic Democrat, to push amnesty. They appeared together in 2015 at an event at which Cupich described opposition to amnesty as racism and Durbin purred about the political benefits of adding millions of new voters to the Democratic ledger.[47]

Cupich is also thick with Chicago's Democratic labor movement. Speaking before the Chicago Federation of Labor, he denounced "right to work" laws. The speech was so tendentiously liberal Hil-lary Clinton could have given it. Making no distinction between his personal politics and Church teaching, he said, "In view of present day attempts to enact so-called right-to-work laws, the church is duty bound to challenge such efforts by raising questions based on longstanding principles. We have to ask, 'Do these measures undermine the capacity of unions to organize, to represent workers and to negotiate contracts? Do such laws protect the weak and vulnerable? Do they promote the dignity of work and the rights of workers? Do they promote a more just society and a more fair economy? Do they advance the common good?'" he said. Above all, he wanted to assure the union activists that "Pope Francis is with you."[48]

That Pope Francis gave one of the most important archdioceses in America to Cupich contained unmistakable meaning for U.S. Democrats. Pope Francis had been advised by conservative Vatican officials not to select Cupich, but he brushed off that advice. Cupich represented for Francis the prototypical bishop: a left-wing political activist who energizes the Church's critics while leaving conservative Catholics out in the cold. In 2016, Pope Francis augmented Cupich's power by adding him to the Congregation for Bishops, which makes him, along with the liberal Cardinal Wuerl, the chief bishop-maker for the United States.[49] Not long thereafter, Pope Francis elevated Cupich to the rank of cardinal.[50] Another revealing appointment cheered by Democrats was Pope Francis's selection of Robert McElroy for the diocese of San Diego, California, in 2014. McElroy is a protégé of the former archbishop John Quinn. McElroy served under Quinn in San Francisco. The liberal Catholic press hailed the McElroy appointment as "the latest sign that Pope Francis intends to make his mark on the Church in America."[51] McElroy has since made headlines by supporting gay rights and sacramental laxity. He has called the catechism's description of homosexual acts as disordered "very destructive" and urged his priests to give Communion to people living in a state of sin. On political matters, he has sounded predictable themes, such as that all parishes in San Diego should install solar-powered systems to counteract global warming and Catholics should support "pathways to citizenship" for illegal immigrants.[52]

"Through his activism, Francis has significantly raised the Church's profile on issues with which it wasn't previously associated in American politics—issues chiefly championed by Democrats," commented the *Atlantic*. "Francis is not an American politician, but his perspective on the state's role in these issues lines up pretty well with that of most American Democrats."[53]

Under the lead of Pope Francis, liberal bishops aren't even bothering to conceal their support for the policies of the left, even on the most neuralgic cultural matters. Retired Washington, DC, cardinal Theodore McCarrick has endorsed gay civil unions, which has only elevated his standing under Francis. "McCarrick is one of a number of senior churchmen who were more or less put out to pasture during the eight-year pontificate of Pope Benedict XVI. But now Francis is pope, and prelates like Cardinal Walter Kasper (another old friend of McCarrick's) and McCarrick himself are back in the mix and busier than ever," writes David Gibson.[54] Indeed, Pope Francis made a McCarrick protégé, Bishop Kevin Farrell, the head of the newly formed Vatican department called the Discatery for the Laity, the Family, and Life in 2016, and later made him a cardinal.

Cardinal Timothy Dolan, asked about the pope's support for gay civil unions on NBC's *Meet the Press*, said Francis was telling Catholics that "we need to think about that and look into it and see the reasons that have driven" the public to accept them. In the wake of the gay-marriage movement's successes, Cardinal Kasper, speaking for many of the Francis-friendly bishops, said, "A democratic state has the duty to respect the will of the people; and it seems clear that, if the majority of the people wants such homosexual unions, the state has a duty to recognize such rights."[55] Pope Francis has called on the bishops to incorporate leftist groups into their chanceries in the form of "social justice" offices. Addressing socialists at a meeting of "popular movements" in 2015, he reassured them that the bishops stand ready to help them: "I am pleased to see the Church opening her doors to all of you, embracing you, accompanying you, and establishing in each diocese, in every justice and peace commission, a genuine, ongoing, and serious cooperation with popular movements. I ask everyone, bishops, priests, and laity, as well as the social organizations of the urban and rural peripheries, to deepen this encounter."

"The Left has its pope," wrote the Stanford economist Thomas Sowell. "Pope Francis is part of a larger trend of the rise of the political left among Catholic intellectuals. He is, in a sense, the culmination of that trend."[56]

"I am not a Catholic nor even a Christian, and I know many American Protestants who, shall we say, were never deeply invested in the moral authority of the pope," writes Robert Tracinski at the *Federalist*, spelling out the stakes for non-Catholics if Pope Francis succeeds in liberalizing the Church. "So what does it matter to us whether or not this pope is surrendering the Church to the left? Historically, it does matter, because in the 20th century the Church helped change the course of history, vastly for the better, by offering ideological and material resistance to Communism. It mattered that there was a large institution with deep historical roots that was independent from the socialist state and politically correct orthodoxy, driven a different set of values. And it's discomforting to think what might happen if that's no longer true."[57]

The implications of this unholy alliance are serious for the world, but they are even more dire for Catholics. Under the left's gradual absorption of the Church, her freedom will continue to wither, as secularists subject the Church to coercive mandates. Owing to the alliance, the left has gained power at the expense of the Church without having to compromise on any of its anti-Catholic positions.

"To f—k your enemies, you must first seduce your allies," Saul Alinsky once bragged to *Playboy* about his political exploitation of the Church.[58] His disciples, such as the late Edward Chambers (a former Catholic seminarian), made it plain that they intended to hijack the Church for political gain: "The Industrial Areas Foundation has been in the field of organizing for nearly forty years. We believe that the best hope for change and social justice is the Church. The churches have the networks, the relationship of loyalty and trust, the money, the values and the untapped talent of the people."

Had Alinsky lived to see the papacy of Francis, he would have laughed at the ease with which his devious work has been advanced in the Church.

# CHAPTER SIX

# The First Radical Green Pope

The Vatican under the frenetic political activism of Pope Francis has become a nest of extreme environmentalists. Operating almost like an annex of Greenpeace and the Sierra Club, Francis's Vatican has held a series of conferences and events that promote the rawest and most aggressive theories of climate change. As the ultra-left *Nation* has pointed out, even the Democrats are "to the right" of Pope Francis on the issue of climate change.[1]

His predecessors kept a prudent distance from day-to-day politics, especially on issues wholly unrelated to faith and morals. But Pope Francis has plunged into them on all matters environmental. He sees himself as a lobbyist for the left's anti–fossil fuels agenda. In this role, he had no reservations about using his papal office to promote a climate change treaty at the UN's Paris conference in 2015.

"In a few days' time an important meeting on climate change will be held in Paris, where the international community as such will once again confront these issues. It would be sad, and I dare say even catastrophic, were particular interests to prevail over the common good and lead to manipulating information in order to protect their own plans and projects," he said.[2]

He mocked a previous UN conference on the environment for not adopting more extreme plans to combat climate change. "Let's hope that governments will be more courageous in Paris than they were in Lima," Pope Francis complained to reporters on his plane during a 2015 trip to the Philippines.[3]

In December 2015, Catholics didn't know whether to laugh or cry when the Vatican used the façade of St. Peter's Basilica as a movie screen for a propagandistic "climate change awareness" film—and did so on a holy day, no less.[4]

"Many enjoyed the spectacle, but equally many others found it highly inappropriate. What caused most of the consternation was that one of Christianity's most sacred and iconic buildings was used as the backdrop to climate change advocacy—a science that remains highly contested—on the Solemnity of the Immaculate Conception," reported Vatican correspondent Edward Pentin. "The event was part-sponsored by the World Bank, well known for its promotion of abortion and contraception."

Archbishop Rino Fisichella, a Vatican official, acknowledged that climate change activists had asked to use St. Peter's Basilica as a backdrop for the film in order to push the UN's climate change conference in Paris.

"The evening of December 8th will conclude in Saint Peter's Piazza with a meaningful and unique presentation entitled 'Fiat lux: Illuminating Our Common Home.' It will be a projection of photographs onto the façade and cupola of Saint Peter's, taken from a repertoire of some of the world's great photographers. These illuminations will present images inspired of mercy, of humanity, of the natural world, and of climate changes," Fisichella told the press.

"The show is sponsored by the World Bank Group (Connect4Climate), by Paul G. Allen's Vulcan Productions, by the Li Ka-shing Foundation and by Okeanos. This event, inspired by the most recent encyclical of Pope Francis, *Laudato si'*, is intended to present the beauty of creation, especially on the occasion of the Twenty-first United Nations Climate Change Conference (Cop 21), which began in Paris last Monday, November 30, and ends on December

11. The show will begin at 19:00. I can assure everyone that it is a unique event for its genre and for the fact that it is being displayed for the first time on such a significant backdrop."[5]

Never had the global left's use of the Vatican as a propaganda tool been more blatant. Once wary of the Vatican, environmentalists now rejoice openly at their unprecedented access to it and the bully pulpit that Pope Francis has offered them. Many of these environmentalists are anti-Catholic Marxists who support aggressive forms of population control.

Angering the faithful, Pope Francis consulted with the rabid environmentalist Hans Joachim Schellnhuber before writing his environmental encyclical *Laudato Si'*.[6] Despite pushing radical population control advocacy to "protect the Earth," Schellnhuber was appointed by Pope Francis to the Pontifical Academy of Sciences. Schellnhuber has said that if climate change goes unchecked, the "carrying capacity of the planet" will fall "below 1 billion." Among his many controversial positions is one that calls for a world government with an "Earth Constitution," a "Global Council," and a "Planetary Court." Schellnhuber was selected by Pope Francis to be one of four presenters at the press conference for the release of *Laudato Si'*.

The Canadian socialist activist Naomi Klein was also tapped by Pope Francis for advice. She said, "When I was first asked to speak at a Vatican press conference on Pope Francis's recently published climate-change encyclical, *Laudato Si'*, I was convinced that the invitation would soon be rescinded." But she discovered that Francis's Vatican agreed with her view that "climate change requires fundamental changes to our economic model."

Klein has marveled at how Pope Francis "is overturning centuries of theological interpretation," and she has bragged about all the radicals like her now happily ensconced within the walls of the Vatican. In the pages of the *New Yorker*, she described how fun it was to hang out at the Vatican with fellow radicals who had helped Pope Francis draft *Laudato Si'*:

My dinner companions have been some of biggest troublemak-
ers within the Church for years, the ones taking Christ's proto-
socialist teachings seriously. Patrick Carolan, the Washington,
D.C.-based executive director of the Franciscan Action Network, is one of them. Smiling broadly, he tells me that, at the
end of his life, Vladimir Lenin supposedly said that what the
Russian Revolution had really needed was not more Bolsheviks
but ten St. Francises of Assisi.

Now, all of a sudden, these outsiders share many of their
views with the most powerful Catholic in the world, the leader
of a flock of 1.2 billion people. Not only did this Pope surprise everyone by calling himself Francis, as no Pope ever had
before him, but he appears to be determined to revive the most
radical Franciscan teachings. Moema de Miranda, a powerful
Brazilian social leader, who was wearing a wooden Franciscan
cross, says that it feels "as if we are finally being heard."

For [Fr. Sean] McDonagh, the changes at the Vatican are
even more striking. "The last time I had a Papal audience was
1963," he tells me over *spaghetti vongole*. "I let three Popes go
by." And yet here he is, back in Rome, having helped draft the
most talked-about encyclical anyone can remember.[7]

Another radical leftist to whom Pope Francis turned for advice on
the environment is Jeffrey Sachs, one of the world's leading cheerleaders for abortion and government-run contraceptive programs.[8]
Sachs, an adviser to the United Nations, has written that killing
unborn children is a "lower-risk and lower-cost option" than population growth. The chancellor for the Pontifical Academy for Social
Sciences, Bishop Marcelo Sánchez Sorono, sits on the Leadership
Council of Sachs's Sustainable Development Solutions Network. In
2016, Sánchez Sorono invited Sachs to accompany Bernie Sanders
to the Vatican.[9]

The once-condemned liberation theologian Leonardo Boff has

said that Pope Francis turned to him for advice on how to redesign the United Nations to fight climate change. Boff said that the pope asked for his input in a unique way: "Indirectly, through the ambassador of Argentina to the Vatican, I was asked by the Pope to send him material about ecology. He said: 'Do not send it to the Vatican, because they will not deliver it to me. Send it to the ambassador who will place it in my hands. Otherwise they will make a sotto sedere, they will sit on it and forget to deliver it.'"[10]

Boff said that the pope "asked for a document that I helped to write, which would be a new configuration of the United Nations," in which he "elaborated a whole conception of a unified planet that distributes the few resources we have in a decent and egalitarian way."

Pope Francis also consulted with Timothy. Wirth, an undersecretary of state under President Bill Clinton who was famous for decorating his Christmas trees with condoms, and UN Secretary-General Ban Ki-Moon, an advocate for population control measures. "We've never seen a pope do anything like this," Wirth enthused. "No single individual has as much global sway as he does."[11]

The Vatican's red carpet was unfurled for officials of the Obama administration as well. Gina McCarthy, the head of Obama's Environmental Protection Agency, turned up in 2014 to tell Pope Francis that Obama appreciated his green activism.[12] "I think the pope knows his own beliefs," she said. "I want him to know that the president is aligned with him on these issues and that we are taking action in the United States."

Vatican officials gave McCarthy a tour of the Holy See's solar panels and environmentally conscious air filtration system in the Sistine Chapel. McCarthy made a revealing comment to the press during her visit about the propagandistic power of a green pope. He can depoliticize the issue for climate change activists, she said. "One of the challenges that I think we face in the U.S. is that climate change is very often viewed as a political issue," said McCarthy. "And environmental issues are not political. I think we need to get this out of the political arena and get it back to the arena we work most effectively on: What's right for our kids, for our families, for public health, and what solutions do we bring to the table that are going to address those?"

McCarthy was oblivious to the irony of Democrats calling for a pope to decide the debate, given the frequency with which they call for a "separation of church and state." Suddenly a close relationship between church and state didn't look so worrisome to liberals. "The faith community's voice is going to be very important here because EPA can talk about the science and reach only so far," she said. "We need to get this to the point where people are as comfortable talking about this as they are other international public health threats."

"Everybody is just looking for the pope to continue to make signals that this is an issue that is important to the Catholic Church and should be important to all of us," said McCarthy. She praised the Catholic Climate Covenant, which is a network of Catholic dioceses, organizations, and schools dedicated to climate change activism.[13]

Pope Francis also made time to meet with actor Leonardo DiCaprio, who gave Francis a book containing a painting that depicts "overpopulation" and other "excesses" on the planet.[14]

Pope Francis often describes himself as a "man of dialogue," but he took no interest in dialoging with global warming skeptics, such as Marc Morano of the Heartland Institute. When he appeared at a 2015 Vatican summit on climate change to ask a question, a security guard shut him down, saying, "You have to control yourself or you will be escorted out of here."[15]

"It wasn't a summit," says Morano in an interview for this book. "It was more like a rebranding party for the Church and the United Nations to merge on climate change. No dissent was going to be tolerated."

"It was a real culture shock," he recalls. "The pope was aligning himself with the most anti-Catholic radicals around, people who want to tear down the Church."

# The Eco-Encyclical

Francis's encyclical on the environment, the first ever written by a pope, was released in May 2015. Its section on climate change turned out to be as radical as conservatives feared. It uncritically drew upon the assumptions and doomsday rhetoric of the warmists.

"It was a cut-and-paste job from the documents of the United Nations," says the physicist Dr. Tom Sheahen in an interview for this book.

The pope made it clear that he was advancing a temporal political goal. He addressed the document to everybody "on the planet" and endorsed the specific climate change initiatives of the United Nations. The encyclical rests on the false premise that resistance to the claims of environmentalism are equivalent to mistreatment of God's creation. What the pope presents as a moral crisis is in fact nothing more than a political dispute. In the encyclical's most controversial sections, Pope Francis treats global warming theory as ironclad fact and gives his blessing to all of the "solutions" proposed by the environmental left to control the climate:

A very solid scientific consensus indicates that we are presently witnessing a disturbing warming of the climatic system. In recent decades this warming has been accompanied by a constant rise in the sea level and, it would appear, by an increase of extreme weather events, even if a scientifically determinable cause cannot be assigned to each particular phenomenon. Humanity is called to recognize the need for changes of lifestyle, production and consumption, in order to combat this warming or at least the human causes which produce or aggravate it.

The passages in the document touching on global warming read like a hybrid of Marx's *Das Kapital* and Al Gore's *Earth in the Balance*. "Climate change is a global problem with grave implications: environmental, social, economic, political and for the distribution of goods. It represents one of the principal challenges facing humanity in our day. Its worst impact will probably be felt by developing countries in coming decades," he wrote.

"Never have we so hurt and mistreated our common home as we have in the last two hundred years," he asserted, adopting a Malthusian tone. He said the earth was becoming an "immense pile of filth." He offered an absurdly one-sided treatment of technology, free markets, and consumerism, conveniently ignoring all of the evidence that those developments had alleviated poverty, improved health, and raised standards of living.

He endorsed a "true world political authority" to enforce "global regulatory norms," saying that "it is remarkable how weak international political responses have been." He called for the phasing out of fossil fuels: "We know that technology based on the use of highly polluting fossil fuels—especially coal, but also oil and, to a lesser degree, gas—needs to be progressively replaced without delay. Until greater progress is made in developing widely accessible sources of renewable energy, it is legitimate to choose the less harmful alternative or to find short-term solutions."

The document is riddled with half-truths and scattershot generalizations, many of which come from deep-seated prejudices against capitalism. He wrote, "The Christian tradition has never recognized the right to private property as absolute or inviolable, and has stressed the social purpose of all forms of private property. Saint John Paul II forcefully reaffirmed this teaching, stating that God gave the earth to the whole human race for the sustenance of all its members, without excluding or favouring anyone."

In fact, Pope John Paul II had defended the free market, saying "Christ does not condemn a simple possession of material goods. Rather, his most severe words are directed against those who use their riches in an egoistic manner, without preoccupying with their neighbor who lacks the indispensable."

No such balance appeared in *Laudato Si'*. Instead, perfectly reasonable human activity, such as turning on air-conditioning, is cast as overconsumption:

> People may well have a growing ecological sensitivity but it has not succeeded in changing their harmful habits of consumption which, rather than decreasing, appear to be growing all the more. A simple example is the increasing use and power of air-conditioning. The markets, which immediately benefit from sales, stimulate ever greater demand. An outsider looking at our world would be amazed at such behavior, which at times appears self-destructive.

Many found this a curious example of overconsumption, given that the lives of millions of people have been saved or improved by air-conditioning. The culture of "overconsumption" and "waste" against which the pope rails has contributed to longer and healthier lives for the poor.

Openly endorsing the anti-growth policies of the Left, Pope Francis cast economic decline in the West as a requirement of justice: "We know how unsustainable is the behavior of those who constantly consume and destroy, while others are not yet able to live in a way worthy of their human dignity. That is why the time has come to accept decreased growth in some parts of the world, in order to provide resources for other places to experience healthy growth."

Socialists found his searing critique of Western capitalism

exhilarating. To the Brazilian socialist sociologist Michael Löwy, no pope had ever denounced capitalism so directly. "For Pope Francis, ecological disasters and climate change are not merely the results of individual behavior, but rather the result of the current models of production and consumption," he said.[16]

The encyclical represented a departure from the pope's normally tolerant attitudes toward the "modern world." On disputed cultural matters, he approaches the modern world very gingerly. "The complaints of today about how 'barbaric' the world is—these complaints sometimes end up giving birth within the church to desires to establish order in the sense of pure conservation, as a defense. No: God is to be encountered in the world of today," he has said. That attitude vanishes in *Laudato Si'*, which amounts to a jeremiad against the modern world.

Addressing a subject on which he enjoys no expertise and that has no bearing on the salvation of souls, he sounded more like Noam Chomsky than St. Francis of Assisi. Adopting the grim faux-scientific tone of Marx, Pope Francis writes in the encyclical:

> Production is not always rational, and is usually tied to economic variables which assign to products a value that does not necessarily correspond to their real worth. This frequently leads to an overproduction of some commodities, with unnecessary impact on the environment and with negative results on regional economies.

No serious economist today gives any credence to such warmed-over Marxist claims. Pope Francis asserts that a free market, because it allows for income inequalities, is not only a threat to the environment but also a cause of war—a link that even the left-leaning *Economist* finds "ultra-radical." It perplexes the *Economist* that Pope Francis "consciously or unconsciously follows Vladimir Lenin in his diagnosis of capitalism and imperialism as the main reason why world war broke out a century ago."[17]

Pope Francis has admitted that his knowledge of economics is thin. "I don't understand it very well," he once said.[18] But that didn't stop him in the encyclical from offering highly specific economic prescriptions.

As a number of economists and political analysts noted, the encyclical, if followed, would hurt the very poor people its advice purports to help.

"Pope Francis—and I say this as a Catholic—is a complete disaster when it comes to his policy pronouncements. On the economy, and now on the environment, the pope has allied himself with the far left and has embraced an ideology that would make people poorer and less free," wrote the economist Stephen Moore. "The pope recently declared: 'The monopolizing of lands, deforestation, the appropriation of water, inadequate agro-toxics are some of the evils that tear man from the land of his birth. Climate change, the loss of biodiversity and deforestation are already showing their devastating effects in the great cataclysms we witness.' This is the language of the radical green movement that is at its core anti-Christian, anti-human being and anti-progress. He has aligned himself with a secular movement that is antithetical to the fundamental theological underpinning of Catholicism—the sanctity of human life and the value of all souls."[19]

"Pope Francis frames his argument in favor of a heavy-handed environmentalism around the idea that climate change hurts the poor the most. Yet he seems to have little notion of what has helped the world's poor more than anything: namely, the march of markets and technology, which has lifted billions out of destitution," wrote Steven Malanga. "As Michael Shellenberger, president of the Breakthrough Institute and co-author of *An Ecomodernist Manifesto*, observed: 'When [the] Pope speaks of 'irrational faith in human progress' I want him to visit the Congo to see what life is like when there is no progress.' "[20]

Cardinal Peter Turkson, the head of the Pontifical Council for Justice and Peace, has been credited with writing one of the encyclical's first drafts. Turkson is famous for his over-the-top pronouncements against capitalism. Among the other papers that have been issued by his pontifical council is one that calls for a "global public authority" to correct the "distortions of capitalist development."[21]

Pope Francis has made it clear that he agrees with Turkson's support for world government. "Interdependence obliges us to think of one world with a common plan," he writes in the encyclical. "It is essential to devise stronger and more efficiently organized international institutions, with functionaries who are appointed fairly by agreement among national governments, and empowered to impose sanctions."

In August 2016, the Vatican announced that Turkson would head up a new Vatican department dedicated to promoting environmentalism and other politically liberal projects described as "Integral Human Development." Pope Francis said that Turkson's dicastery would focus on "migrants, those in need, the sick, the excluded and marginalized, the imprisoned and the unemployed, as well as victims of armed conflict, natural disasters, and all forms of slavery and torture."[22]

## The Church of Jeffrey Sachs

In many dioceses, the Church has gone intensely green under Francis. Rosary groups have given way to recycling clubs, and priests are more likely to question Catholics for their "carbon footprint" than their abortions. It is now common to see "justice and peace" diocesan offices calling on Catholics to "go vegetarian," "take shorter showers," and "use both sides of paper." In March 2016, the governorate of the Vatican City State announced that it was going to "repurpose" the floral arrangements from the Easter Mass and announced that it would set up an "ecological island" at the Vatican to serve as a compost station for waste. To promote "climate change awareness" on March 19, Pope Francis ordered the cupola of St. Peter's Basilica and Bernini's colonnade to go dark for an hour and urged the faithful to turn off all nonessential lights.[23]

Eyeing the Church's enormous resources, environmentalists have convinced many Catholics organizations to divest from coal, oil, and gas companies and to go solar. In the Philippines, thousands of Catholics, led by their bishops, marched against fossil fuels. The 2016 event was organized by Greenpeace and other radical groups.[24]

The coordination between the environmental left and the Church has never been more obvious, with environmentalists putting out memes about the need for Catholic institutions to "free" themselves from fossil fuels. That such efforts will increase unemployment doesn't seem to disturb a pope who claims unemployment as one of his key issues. Nor does he feel any reservations about using the donations he has inherited from previous generations for an overtly political cause. Catholics have donated to the Church over the years on the assumption that that money would go to the promotion of the Catholic faith, not end up in an ideological slush fund directed by activists like Jeffrey Sachs.

The Vatican is now looking at making classes in "ecology" a requirement for all seminarians. Many seminaries across the world have already adopted such classes, in light of the pope's call that "seminaries and houses of formation will provide an education in responsible simplicity of life."

According to *La Stampa*, "Seven Catholic seminaries offer courses on faith and ecology." In the US, they are the Catholic Theological Union in Chicago; Catholic University of America: School of Theology and Religious Studies in Washington D.C.; Oblate School of Theology in San Antonio, Texas; Saint Paul Seminary School of Divinity at Saint Thomas University in St Paul, Minnesota, it reported. "The Pontifical universities in Rome that have introduced such courses include the Gregorian University, St. Anselmo and the Salesian Pontifical University."[25]

In September 2016, Pope Francis stunned Catholics by suggesting that environmentalism be added to the spiritual and corporal works of mercy. In a message on the "world day of prayer for the care of creation," he wrote:

> The Christian life involves the practice of the traditional seven corporal and seven spiritual works of mercy. "We usually think of the works of mercy individually and in relation to a specific initiative: hospitals for the sick, soup kitchens for the hungry, shelters for the homeless, schools for those to be educated, the confessional and spiritual direction for those needing counsel and forgiveness... But if we look at the works of mercy as a whole, we see that the object of mercy is human life itself and everything it embraces."
>
> Obviously "human life itself and everything it embraces" includes care for our common home. So let me propose a complement to the two traditional sets of seven: may the works of mercy also include care for our common home.
>
> As a spiritual work of mercy, care for our common home calls for a "grateful contemplation of God's world" (Laudato Si', 214) which "allows us to discover in each thing a teaching which God wishes to hand on to us" (ibid., 85). As a corporal work of mercy, care for our common home requires "simple daily gestures which break with the logic of violence, exploitation and selfishness" and "makes itself felt in every action that seeks to build a better world" (ibid., 230–231).

He also said that Catholics should go to confession if they fail to uphold the injunctions of environmentalism:

> After a serious examination of conscience and moved by sincere repentance, we can confess our sins against the Creator, against creation, and against our brothers and sisters. "The

Catechism of the Catholic Church presents the confessional as the place where the truth makes us free." We know that "God is greater than our sin," than all our sins, including those against the environment. We confess them because we are penitent and desire to change. The merciful grace of God received in the sacrament will help us to do so.

Examining our consciences, repentance and confession to our Father who is rich in mercy lead to a firm purpose of amendment. This in turn must translate into concrete ways of thinking and acting that are more respectful of creation. For example: "avoiding the use of plastic and paper, reducing water consumption, separating refuse, cooking only what can reasonably be consumed, showing care for other living beings, using public transport or car-pooling, planting trees, turning off unnecessary lights, or any number of other practices" (Laudato Si', 211). We must not think that these efforts are too small to improve our world. They "call forth a goodness which, albeit unseen, inevitably tends to spread" and encourage "a prophetic and contemplative lifestyle, one capable of deep enjoyment free of the obsession with consumption" (ibid., 212, 222).

After Donald Trump won the U.S. presidency, Cardinal Joseph Tobin called on the U.S. bishops to increase their climate change activism, "given the possibility that the administration isn't going to be very interested in the questions that Pope Francis is interested in."[26]

## Don't Breed "Like Rabbits"

Environmentalists often chafed under the rhetoric of Pope John Paul II, who decried the left's "culture of death," and Pope Benedict XVI, who described its politics as a "dictatorship of relativism." But

Pope Francis has avoided those phrases. Environmentalists have breathed easier knowing that any opposition from Francis's Vatican on contested moral issues will be minimal. At the beginning of the papacy, they cheered his comment that the Church is too "obsessed" with abortion and artificial birth control—stances that environmentalists regard as a major obstacle to their climate change agenda. In *Earth in the Balance*, Al Gore wrote that environmentalists support a "Global Marshall Plan" with "fertility management" at the core of the plan—fertility management being a euphemism for widespread abortions and ubiquitous government-regulated contraceptive use.[27]

Francis's predecessors unequivocally condemned the sexual revolution, but he has been far more elliptical on the subject. While he hasn't promoted the population control agenda of the Al Gores, he does allow himself heterodox musings from time to time that undercut the Church's opposition to it.

In early 2015, for example, Francis appalled conservative Catholics with large families, and delighted environmentalists who call for small families, when he told the press that Catholics shouldn't "be like rabbits."[28] "Good Catholics," he said, should practice "responsible parenthood." Catholic married couples who conscientiously follow the Church's prohibition on artificial birth control were aghast, and even liberal Catholics acknowledged that Pope Francis had adopted a startlingly novel line. "As a Catholic, it's kinda shocking to hear @Pontifiex say, 'Catholics must not breed like rabbits.' Really?" tweeted CNN anchor Carol Costello.[29]

Nor could conservative Catholics believe their ears when Pope Francis expanded on his remark by recalling the time he rebuked one of his parishioners—a mother who had had seven children by caesarean sections—for "tempting God." She was guilty of "irresponsibility," he said.[30]

Past popes quoted the scriptural admonition "Be fruitful and multiply," but Pope Francis has sent mixed signals on family size. In

recent decades, the size of families for many Catholics has shrunk—
a trend with which Pope Francis appears comfortable. Around the
time he was telling Catholic couples not to be like "rabbits," he
pointed to a finding of modern demographers: "I believe that three
children per family, from what the experts say, is the key number for
sustaining the population."[31]

The British Catholic organization Voice of the Family expressed
concern that *Laudato Si'* omitted any traditional defense of the
Church's teaching on artificial birth control. Voice of the Family
official Maria Madise noted that at a time when "contraception and
environmentalism so often go hand-in-hand" Pope Francis declined
to reaffirm "Church teaching on the primacy of procreation." The
organization has also expressed concern that Pope Francis's repre-
sentatives to the United Nations are consenting to the UN agenda in
favor of abortion and free contraception.

"There has been extensive collaboration between other Holy
See bodies and powerful proponents of abortion, contraception
and population control during the current pontificate, under the
guise of promoting sustainable development," according to the
group. It points in particular to a 2016 speech in which Monsignor
Jean-Marie Mupendawatu, secretary of the Pontifical Council for
Pastoral Assistance to Health Care Workers, endorsed the UN's sustainable development goals, even though one of them is "universal
access to sexual and reproductive health care services."[32]

In his post-synodal exhortation *Amoris Laetitia*, Pope Francis
makes passing mention of *Humanae Vitae* without quoting its direction condemnations of artificial birth control. He also belittles the
Church for its past teaching on marriage: "we often present marriage in such a way that its unitive meaning, its call to grow in love
and its ideal of mutual assistance are overshadowed by an almost
exclusive insistence on the duty of procreation."

Where his predecessors condemned artificial birth control in
all cases as an "intrinsically disordered" act, Pope Francis has said

that it is permissible under certain circumstances. On a flight back from Mexico in 2016, he approved of contraceptive use by women infected with the Zika virus.[33] In the course of his remarks, he falsely claimed that Pope Paul VI had approved of contraceptive use in the 1960s by missionaries in Africa who were in danger of rape. This falsehood was pointed out to Francis's press secretary, but he didn't bother to clarify the pope's remark. He just reiterated it: "So contraceptives or condoms, especially in cases of emergency and seriousness, may also be the subject of a serious conscience discernment. This is what the pope said."[34]

Once again, the situation ethics of the Church's first Jesuit pope confused the faithful and gratified the Church's critics, who gleefully observed that if contraceptive use is justified for Zika, then the pope must surely also condone it for the even deadlier AIDS virus.

## The Darwinist Pope

The first radical green pope is also impressing the environmental left with his support for Darwinism. Leading Darwinists have called mainstream evolutionary theory—which holds that species form as a result of random mutations and natural selection—the "greatest engine of atheism ever invented," insofar as it provides a creation story without a creator.[35] Understanding the atheistic implications of the theory, the Church has long viewed Darwinism with suspicion. But Pope Francis doesn't. In the contemporary clash between Darwinism and "intelligent design," Pope Francis sides with the Darwinists.

Pope Francis has lectured Catholics on the need to embrace a conception of God that comports with Darwinian theory. "Pope Francis: God is not 'a magician, with a magic wand,'" ran a headline in October 2014. Reporters noted that his deference to Darwinism represents a significant "rhetorical break" with his predecessors.[36]

"When we read about Creation in Genesis, we run the risk of imagining God was a magician, with a magic wand able to do everything. But that is not so," Pope Francis said in a speech before the Pontifical Academy of Sciences. "[God] created human beings and let them develop according to the internal laws that he gave to each one so they would reach their fulfillment. Evolution in nature is not inconsistent with the notion of creation, because evolution requires the creation of beings that evolve."

Pope Francis, from time to time, indicates that he doesn't share the Church's traditional understanding of Christ's miracles, a position explained by his exaggerated respect for the rationalism of modern science and his weakness for trendy currents within modern biblical scholarship. For example, Pope Francis has interpreted Christ's miracle of the loaves and fishes as nothing more than a metaphor. On multiple occasions, he has said that the "miracle" wasn't a physical event but a lesson of "sharing" that Christ had imparted to the crowd, which inspired them to take food out that they were hoarding and give it to those nearby. He has called it a "parable" and that it was "not magic or sorcery." In one homily he said, "Jesus managed to generate a current among his followers: they all went on sharing what was their own, turning it into a gift for the others; and that is how they all got to eat their fill. Incredibly, food was left over: they collected it in seven baskets."

That sermon, as one priest put it, "leaves us to draw the inescapable conclusion that, along with so many modern historical-critical biblical scholars, he has taken on board the well-known, century-old rationalistic 'demythologization' of this Gospel miracle. So we are left to wonder what other miracles of Jesus he may think require the same treatment."[37]

For Vatican officials these days, theistic Darwinism, even though it remains a contested theory, is treated like catastrophic man-made global warming—as unquestionably factual. (Pope Francis's chancellor of the Pontifical Academy of Sciences has ludicrously said that the pope's support for the global warming claims carries the same moral and magisterial weight as the Church's opposition to abortion.[38]) The number two official at the Congregation for the Doctrine of Faith, Archbishop Augustine Di Noia, said at a lecture in New York City in 2016 that "we can't ignore what evolutionary science is telling us." But Fr. Michael Chaberek, a Dominican and author of *Catholicism and Evolution: A History from Darwin to Pope Francis,* believes that Pope Francis and his aides are sowing "confusion" on the issue by treating Darwinism as a fact. He argues that this unwarranted deference to Darwinian science threatens to corrupt the Church's understanding of creation and the doctrine of Original Sin.

"Even in the seminaries and theological departments, the classic theological treatise 'On Creation' (De Deo Creante or De Creatione) has been replaced with the teaching about different science-faith models and vague speculations about 'God working entirely through secondary causes,'" he has said. "In Biblical scholarship the historical and literal meaning of Genesis (1–3) was abandoned, giving place to all kinds of reductive interpretations. But new science shows how little the Darwinian mechanism can actually accomplish."[39]

In *Laudato Si',* Pope Francis makes admiring mention of the Jesuit Pierre Teilhard de Chardin, a Darwinist who was disgraced by his association with Piltdown Man, an "early human discovery" that turned out to be a hoax. The writings of Teilhard were repeatedly censured by the Church. But Francis cites him as an impeccably orthodox source, writing in *Laudato Si'* of his "contribution" to the Church's understanding of creation.[40]

A scientist interviewed for this book called Pope Francis's slavish adherence to "unfettered Darwinism" a "cover-your-ass strategy" designed to placate a Western elite quick to call the Church anti-science.

Like the climate change activists, the Darwinists see the pope's support as a propaganda coup and have incorporated it into their politics. "The Pope would like you to accept evolution," intones *Smithsonian Magazine*.[41] In 2016, in keeping with his enthusiastic embrace of Darwinism, Pope Francis lifted the Congregation for the Doctrine of the Faith's sanction on a scholar, Ariel Álvarez Valdés, who denies the historicity of Adam and Eve.

By placing the Church at the front of the left's environmentalist juggernaut, Pope Francis has become a superstar in the eyes of the Western intelligentsia. But many Catholics in the pews view it as one more frivolous abuse of his authority. On the moral issues a pope should address, he falls silent. On contentious political issues, he couldn't be more voluble.

A study released by the University of Pennsylvania's Annenberg Public Policy Center in 2016 suggested that the pope's encyclical on global warming had left faithful Catholics and non-Catholics cold. Texas Tech professor Nan Li, who led the study, concluded, "While Pope Francis's environmental call may have increased some individuals' concerns about climate change, it backfired with conservative Catholics and non-Catholics, who not only resisted the message but defended their pre-existing beliefs by devaluing the pope's credibility on climate change."[42] "The Church has got no mandate from the Lord to pronounce on scientific matters," said Australian cardinal George Pell, in an implicit rebuke to the pope's environmentalism.[43]

In his attempt to pressure Catholics into embracing the radical green movement, Pope Francis is creating needless divisions within the Church, handing a propaganda tool to her moral enemies, and exposing the Church to future embarrassment when the "science" behind global warming claims is discredited. Where other popes sought to save souls, he prefers the more fashionable cause of "saving the planet."

# CHAPTER SEVEN

# The Open-Borders Pope

Render unto Caesar the things that are Caesar's and unto God the things that are God's," Jesus Christ told his disciples. Traditionally, the Church has interpreted this to mean that Catholics are duty-bound to obey the state's just laws, including its immigration laws. To the cheers of the left, Pope Francis has broken with this tradition, openly encouraging defiance of national borders. His pontificate has been a bewildering spectacle of stunts and speeches designed to advance the cause of open borders and illegal immigration.

In 2016, seeking to sanctify illegal immigration, Pope Francis traveled to the border between Mexico and America to hold a Mass. A needlessly provocative gesture, the Mass in Ciudad Juárez, Mexico, had the predictable effect of dividing Catholics and galvanizing liberals. The pope used soft and platitudinous language to present illegal immigration in the most benign terms. He called it "forced migration."

"The human tragedy that is forced migration is a global phenomenon today," he said during his homily at the Mass. "This crisis, which can be measured in numbers and statistics, we want to instead measure with names, stories, families." They are "brothers and sisters excluded as a result of poverty and violence, drug trafficking and criminal organizations." He made no mention of the problems associated with illegal immigration or the duties of the state to address those problems. Gazing over at the U.S. border fence, he made a sign of the cross and gave his blessings to the illegal immigrants.[1]

His one-sided characterization of the immigration debate was seen by Democrats as a political windfall in an election year. But Republicans pushed back against it.

"I don't think he understands the danger of the open border that we have with Mexico," said Donald Trump during the Republican presidential primaries. The pope, in reply, called Trump "not Christian" for proposing to build a wall along the southern border.[2]

"It is stunning," said former Arkansas governor Mike Huckabee. "I don't ever remember in my lifetime that a pope has ever injected himself into the specifics of an American presidential election and specifically calling out of a candidate."[3]

The pope's criticism encouraged left-wing bishops to launch attacks on Trump. Santa Fe archbishop John Wester said, "I think some of the rhetoric coming out of [the Trump] campaign is deplorable." He dismissed Trump's position as "scapegoating and targeting people like the immigrant, the refugee and the poor."[4]

But in a measure of his wilting support among conservatives, the pope's criticism of Trump only enhanced Trump's appeal in the Republican primaries. Mary Matalin, a Republican strategist who opposed Trump in the primaries, found the pope's broadside unhelpful. "The pope should stay out of politics," she said.[5] "He gave Trump a big, fat, wet kiss, whether he meant to or not." After Jeb Bush lost the South Carolina primary, he blamed his defeat in part on the pope's open-borders activism. When asked by MSNBC what contributed to his loss, Bush replied, "The pope intervening in American politics."

The pope's questioning of Trump's faith was ironic, given his unwillingness to question the faith of pro-abortion Catholic politicians, not to mention the faith of third-world dictators. Rush Limbaugh noticed the latter, saying: "Has he questioned the faith of the Castro brothers? Has the Pope questioned the faith of any communist leaders?...Has he ever said that Mao Tse-tung, that Fidel Castro, that Raul Castro, any other communist is not a Christian? Why Donald Trump? 'Cause Trump wants to build a wall?"

The pope's anti-Trump outburst highlighted his tendency to prioritize political rather than religious issues. He reserves his rhetorical fire not for defiant members of his flock but for easy targets reviled by the liberal elite. Many theological subjects leave him cold, but immigration politics draws out his passions. (After Trump won the presidency in 2016, Pope Francis immediately called on the U.S. bishops to ramp up their amnesty advocacy, "mindful of the contribution that the Hispanic community makes to the life of the nation.")

"Let everyone come," he said in 2016 while surrounded by amnesty advocates whom he had invited to join him on the steps of St. Peter's Basilica in a spontaneous gesture.[6] His open-borders ideology is closely connected to his anti-capitalist, third-worldist view that poor countries have a right to the wealth of richer countries. It also flows from his confidence in international institutions and dim view of national sovereignty, which he sees as an impediment to world progress. In *Laudato Si'*, he calls for "stronger and more efficiently organized international institutions" to address matters related to "migration."

Just as he has called on wealthy countries to forgive the debts of poorer countries, so he also believes that wealthy countries have a duty to open their borders to immigrants from those countries. Were the goods of the earth more "equitably" distributed, he argues, people wouldn't need to migrate.

"These poor people are fleeing war, hunger, but that is the tip of the iceberg. Because underneath that is the cause; and the cause is a bad and unjust socioeconomic system," he has said.[7] In other words, if the poor have a right to the property of the rich, then it follows that they also have a right to citizenship in their countries.

His speeches are replete with "apologies" and appeals to the third world, without any scrutiny of the internal causes of poverty in those countries. "I want to be a spokesman for the deepest longings of indigenous peoples," he says. In this role, he has castigated the Church for evangelizing indigenous peoples: "I say this to you with regret: many grave sins were committed against the native peoples in the name of God."[8] He often condemns "new forms of colonialism" even as he operates like a lobbyist for paternalistic forms of liberal neocolonialism that come from the United Nations.

Capitalism, according to his way of thinking, is never a solution to poverty but a cause of it. He has devoted much of his pontificate to "Catholic social justice," which amounts to reflexive advocacy for government-planned economies. His repetitive use of such ostensibly harmless phrases as the "preferential option for the poor" do not refer simply to charity toward the poor, which is undeniably Christian, but to pervasive government regulation of private property and business in the name of the poor, which is socialist.

"He's very concerned for the poor, but I'm worried whether he has a very good theory for how you get the poor out of poverty," says the theologian Michael Novak.[9]

Home Depot founder Kenneth Langone, who has complained that his efforts to raise money for the Church have been hurt by the pope's socialist rhetoric, attributes it to the "pope's experience in Argentina."[10]

In 2013, Pope Francis made a visit to the Italian island of Lampedusa, where at an open Mass near its harbor he praised illegal immigrants for trying to "find some serenity and peace." He called opposition to illegal immigration the "globalization of indifference" and likened critics of illegal immigration to Cain and King Herod.[11]

"Herod sowed death to protect his own comfort, his own soap bubble. And so it continues," he said. "Let us ask the Lord to remove the part of Herod that lurks in our hearts; let us the Lord for the grace to weep over our indifference, to weep over the cruelty of our world, of our own hearts, and of all those who in anonymity make social and economic decisions which open the door to tragic situations like this."

The crossing from Africa to Lampedusa is fraught with danger. "More than 6,000 people are believed to have drowned in the waters around Lampedusa between 1994 and 2012," reports the *Los Angeles Times*. "The United Nations recorded 500 deaths of migrants attempting to cross the Mediterranean during 2012."[12] In light of these numbers, Italian politicians warned the Holy Father that his Mass and his romanticized view of illegal immigration would only encourage more dangerous crossings. He waved off those objections.

## The Pope Encourages Eurabia

In 2016, as a wave of illegal immigrants from Islamic countries crashed upon the shores of Europe, Pope Francis called on all Catholic parishes to open their doors to them.

"Faced with the tragedy of tens of thousands of refugees who are fleeing death by war and by hunger, and who are on a path toward a hope for life, the Gospel calls us to be neighbors to the smallest and most abandoned, to give them concrete hope," he said. "May every parish, every religious community, every monastery, every sanctuary in Europe host a family, starting with my diocese of Rome," he said.[13]

At an Italian parish, which had opened its doors to Islamic immigrants after the pope's directive, the Catholic organization Caritas lectured Catholics on the need to avoid pious practices such as reciting the rosary, lest it disturb the "migrants." "Pray in silence," Catholics were instructed.[14]

One of the top bishops in Hungary, a country reeling from the crush of illegal immigrants, told the press that he found the pope's instruction mystifying. "They're not refugees. This is an invasion," said Bishop Laszlo Kiss-Rigo, whose diocese stretches across the southern part of Hungary. "They come here with cries of 'Allahu Akbar.' They want to take over."[15]

"On the question of taking in immigrants Pope Francis is wrong," Jarosław Gowin, a Polish Catholic politician, said. "In no case should we take in Muslims."[16]

In stark contrast to his predecessors, Pope Francis has shown no interest in reviving a historically Christian Europe against a potential Eurabian future. Pope Francis subscribes to the left's suicidally softheaded explanation for the rise of Islamic terrorism in Europe. He blames it not on Islamic radical ideology but on the West's unwillingness to "integrate" Muslims and open its borders to them.

"Coming back to the migrant issue, the worst form of welcome is to 'ghettoize' them. On the contrary, it's necessary to integrate them. In Brussels, the terrorists were Belgians, children of migrants, but they grew up in a ghetto," according to the pope.[17]

Conservative Catholics in Europe, like their counterparts in America, find the pope's politically correct grandstanding on the issue of Islamic refugees baffling and divisive.

Viktor Orbán, the prime minister of Hungary, a largely Catholic country, has warned that Europe's Christian identity is vanishing under an ethos that privileges "those arriving [who] have been raised in another religion, and represent a radically different culture."[18]

Cardinal Dominik Duka, the archbishop of Prague, has tried to explain the pope's boosterism for illegal immigration as a by-product of his Latin American roots. In an interview with the Czech Republic daily newspaper *Lidove noviny*, Duka said, "The sensitivity of Pope Francis on social issues is different from ours in Europe. He comes from Latin America where the gap between rich and poor is much bigger, as a result of its Indian cultures."

Duka sees the pope's enthusiasm as naïve and unfair to Christians on the continent. Throwing open the doors of Europe to illegal immigrants is a formula for an "enormous humanitarian and economic catastrophe," all for the sake of accommodating members of a "completely different culture and civilization," he said.[19]

Would Pope Francis, some wonder, even want a secularized

Europe to return to Christianity? He sounds at best agnostic on this subject. In 2016, a group of liberal Europeans awarded Pope Francis the Charlemagne Prize. He used his acceptance speech not to call for the restoration of Christianity but for the spread of a "new European humanism" open to illegal immigration and socialism:

> I dream of a Europe where being a migrant is not a crime but a summons to greater commitment on behalf of the dignity of every human being. I dream of a Europe where young people breathe the pure air of honesty, where they love the beauty of a culture and a simple life undefiled by the insatiable needs of consumerism, where getting married and having children is a responsibility and a great joy, not a problem due to the lack of stable employment. I dream of a Europe of families, with truly effective policies concentrated on faces rather than numbers, on birth rates more than rates of consumption.[20]

In an interview with *La Croix*, the French Catholic newspaper, Pope Francis broke with his predecessors in denouncing Christian confessional states (states that give a privileged position to Christianity in their constitutions) and gave his blessing to the post-Enlightenment concept of the secular nation-state.

His remarks revealed why the prospect of Eurabia doesn't bother him. What his predecessors called indifferentism—the heretical notion that all religions are of equal value—crept into his remarks.

"States must be secular. Confessional states end badly. That goes against the grain of history," he said. "We are all equal as sons (and daughters) of God and with our personal dignity. However, everyone must have the freedom to externalize his or her own faith. If a Muslim woman wishes to wear a veil, she must be able to do so; similarly, if a Catholic wishes to wear a cross."[21]

On his return to Rome from a visit to the Greek island of Lesbos in 2016, the pope brought back with him three Muslim families. In a sad irony, he left behind a Christian family, whose papers, according to the Vatican, weren't in order, even though he had just been waxing indignant about indifference to the "undocumented." That generated a spate of embarrassing stories for the Vatican.

"Pope Francis reneges on offer to take in Christian refugees," headlined a story in the *New York Post*. It reported that "A Christian brother and sister from Syria felt blessed to have been among the dozen refugees selected to start a new life in Italy—but now say their savior, Pope Francis, abandoned them on a Greek island, according to a [*Daily Mail*] report."

"Roula and Malek Abo, who had been housed in a refugee camp on Lesbos, said they thanked their lucky stars when they found out the Vatican had selected them during the pontiff's visit to the island last week," it continued. "Their dreams were shattered, though, when they were informed the following day that they would not be traveling to Rome. Instead, three Muslim families were taken. Asked why they were all Muslim, Francis said there was something wrong with the papers of a Christian family on the list."[22]

Conservatives who seek to rebuild a "Christian Europe" embarrass Pope Francis, as he explained in his interview with *La Croix*: "We need to speak of roots in the plural because there are so many. In this sense, when I hear talk of the Christian roots of Europe, I sometimes dread the tone, which can seem triumphalist or even vengeful. It then takes on colonialist overtones."

Christianity's influence over Europe should be reduced to humanitarian service, he argued: "Christianity's duty to Europe is one of service. As Erich Przywara, the great master of Romano Guardini and Hans Urs von Balthasar, teaches us, Christianity's contribution to a culture is that of Christ in the washing of the feet. In other words, service and the gift of life. It must not become a colonial enterprise."[23]

In 2016, during a visit to Poland, he urged the faithful to give up their objections to illegal immigration. His words sounded like they had been borrowed from the lyrics of John Lennon: "People may judge you to be dreamers, because you believe in a new humanity, one that rejects hatred between peoples, one that refuses to see borders as barriers and can cherish its own traditions without being self-centered or small-minded."[24]

At a time when jihadists are cutting off the heads of priests and calling for the destruction of the Catholic Church, the pope's naïve amnesty advocacy has left many conservative bishops appalled. "I would expect a more firm defense of Christians," the Italian bishop Andrea Gemma said. "I would like a pope more energetic in defense of our principles and our faith."[25]

## The Clericalism of Amnesty Advocacy

Previous popes treated the debate over immigration law as a matter on which reasonable Catholics can disagree. But under Pope Francis the entire weight of the Catholic Church has fallen on one side of the debate, and politically liberal bishops feel increasingly empowered to impose their personal opinion in favor of amnesty on their flocks.

British bishops cast Britain's departure from the European Union as "xenophobia."[26] The United States Conference of Catholic Bishops has a web page titled "Catholic Church's Position on Immigration Reform," which represents nothing more than the left-wing politics of the bishops. It offers a "parish kit" for advancing amnesty, offers an "intercessory prayer" for amnesty, and directs priests to a "sample homily on migration related issues from Cardinal McCarrick," which "may provide some insights on creating a homily related to immigration."

After the U.S. Supreme Court blocked President Obama's blatantly unconstitutional order to grant amnesty to four million illegal immigrants, the U.S. bishops blasted the decision: "The decision is a huge disappointment; it means millions of families will continue to live in fear of deportation and without the immediate ability to improve their lives through education and good jobs."[27]

There is no doctrinal authority for such statements. They simply reflect the ideological preferences of influential bishops. The *Catechism of the Catholic Church* contains no justification for illegal immigration. It says that the "political authorities" have the right to secure the borders of their countries and that they may make the "exercise of the right to immigrate subject to various juridical conditions."

In 2016, Pope Francis baffled Church observers by making a relatively obscure archbishop, Joseph Tobin of Indianapolis, a cardinal. The liberal Catholic press saw the elevation as a reward in part for Tobin's strong support for illegal immigration. In 2015, Tobin had sparred with then Indiana governor Mike Pence over the issue of Syrian refugee resettlement, defying Pence's order to cease resettlement in the wake of terrorist attacks and reports of porous vetting. Tobin cast his defiance in lofty terms. Helping the Syrian refugees, he said, "is an essential part of our identity as Catholic Christians, and we will continue this life-saving tradition."[28]

Beneath the misleading rhetoric about Christian identity lay a more compelling reason for Tobin's stance: the Catholic Church in America has received tens of millions of dollars from the Obama administration to resettle migrants. Flush with government grants, the U.S. bishops have stepped up their lobbying, even calling on Catholics to write "a letter to President Obama, urging him expand U.S. resettlement efforts of Syrian refugees."[29]

Francis-favored bishops, such as San Diego's Robert McElroy, regularly rip into critics of their amnesty advocacy. McElroy has castigated Catholics concerned about the creeping Islamization of the West. "We are witnessing in the United States a new nativism, which the American Catholic community must reject and label for the religious bigotry which it is," he said at a 2016 forum.[30]

Groups such as Dioceses Without Borders are springing up as the Church under Francis becomes indistinguishable from the National Council of La Raza lobby. In 2016, Pope Francis appointed a progressive French prelate, Christophe Pierre, to be his nuncio in the United States. One of his first newsmaking events was to say a Mass near the U.S.-Mexican border in Nogales, Arizona, which served as a political rally for "needed immigration reform" and the dissolution of "barriers."[31] After Donald Trump won the presidency, Pierre called on the U.S. bishops to "assume a prophetic role" in response and to step up their amnesty advocacy. He said the "pope is more prophetic than the Catholic bishops here today."[32]

Pope Francis frequently denounces clericalism (the extension of Church authority to matters beyond it), but he ignores the rank clericalism of politically liberal clerics imposing their opinions on the flock. He is constantly blurring the line between official Church teaching and his personal political opinions. Pope Benedict XVI warned against this form of clericalism when he said that a pope "is not an absolute monarch whose thoughts and desires are law." He said that a pope "must not proclaim his own ideas, but rather constantly bind himself and the Church to obedience to God's Word, in the face of every attempt to adapt it or water it down, and every form of opportunism."

Much of this pontificate has revolved around exactly that kind of clericalism. Pope Francis never hesitates to use his office as a platform for opining on political matters. "The Church must be involved in the great political issues of our day," he has said. "A good Catholic meddles in politics." At a press conference in 2015, he was asked if he is improperly passing off his political opinions as Church teaching. He scoffed at the suggestion and said innocently: "I am sure that I haven't said anything more than what is contained in the Church's social teaching."[33]

Imagine the cries of clericalism one would hear from liberals if Catholic bishops hosted web pages and "parish kits" in favor of

Republican policies on taxation. Yet they don't hesitate to do the same on the disputed issue of illegal immigration.

In his 2015 speech before the U.S. Congress, Pope Francis made a call for amnesty and tacitly accused those with principled objections to it as inhumane. "Thousands of persons are led to travel north in search of a better life for themselves and for their loved ones in search of greater opportunities in North America," he said. "Is this not what we want for our own children? We must not be taken aback by their numbers, but rather view them as persons, seeing their faces and listening to their stories, trying to respond as best we can to their situation. To respond in a way which is always humane, just and fraternal."

Pope Francis is fond of quoting Jesus Christ's description of the Pharisees as those who lay heavy burdens on people without carrying those burden themselves. But he is oblivious to his own tendency toward that on issues like amnesty, where he is demanding that countries adopt an unrealistic policy that the Vatican state itself rejects. Safely behind the walls of the Vatican, he declares to world leaders that they must tear theirs down.

# CHAPTER EIGHT
# The Pacifist Pope

The Church has long supported the morality of the death penalty, the "just war doctrine," and resistance to tyrants. At the level of official teaching, the Church has always rejected the superficial claims of pacifism, which spring not from the moral absolutes of the Christian tradition but from the relativism contained within post-Enlightenment moral and political philosophy.

Francis is the first pope to flirt seriously with these claims. He supports a pacifism fashionable in European liberal circles and leftist Latin American ones. He is entertaining proposals to discard the Church's "just war" doctrine and has set up a commission to examine altering her teaching on capital punishment.

His musings on pacifism have been "silly," says a former high-ranking Church official interviewed for this book. "He has been cursed by his background."

"States kill when they apply the death penalty, when they send their people to war or when they carry out extrajudicial or summary executions," he asserted in one statement, as if a military draft and capital punishment fall on the same continuum as state-sponsored terrorism. That appeared in a letter to the president of the International Commission Against the Death Penalty in which he quoted the Russian author Fyodor Dostoyevsky as saying that "to kill one who killed is an incomparably greater punishment than the crime itself."[1]

Many of his statements constitute little more than pacifist polemics. "War is always a defeat for humanity," he has said categorically. Gone are the careful distinctions between just and unjust wars made by his predecessors.

Stopping the wicked from slaughtering the innocent, according to the Catholic tradition, is an expression of Christian love, not a denial of it. Yet his sweeping statements appear to rest upon that assumption.

"Violence is not answered with violence, death is not answered with the language of death," he has said. "In the silence of the Cross, the uproar of weapons ceases and the language of reconciliation, forgiveness, dialogue, and peace is spoken. This evening, I ask the Lord that we Christians, and our brothers and sisters of other religions, and every man and woman of good will, cry out forcefully: violence and war are never the way to peace!"[2]

## The Pope Opposes Lifetime Imprisonment

Even a concept as uncontroversial as lifetime imprisonment for serial killers has been rejected by this pope. Not even the most liberal of liberal Democrats in the United States take his absolutist stance against lifetime imprisonment. Indeed, most of them argue against the death penalty on the grounds that lifetime imprisonment provides an adequate means of protecting society from violent criminals.

Some opponents of the death penalty have expressed unease about the pope's opposition to lifetime imprisonment. They fear that it could end up strengthening public support for the death penalty, which already enjoys strong majority approval in the United States, including from Catholics.

Undaunted, Pope Francis has said to murderers and other capital offenders that they not only don't deserve the death penalty but that states owe them freedom from lifetime imprisonment. He has become a crusader for "prisoners' rights," casting lifetime imprisonment as a "form of torture" and a "hidden death penalty."[3]

He has made the quirky proposal that more prisons be run by female wardens. "When I go to a city, I like to visit prisons; I have already visited a number of them. Without wishing to detract from anyone, I would say that my general impression is that prisons run by women are better run," he said to a group of judges in 2016. "When it comes to reinsertion, women have a particular, almost natural, knack for putting people in the right place; some might think it is because they are mothers. But it is curious. I mention it as a personal experience which may be worth thinking about. Here in Italy, many prisons are run by women. Many of them are young; they are respected and enjoy a good rapport with the prisoners."[4]

In November 2016, he held a "jubilee of prisoners" at St. Peter's Basilica. Other popes have visited prisoners and said Masses at prisons. But Pope Francis, displaying his love of novel and provocative gestures, is the first pope to ask prisons to release prisoners for an outing to the Vatican. "For the first time it will be possible for a large number of detainees from different parts of Italy and other countries to be present in St. Peter's Basilica to live the Jubilee with Pope Francis," Archbishop Rino Fisichella told the press.[5] At the event, which included a Mass, Pope Francis called for prisoner amnesty and criticized a lock-them-up mentality among the public: "Sometimes, a certain hypocrisy leads to people considering you only as wrongdoers, for whom prison is the sole answer. We don't think about the possibility that people can change their lives. We put little trust in rehabilitation... into society. But in this way we forget that we are all sinners and often, without being aware of it, we too are prisoners."[6]

The Church has long justified the death penalty on the grounds of "retributive justice." But Pope Francis insists on describing retributive justice as "vengeance." He regularly maligns the motives of those who support the death penalty, which is a condemnation that falls as much on his predecessors as contemporary supporters of the death penalty.

"No matter how grave the crime committed," the death penalty is never justified, he said to an anti-death penalty congress in Norway.[7]

This view contradicts the constant teaching of the Church on this issue. The late cardinal Avery Dulles did a study of this question and found that the Church "never" morally opposed the death penalty and that all the way up until the twentieth century the Vatican state had the death penalty on its books. Wrote Dulles:

> Throughout the first half of the twentieth century the consensus of Catholic theologians in favor of capital punishment in extreme cases remained solid, as may be seen from approved textbooks and encyclopedia articles of the day. The Vatican City State from 1929 until 1969 had a penal code that included the death penalty for anyone who might attempt to assassinate the pope. Pope Pius XII, in an important allocution to medical experts, declared that it was reserved to the public power to deprive the condemned of the benefit of life in expiation of their crimes.[8]

Rejecting this tradition, Pope Francis, in a speech to delegates from the International Association of Penal Law, spoke about opposition to the death penalty as a Christian duty:

> All Christians and people of good will are called today to struggle not only for abolition of the death penalty, whether legal or illegal, and in all its forms, but also to improve prison conditions, out of respect for the human dignity of persons deprived of their liberty. And this I connect with life imprisonment. Life imprisonment is a hidden death penalty.[9]

Under the Vatican state's penal code, as Pope Francis likes to say, lifetime imprisonment no longer exists. Similar to his extreme stance on the issue of climate change, the pope, on issues of crime and punishment, has gone beyond even the conventionally liberal position to the most radical one. This explains the over-the-top praise that he receives from the European left, which has succeeded in convincing judges to outlaw lifetime imprisonment. It never dreamed a pope would so perfectly conform to their agenda.

At times the pope almost sounds like a parody of a 1960s-style pacifist. He once sweepingly condemned the arms trade by saying, "It is hypocritical to talk about peace and make weapons." Even as oversimplifications in today's vapid political discourse go, that over-simplification staggered conservatives.[10] Just as the pope casually equates capitalism with greed, so he equates weaponry with blind violence. He has called the arms trade an "industry of death" and said that it is "furthering a cycle of hate, fratricide, violence." That weapons protect innocent people from the violent rarely figures into his analysis.

The day after an Islamic terrorist fired upon hundreds of people at a homosexual nightclub in Orlando, Florida, in 2016, causing the deadliest mass shooting in modern American history, the pope condemned the arms trade.[11] He preferred to engage that subject rather than the spread of radical Islam. (A Francis-friendly bishop in America, Robert Lynch, meanwhile blamed "our own" religion for the violence, saying that Catholicism bred "contempt" for the "LGBT" community.)

"Now the Pope is lashing out at guns, not Islamism. He says guns circulate too freely. Doesn't he know that ISIS hits soft targets, not hard ones like the Vatican?" said Fox News commentator Greg Gutfeld. "If the Vatican were as unarmed as Pulse, the club, the pope would not be alive. But ISIS knows that the Pope is surrounded by a military force consisting of 100 plus ex-Swiss soldiers who carry muskets but also sub-machine guns, with heavily armed agents nearby. If that club, Pulse, had three percent of the Pope's arms, he wouldn't lecturing on guns. The Pope complained that aid and food in few support countries are often blocked, but guns are not. Doesn't he see that if it weren't for armed men from our country, most aid would get nowhere? He says he is pro-life, not here I'm afraid."[12]

So frequent are the pope's denunciations of the arms trade that the gun-control lobby in the United States has turned him into a poster boy for their cause in fundraising letters. Following his lead, the U.S. bishops have backed President Obama's gun control proposals. "It is time to heed the words of Pope Francis and take meaningful and swift action to address violence in our society. We must band together to call for gun-control legislation," Chicago archbishop Blase Cupich wrote.[13]

## All Wars Are Unjust?

In keeping with the pope's oversimplified hostility to arms, the Vatican is now flirting with a plan to eliminate the Church's centuries-old just war doctrine. That doctrine has been defended by countless popes and was carefully articulated by such doctors of the Church as St. Augustine and St. Thomas Aquinas. But Pope Francis sees it as just one more disposable tradition.

In 2016, his Pontifical Council for Justice and Peace teamed up with the pacifist organization Pax Christi International to hold a three-day conference trashing the Church's traditional understanding of just war.[14] "I came a long distance for this conference, with a very clear mind that violence is outlived," said Archbishop John Baptist Odama of Gulu, Uganda. "It is out of date for our world of today."

The participants have called on Pope Francis to pen an encyclical endorsing pacifism. "There is no 'just war,'" they declared in a statement. "Too often the 'just war theory' has been used to endorse rather than prevent or limit war. Suggesting that a 'just war' is possible also undermines the moral imperative to develop tools and capacities for nonviolent transformation of conflict."

They want the Church to trade her just war teaching for a "just peace" one. "We need a new framework that is consistent with Gospel nonviolence," they said. "We propose that the Catholic Church develop and consider shifting to a Just Peace approach based on Gospel nonviolence."

Officials close to Pope Francis have encouraged this talk. Cardinal Peter Turkson, who helped ghostwrite Francis's environmentalist statements, has said that the position of the group is "very legitimate."

In fact, it is baldly heretical. The *Catechism of the Catholic Church* states that "it sometimes becomes necessary to use force to obtain the end of justice. This is the right, and the duty, of those who have responsibilities for others, such as civil leaders and police forces."

## Coddling Dictators

The pacifism of this pontificate is also seen in its diplomacy, which has been marked by the coddling of communist dictators and excuse-making for Islamic radicals. In 2015, Pope Francis perplexed many by rolling out the red carpet for Raúl Castro, the murderous leader of Cuba's communist regime.

"The warmth and hospitality that Pope Francis showed to Raúl Castro at the Vatican last week has baffled many Catholics—and for good reason. The dictator went to Rome for a PR boost. The pontiff obliged him," wrote Mary Anastasia O'Grady in the *Wall Street Journal*. "The Holy Father is a native of 20th-century Argentina, ideologically defined by nationalism, socialism, corporatism and anti-Americanism. It wouldn't be surprising to learn that this influences his views toward the U.S. and the island 90 miles from its shores."

O'Grady argues that the pope's much-ballyhooed role as a "broker" in hastening normalized relations between the United States and Cuba is a boon not to dissidents but to the Castro brothers, who desperately needed the U.S. embargo lifted in order to prolong their regime.

"When the Cuban dictatorship lost its Soviet sugar daddy in the early 1990s, it nearly crumbled. Last year deep economic troubles again looked as if they might force change. As Venezuelan oil subsidies to Havana slowed, the rotting system teetered on the edge of collapse," she wrote. "It was an opportunity for the church to show solidarity with the powerless Cuban people—or at least stand back. Instead the Vatican stepped in to help the Castros. In December we learned that Pope Francis brokered the Obama-Castro thaw, which while unlikely to spur improvements in human rights is already generating new interest in investing with the military government."[15]

Even the politically liberal *Washington Post* was appalled the following year by the pope's feel-good visit to the brothers Castro in Cuba. In an editorial titled "Pope Francis Appeases the Castros in Repressive Cuba," the *Post* ripped into his sycophantic diplomacy:

The pope is spending four days in a country whose Communist dictatorship has remained unrelenting in its repression of free speech, political dissent and other human rights despite a warming of relations with the Vatican and the United States. Yet by the end of his third day, the pope had said or done absolutely nothing that might discomfit his official hosts.

Pope Francis met with 89-year-old Fidel Castro, who holds no office in Cuba, but not with any members of the dissident community—in or outside of prison. According to the Web site 14ymedio.com, two opposition activists were invited to greet the pope at Havana's cathedral Sunday but were arrested on the way. Dozens of other dissidents were detained when they attempted to attend an open air Mass. They needn't have bothered: The pope said nothing in his homily about their cause, or even political freedom more generally.[16]

Raúl Castro's gift to Pope Francis—a crucifix made from the wooden oars of a "migrant's" boat—grated on the dissidents, many of whom had seen relatives drown after fleeing communist Cuba.

Liberation theologians friendly with the Castro brothers, such as the Brazilian Frei Betto, have met with Pope Francis and received encouragement from him. When Pope Francis gave a copy of *Evangelii Gaudium* (an apostolic exhortation in which he condemns "trickle-down" economics) to Raúl Castro, he said to him, "There are here some declarations that you will like!"

Raúl Castro said to Pope Francis: "If you continue talking like this...I will return to the Catholic Church. I am not joking. I may convert again to Catholicism, even though I am a Communist."[17]

O'Grady argues that Pope Francis has been a morale boost for left-wing strongmen like Ecuador's Rafael Correa, who used the pope's visit to his country to highlight the pope's support for socialism. "This pope is very political and his politics, if we take him at his word, favor statist solutions to poverty. In terms of appearances that puts him on the same side of many policy debates as the region's socialist tyrants," she wrote. "The populist Mr. Correa smells opportunity. In the lead up to the visit, he posted billboards in Guayaquil and Quito featuring his government's logo encircling a photo of the pontiff next to what appears to be a Francis quote that reads 'one must demand the redistribution of wealth.' State television and radio delivered a similar message."[18]

The pope's support for left-wing Latin American populism has led the *Economist* to call him the "Peronist pope." He routinely mistakes the Church's insistence on charity toward the poor for an endorsement of socialism. "If you were to read one of the sermons of the first fathers of the church, from the second or third centuries, about how you should treat the poor, you'd say it was Maoist or Trotskyist," he has mused absurdly.[19] The church fathers were sermonizing about the corporal works of mercy, not advancing government-planned economies.

The pope has said nothing about the plight of the poor under socialism in Latin America, preferring instead to attribute their problems to "unseen forces" that worship a "deified market." The moral causes of poverty, such as rising illegitimacy, don't appear to play any role in his analysis either.

Pope Francis has also lent his prestige to the cause of Palestinian activists, many of whom have terrorist ties. Rankling Israelis, he has called Palestine's president, Mahmoud Abbas, a "man of peace." On another occasion, reporters heard him describe Abbas, a patron of terrorists, as an "angel of peace."[20]

Pope Francis's 2014 visit to Palestine was seen by Palestinian activists as a remarkable propaganda victory. Befuddling even Vatican correspondents, the pope during his visit abruptly ordered his popemobile stopped so that he could go out and pray before a wall separating Jerusalem from the West Bank town of Bethlehem.

"He got down from the Popemobile and walked up to the wall," Fr. Federico Lombardi, the Vatican spokesman, explained to confused members of the press. "He remained there for some minutes, praying silently. He then touched the wall with his forehead."

Palestinian activists saw it as vindication of their grievances against the Israelis. Israeli government officials, who saw it in the same light, were not pleased. "[The Palestinians] are turning the visit into a whole propaganda stunt but that's what they do and the Vatican plays along with it and so be it. We will find the time to speak with the Vatican through diplomatic channels about this," said an Israeli foreign ministry official.

One of the pope's closest advisers, Cardinal Rodríguez, is a loud critic of Israel. He once cast the media's coverage of the sex abuse scandal in the Church as payback for the support that the Vatican has extended to Palestinians:

It certainly makes me think that in a moment in which all the attention of the mass media was focused on the Middle East, all the many injustices done against the Palestinian people, the print media and the TV in the United States became obsessed with sexual scandals that happened 40 years ago, 30 years ago. Why? I think it's also for these motives: What is the church that has received Arafat the most times and has most often confirmed the necessity of the creation of a Palestinian state? What is the church that does not accept that Jerusalem should be the indivisible capital of the State of Israel, but that it should be the capital of the three great monotheistic religions?[21]

## The Pope Appeases Communist China

In 2015, Pope Francis denied a private audience to the Dalai Lama, out of fear of offending Chinese communists in Bejiing. The Dalai Lama's request was declined "for obvious reasons concerning the delicate situation," said a Vatican spokesman.[22]

The Chinese communists have long subjected the Catholic Church to brutal persecution and state control, a problem that has worsened under the pontificate of Francis. "Yes, the Chinese government's control over the Church in China has absolutely increased since the beginning of Pope Francis's pontificate," says Joseph Kung, who monitors religious persecution in China, in an interview for this book.

Cardinal Joseph Zen of Hong Kong has complained that Pope Francis is kowtowing to the communists, which has only made it easier for the Chinese government to dominate the Church.

"I have searched at length for some good news, but have found none," he wrote in January 2016. "I remember that at the beginning of last year the newspaper Wen Wei Po announced jubilantly that 'relations between China and the Vatican will soon have a good development.' Soon after, the Vatican Secretary of State said that 'the prospects are promising, there is a desire for dialogue on both sides.' I had my doubts about this unexpected wave of optimism, I saw no basis for this optimism."

He then detailed the persecution of the Church: "More than a thousand crosses were removed from the top of the churches (in some cases the churches themselves have been destroyed)... Several seminaries have been closed. Students of the National Seminary in Beijing were forced to sign a declaration of loyalty to the Independent Church, promising also to concelebrate with illegitimate bishops (otherwise they would not receive a diploma at the end of their studies). The Government is continuously strengthening a church that now objectively is already separated from the universal Catholic Church; with enticements and threats they induce the clergy to perform acts contrary to the doctrine and discipline of the Church, denying their conscience and their dignity."

Zen fears that Pope Francis is on the verge of letting the Chinese Communists select bishops for the Church. The Chinese communists, who exert control over the Church through a front called the Chinese Catholic Patriotic Association, are demanding "democratic" elections and Francis may grant them, wrote Zen: "Do our officials in Rome know what an election is in China? Do they know that the so-called Episcopal Conference is not only illegitimate, but simply does not exist? What exists is an organism that is called 'One Association and One Conference,' namely the Patriotic Association and the Bishops' Conference always work together as one body, which is always chaired by government officials (there are pictures to prove it, the Government does not even try more to keep up appearances, it starkly flaunts the fact that they now manage religion!). Signing such an agreement means delivering the authority to appoint bishops into the hands of an atheist government."[23]

The Chinese communists have taken a keen interest in Pope Francis, sending spies to the Vatican to collect secrets on him. That practice was revealed in the course of a Vatican trial over leaks in which a Spanish monsignor was found to have offered a bogus medical report on Pope Francis to Chinese espionage agents.[24]

Pope John Paul II biographer George Weigel also worries that the Vatican is capitulating to the Chinese Communists:

> This passion among Vatican diplomats for getting a deal done with the PRC [People's Republic of China] has always puzzled me. It would almost certainly mean severing diplomatic relations with the Republic of China on Taiwan, the first democracy in Chinese history. If Taiwan is thrown over the side for the sake of a deal with Beijing, what signal does that send to the world, and to Chinese democrats and human-rights activists on the mainland—including Christians—about the Catholic Church's commitment to free societies? Moreover, one can't draw a lot of satisfaction from recent Vatican attempts to get along by going along with dictators and authoritarians. Being nice to the brothers Castro has done nothing for a human-rights situation in Cuba that has actually gotten worse.[25]

In July 2016, Reuters reported that Pope Francis was considering pardoning eight "bishops" appointed by the Chinese communists in bald violation of canon law (which reserves the appointment of bishops to the pope).[26] Later that year, the Vatican entertained an appointment-sharing agreement with the Chinese government. This has left Cardinal Zen so dispirited that he is counseling Chinese Catholics to resist the pope: "We will have to refuse to take that step just because it formally contradicts the petrine authority. Yes, in the case under consideration (in this moment we still strongly hope that it does not happen) we will have to be loyal to the Pope (the Papacy, the authority of the Vicar of Christ) in spite of the Pope."[27]

To the *Wall Street Journal,* Zen said "Pope Francis has no real knowledge of communism" and attributes his tendency to romanticize it to his Argentinian background: "So the Holy Father knew the persecuted communists, not the communist persecutors. He knew the communists killed by the government, not the communist governments who killed thousands and hundreds of thousands of people. I'm sorry to say that in his goodwill he has done many things which are simply ridiculous."[28]

"Times and situations have changed," Pope Francis has said by way of explaining his departures from previous Church teaching. In other words, deference to the fads of modern culture, rather than respect for the Catholic intellectual and magisterial tradition, is driving his pacifism.

# CHAPTER NINE

# "I Don't Want to Convert You"

Like his fellow liberal Jesuits, Pope Francis often seems to exude enthusiasm for every religion except his own. In his extreme ecumenism, he is conforming to the lowest-common-denominator culture of a post-Christian age. As Vatican correspondent Sandro Magister has put it, "Christianity matters less" under Pope Francis.[1] Even as Pope Francis pours scorn upon traditional Catholicism — he regularly caricatures conservative Catholics as heartless "Pharisees" — he heaps praise upon Protestantism, non-Christian religions, and atheism.

The Western media has been enamored with the ecumenism of this pope since the beginning of his pontificate when, at his first press conference, he spoke of his respect for "non-believers." The left-leaning Religion News Service was so struck by his lack of interest in Catholic evangelization that it asked in a headline: "Is Francis the First Protestant Pope?"[2]

Pope Francis is particularly quick to defend and bolster Islam, a historic adversary of the Church. He repeatedly calls it a "religion of peace," even as Islam's persecution of Catholics intensifies and its radical branches spread terrorism throughout the world.

"Our respect for true followers of Islam should lead us to avoid hateful generalizations, for authentic Islam and the proper reading of the Quran are opposed to every form of violence," Pope Francis wrote in *Evangelii Gaudium*.

Speaking to Sun TV, Robert Spencer, an expert on Islam, responded to the pope's statement: "I don't hesitate to say that this statement is flatly wrong, it's misleading and it's a shame because it gives the Christians who are being persecuted by Muslims in Nigeria, in Egypt, in Syria, in Iraq and elsewhere no support; it doesn't give them any help to deny and dissemble about the root cause of why they are being persecuted in the first place."

Pope Francis hews closely to the fashionable liberal talking points about Islam. In an anticipation of his liberal papacy, he had joined the Western liberal elite in denouncing Pope Benedict XVI for a speech critical of Islam that he delivered at the University of Regensburg. Yet nothing Pope Benedict XVI said about Islam in that speech was untrue. Indeed, the violent Islamic response to his comments only confirmed their validity.

In 2014, Catholics witnessed the curious spectacle of Pope Francis commending the reading of the Qur'an, a book that his predecessors viewed as a source of rank heresy. Placing Christianity and Islam on the same level, Pope Francis said to an audience composed of Christians and Muslims: "Sharing our experience in carrying that cross, to expel the illness within our hearts, which embitters our life: it is important that you do this in your meetings. Those that are Christian, with the Bible, and those that are Muslim, with the Quran. The faith that your parents instilled in you will always help you move on."[3]

In a 2016 interview with the French newspaper *La Croix*, Pope Francis outrageously likened the concept of jihad within Islam to the preaching of the Gospel in Christianity. "It is true that the idea of conquest is inherent in the soul of Islam. However, it is also possible to interpret the objective in Matthew's Gospel, where Jesus sends his disciples to all nations, in terms of the same idea of conquest," he said.[4]

In a previous interview, he compared conservative Christians to jihadist Muslims: "You just can't say that, just as you can't say that all Christians are fundamentalists. We have our share of them [fundamentalists]. All religions have these little groups," he said. "They [Muslims] say: 'No, we are not this, the Koran is a book of peace, it is a prophetic book of peace.'"[5]

## An Apologist for Islam

The Islamic persecution of Christians is a subject that Pope Francis has largely avoided out of a politically correct fear of offending Muslims.

"On Islam the Catholic Church stammers, the more so the higher up the ladder one goes," wrote Sandro Magister in 2014. "[Pope Francis] remained silent on the hundreds of Nigerian schoolgirls abducted by Boko Haram. He remained silent on the young Sudanese mother Meriam Ibrahim, sentenced to death solely for being Christian and finally liberated by the intervention of others. He remains silent on the Pakistani mother Asia Bibi, who has been on death row for five years, she too because she is an 'infidel,' and does not even reply to the two heartrending letters she has written to him this year, before and after the reconfirmation of the sentence."[6]

His references to the persecution of Christians have tended to be opaque and rare, and do not even remotely approach the urgent status he has given to such comparatively trivial subjects as climate change and amnesty.

Judge Jeanine Pirro of Fox News, among other commentators, finds the pope's unwillingness to prioritize Christian persecution frustrating. "I am a Catholic," she said in July 2014. "And I mean no disrespect, but it is time for the papacy and Pope Francis in particular to start protecting his Christian flock. This month, Pope Francis preached that immigrant children in facilities around the United

States should be 'welcomed and protected.' Your holiness, they're in the United States. They are protected. They are being given food, and clothing and shelter. No children are being killed by the United States. Christian children are being killed in the Middle East! And while we appreciate your prayer for those in the Middle East last week, it's just not enough!"[7]

After Islamic terrorists shot up the offices of the satirical newspaper *Charlie Hebdo* in 2015, killing ten journalists, Pope Francis felt the need not to defend free speech or the Christian West but to defend Islam. "You cannot provoke. You cannot insult the faith of others. You cannot make fun of the faith of others," he said. People should "expect a punch," he said, if they offend others.[8]

The pope's comments sparked outrage in conservative circles, prompting articles about the pope "blaming" the cartoonists for "provoking the attack." Conservatives ruefully noted that the pacifist pope, normally so eager to lecture others on the need to turn the other cheek, had finally found a form of violence that he could condone.

The Vatican's newspaper *L'Osservatore Romano* often runs pieces in defense of Islam and treats Western criticism of it as "blasphemous," a claim that would only make sense if Catholicism viewed Islamic doctrines as true and divinely inspired. Catholicism never has. As St. Thomas Aquinas wrote of Muhammad, "He seduced the people by promises of carnal pleasure to which the concupiscence of the flesh goads us." Along with countless popes, Aquinas regarded Islam as a combination of half-truths, "fables, and doctrines of the greatest falsity," without the slightest odor of sanctity about them: "Muhammad said that he was sent in the power of his arms—which are signs not lacking even to robbers and tyrants."[9]

"Religions don't want war," Pope Francis declared after jihadists cut off the head of a Catholic priest in France in July 2016. The motivation for that act of terrorism was baldly Islamic. The ISIS terrorist who slit the priest's throat yelled "Allahu Akbar." Yet the pope refused to attribute it to "Islamic violence." "I don't like to talk about Islamic violence, because every day, when I read the newspaper, I see violence," he said. He then offered an off-the-wall explanation for terrorism rooted in the "idolatry" of capitalism: "As long as the god of money is at the center of the global economy and not the human person, man and woman, this is the first terrorism."[10]

Pope Francis rarely misses an opportunity to serve as an apologist for Islam or tut-tut Christians who dare to criticize it. After a jihadist almost shot up the Muhammad Art Exhibit in Texas, the Vatican condemned the event as an irresponsible exercise of free speech.[11] During a 2016 visit to the Muslim Dome of the Rock in Jerusalem, Cardinal Reinhard Marx, a member of the pope's inner circle, removed his pectoral cross, lest it offend Muslims.[12]

"It's ironic that a Catholic can get a better grasp of the Islamic threat by listening to a short speech by [Egyptian] President el-Sisi than by listening to a hundred reassuring statements from Catholic bishops," writes author William Kilpatrick, referring to el-Sisi's comments about problems within Islam. "The let's-be-friends approach has been in place even since Vatican II, but other than dialoguers congratulating themselves on the friendships they have made, it hasn't yielded much in the way of results. Christians in Muslim lands are less safe than they have been for centuries."[13]

## The Pope's Praise of Atheists

The pope's pandering to Islam has disoriented the faithful but earned him accolades from Western liberals. He is also generating praise from them for his curious sympathy for atheism. Francis is the first pope to pride himself on not trying to convert atheists to belief in God.

"When I speak with atheists, I will sometimes discuss social concerns, but I do not propose the problem of God as a starting point, except in the case that they propose it to me," he has said. "I do not approach the relationship in order to proselytize, or convert the atheist; I respect him and I show myself as I am. Where there is knowledge, there begins to appear esteem, affection, and friendship. I do not have any type of reluctance, nor would I say that his life is condemned, because I am convinced that I do not have the right to make a judgment about the honesty of that person; even less, if he shows me those human virtues that exalt others and do me good."[14]

In a 2013 interview with the atheistic ex-Catholic Eugenio Scalfari, Pope Francis said that he had no interest in converting him and that atheists should just follow their own consciences. Don't trouble yourself with the "solemn nonsense" of those Catholics who expect you to convert, Pope Francis told him. "The most surprising thing he told me was: 'God is not Catholic,'" Scalfari said after the interview.[15]

"God's working in non-Christians tends to produce sacred expressions which in turn bring others to a communitarian experience of journeying towards God," Pope Francis asserted in *Evangelii Gaudium*, a comment that past popes would have found inexplicable.

Scalfari told Francis that he never envisioned a pope who could embrace relativism and atheism: "Your Holiness, you wrote that in your letter to me. The conscience is autonomous, you said, and everyone must obey his conscience. I think that's one of the most courageous steps taken by a Pope." Pope Francis was flattered by this review of his courage and said in response, "And I repeat it here. Everyone has his own idea of good and evil and must choose to follow the good and fight evil as he conceives them. That would be enough to make the world a better place."[16] To orthodox Catholics, this sounded like raw relativism.

Scalfari has been playing Boswell to Francis's Samuel Johnson. Pope Francis was so happy with his first interview with Scalfari that he had the Vatican publishing house issue it as a book. If a future pope ever revives the *Index of Forbidden Books*, that book may appear on the list. Many of Francis's answers to Scalfari's self-indulgent questions were unfathomable for a priest to make, much less a pope. (In 2016, Pope Francis gave yet another interview to Scalfari, in which he said, "If anything, it is the communists who think like Christians." The fact that Pope Francis continues to give interviews to Scalfari makes it impossible to sustain the charge, made by some apologists for the pope, that Scalfari is misrepresenting him.)

In a 2013 homily, Pope Francis said, "The Lord has redeemed all of us, all of us, with the Blood of Christ: all of us, not just Catholics. Everyone! 'Father, the atheists?' Even the atheists. Everyone!"[17]

HBO's Bill Maher was so impressed by this statement that he declared, "I think the pope is an atheist" and that the pope's emphasis on political liberalism rather than Catholic theology put him in mind of his experience with atheistic priests: "[It] made me think—I remember when I was making 'Religulous' and we talked to a lot of priests, and we found out that a lot of priests really aren't believers... they do it because it's a way to help people and they know they can't tell the masses that it's all a crock."[18]

Pope Francis appears to entertain theological novelties about both heaven and hell. While saying confidently that atheists can go to heaven, he has flirted with theological concepts suggesting that no one goes to hell. The wicked, he told an Italian interviewer, don't suffer punishment but "annihilation," which means "their journey is finished."[19] On another occasion, he said that hell may be empty of all sinners, since "if you were a terrible sinner, who had committed all the sins in the world, all of them, condemned to death, and even when you are there, you were to blaspheme, insults...and at the moment of death, when you were about to die, you were to look to Heaven and say, 'Lord...!', where do you go, to Heaven or to Hell? To Heaven!" In *Amoris Laetitia*, he again suggested that no one goes to hell by writing that "the way of the Church is not to condemn anyone forever." He has also astonished Catholics by speaking of Judas sympathetically, as a "poor, repentant man."[20]

## The Pope Celebrates Martin Luther

On several occasions, Pope Francis has told Protestant leaders that they should remain Protestants. "I'm not interested in converting Evangelicals to Catholicism. I want people to find Jesus in their own community," he told a group of Protestants in 2014.[21] After his late friend Tony Palmer, an Anglican bishop, expressed an interest in converting to Catholicism, he discouraged him, saying that he should remain among the Protestant "bridge-builders." In a foreshadowing of that attitude, he had opposed the decision of Pope Benedict XVI to set up an "ordinariate" for Anglicans interested in converting to Catholicism. At the time, Bergoglio told the top Anglican leader in Buenos Aires, Greg Venables, that the ordinariate "was quite unnecessary" and that they should stay "as Anglicans."[22]

The pope is not seeking to convert Protestants but to apologize to them. In 2014, he baffled the Catholic community in Caserta, Italy, by visiting a Pentecostal congregation and apologizing to it for the Church's past evangelical activities.

"Someone will be surprised: 'The pope went to visit the evangelicals?' But he went to see his brothers," he said, delighting in his maverick reputation. "Among those who persecuted and denounced Pentecostals, almost as if they were crazy people trying to ruin the race, there were also Catholics. I am the pastor of Catholics, and I ask your forgiveness for those Catholic brothers and sisters who didn't know and were tempted by the devil."

Sandro Magister reports that Pope Francis had planned to ignore the Catholic community in Caserta during his visit, but when the bishop caught wind of his visit to the Pentecostals the pope was forced to change his plans:

> When the news got out, and was confirmed by Fr. Federico Lombardi, that Pope Francis intended to make a private visit

to Caserta to meet with a friend, the pastor of a local Evangelical community, the city's bishop, Giovanni D'Alise, was thunderstruck. He hadn't been told a thing. Moreover, the pope had planned his visit to Caserta for the same day as the feast of Saint Anne, the city's patron. Seeing themselves snubbed, some of the faithful threatened an uprising. It took a good week to convince the pope to change his schedule and divide the trip into two phases: the first a public one with the faithful of Caserta on Saturday, July 26, and the second in private with his Evangelical friend on the following Monday.[23]

The pope's lack of interest in converting anyone has led commentator Ann Coulter to joke, "If you're the head of the Catholic Church and your position is, 'ah, join any church. In fact, you don't even have to be a Christian.' Maybe, you know, you can get a show on CNN, but maybe you shouldn't be the head of the Catholic Church."[24]

Pope Francis goes out of his way to prop up the Church's historic opponents. Who could have imagined any other pope than this one celebrating the 500th anniversary of the Protestant Reformation? In October 2016, Pope Francis traveled to Sweden to participate in a Catholic-Lutheran service that commemorated the beginning of Martin Luther's revolt against Catholicism. According to *L'Osservatore Romano*, the idea for the joint commemoration came from Pope Francis, not from the Lutherans. (Before it, he revealed to an interviewer that "I wasn't planning to celebrate a Mass for the Catholics on this trip" lest it undercut "the ecumenical witness." He later changed his mind after a "fervent request" from Scandinavian Catholics.)

In anticipation of the trip, Pope Francis praised Luther, describing him as a "reformer." He didn't mention Luther's sweeping rejection of Catholic doctrine and sacraments, reserving his criticism not for Luther but for the Church. "I believe the intentions of Martin

Luther were not wrong," he said.[25] It has become fashionable in Vatican circles to shower lavish praise upon Martin Luther. When city officials in Rome were debating whether or not to name a town square after Luther in 2015, Pope Francis's aides readily supported the idea.[26]

"Luther Was Right, Says the Pope's Preacher," ran a headline in the UK's *Telegraph*. Fr. Raniero Cantalamessa, the preacher to the papal household, has mystified Catholics with his paeans to Luther. The Church is "indebted" to Luther's theology, according to Cantalamessa. In deference to Protestants, the pope's preacher has also advised Catholics to tone down their devotion to the Virgin Mary. "Mariology in recent centuries has become a non-stop factory of new titles, new devotions, often in polemic against Protestants," he said.[27]

In 2016, the Vatican announced that a Protestant theologian, Marcelo Figueroa, would edit the Argentine version of its newspaper *L'Osservatore Romano*. Figueroa is a friend of Pope Francis. The German bishops, in anticipation of the commemoration of Luther's revolt, called Luther a "religious pathfinder, Gospel witness, and teacher of the faith."[28] On October 13, 2016, in an event that played out almost like an *Onion* parody at the Vatican, a group of Lutherans presented a smiling Pope Francis with a copy of Martin Luther's "95 Theses" against the Church.[29]

At that event, a young Catholic girl asked the pope, "My friends do not go to Church, but they are my friends. Do I have to help them to go to Church or is it enough that they remain good friends?" Don't bother, the pope replied: "It is not licit that you convince them of your faith; proselytism is the strongest poison against the ecumenical path."[30] Former Protestants who have entered the Catholic Church find the Vatican's promotion of Luther absurd and consider the pope's blunt statement—"And today Lutherans and Catholics, Protestants, all of us agree on the doctrine of justification"—false.

"The Protestant movement sparked by Martin Luther was not

a legitimate reformation of the church," writes Fr. Dwight Longenecker. "It was an open rebellion against the Catholic Church that
ended not just in one schism, but in thousands. It also led to civil
unrest, bloodshed, rebellion and revolution that tore Christendom
apart."

Richard Ballard, a former Lutheran pastor who now serves as a
Catholic deacon, told Longenecker that the pope's claim of theological unity between Lutherans and Catholics on the doctrine of
justification is simply not true.

"According to orthodox Catholic theology, Luther did err," he
says. "Catholics insist good works (empowered by God's grace) are
meritorious and that they contribute to the process of the soul's salvation and purification. Lutherans still cling to the notion of salvation by 'faith alone' and thus negate the importance of good works
in the economy of salvation."[31]

Lutheran leaders, meanwhile, marvel at the Vatican's promotion
of Luther. "In the 1980s no one would have believed that Lutherans and Catholics were capable of reaching an agreement on the
justification question, as was the case in 1999 and just a few years
ago, had someone spoken about a joint commemoration of the
500th anniversary of the Martin Luther's Reformation, many would
have believed it to be impossible," Reverend Martin Junge, General
Secretary of the of the Lutheran World Federation, said before the
pope's trip to Sweden.[32]

In his own lifetime, Luther was condemned by Pope Leo X in
scalding terms: "we condemn, reprobate, and reject completely the
books and all the writings and sermons of the said Martin, whether
in Latin or any other language, containing the said errors or any one
of them; and we wish them to be regarded as utterly condemned,
reprobated, and rejected."

To commemorate the Reformation, the Vatican issued a document rehabilitating Luther at the expense of Pope Leo X and the
Council of Trent (which condemned Luther's theology):

To fulfill his "pastoral office," Pope Leo X felt obliged to protect the "orthodox faith" from those who "twist and adulterate the Scriptures" so that they are "no longer the Gospel of Christ." Thus the pope issued the bull Exsurge Domine (15 June 1520), which condemned forty-one propositions drawn from various publications by Luther. Although they can all be found in Luther's writings and are quoted correctly, they are taken out of their respective contexts...The Council of Trent, although to a large extent a response to the Protestant Reformation, did not condemn individuals or communities but specific doctrinal positions. Because the doctrinal decrees of the Council were largely in response to what it perceived to be Protestant errors, it shaped a polemical environment between Protestants and Catholics that tended to define Catholicism over and against Protestantism.

The pope during his trip to Sweden spoke of "unity." But in what did it consist? Mainly, a shared commitment to left-wing politics. The liberal Lutherans with which the pope met in Sweden reject the Church's teachings on abortion, gay marriage, contraception, female priests, and many other issues. But they do agree with him on climate change, as he made clear in his remarks: "I share your concern about the abuses harming our planet, our common home, and causing grave effects on the climate. As we say in our land, in my land: 'In the end, it is the poor who pay for our great festivity.' As you rightly mentioned, their greatest impact is on those who are most vulnerable and needy; they are forced to emigrate in order to escape the effects of climate change."

Pope Francis signed a joint statement with the Lutheran World Federation that gushed over the "spiritual and theological gifts of the Reformation" and committed Catholics to working with Lutherans in defense of illegal immigrants and against the "insatiable greed" of planet-destroying capitalists.

He also proposed during the trip that environmentalism be added to the Beatitudes, which caused the *Wall Street Journal* to remark: "his suggestion that Jesus' words don't merely need reinterpretation but updating was a rhetorical move only slightly less ambitious than proposing an Eleventh Commandment."[33]

Previous popes would have found the idea of a pope celebrating Luther's revolt unfathomable. In 1928, Pope Pius XI condemned the very ecumenism in which Pope Francis routinely engages, saying that it only serves to weaken the Church and compromise her teachings:

> Is it not right, it is often repeated, indeed, even consonant with duty, that all who invoke the name of Christ should abstain from mutual reproaches and at long last be united in mutual charity?... [I]n reality beneath these enticing words and blandishments lies hid a most grave error, by which the foundations of the Catholic faith are completely destroyed... it is clear why this Apostolic See has never allowed its subjects to take part in the assemblies of non-Catholics: for the union of Christians can only be promoted by promoting the return to the one true Church of Christ of those who are separated from it, for in the past they have unhappily left it. To the one true Church of Christ, we say, which is visible to all, and which is to remain, according to the will of its Author, exactly the same as He instituted it.

Future historians will find it difficult to explain how the papacy went from making statements such as that one to commemorating the Reformation. While most churchmen remained tight-lipped about the pope's trip to Sweden, a few admitted it was inexplicable. "This pope is an indifferentist," said a senior churchman interviewed for this book.

"We have already had an infallible response to the errors of

Martin Luther: the Council of Trent," said Bishop Athanasius Schneider from Kazakhstan during a talk in Washington, DC. "The teaching of the Council of Trent about the errors of Luther, I repeat, are infallible, ex cathedra. And the comments of the pope in the plane are not ex cathedra."[34]

"We Catholics have no reason to celebrate October 31, 1517, the date that is considered the beginning of the Reformation that would lead to the rupture of Western Christianity," said German cardinal Gerhard Müller before the pope's trip. "If we are convinced that divine revelation is preserved whole and unchanged through Scripture and Tradition, in the doctrine of the Faith, in the sacraments, in the hierarchical constitution of the Church by divine right, founded on the sacrament of holy orders, we cannot accept that there exist sufficient reasons to separate from the Church."[35]

## "One Hell of an Ecumenical Mess"

The religious relativism of Pope Francis is complicating his relationship with conservatives, both non-Catholic and Catholic. In 2016, it appeared that the Society of Pius X was on the verge of returning to a regular canonical relationship with the Church. But the doctrinal confusion of this pontificate has caused the traditionalist group to hesitate. Bishop Bernard Fellay, the leader of the order, has said that it has been discouraged by the "great and painful confusion that currently reigns in the Church."

As long as "errors that have made their way into it and are unfortunately encouraged by a large number of pastors, including the pope himself" persist, the order will not submit to Rome's direction, he said.[36] In the summer of 2014, the aforementioned Tony Palmer died in a motorcycle accident. In defiance of canon law, Pope Francis told Catholic officials to give the Anglican Palmer a Catholic burial as a fellow "bishop." A witness at the funeral held in Bath, England, at St. John the Evangelist Roman Catholic Church reported how the highly unorthodox Catholic funeral transpired:

> Fr. David told us that because Tony was not a Roman Catholic he had to ask his bishops permission to celebrate the requiem and though Tony's wife and children are Roman Catholics, permission still had to be given for the requiem. The bishop agreed but said that Tony could not be buried as a bishop as he was not a Roman Catholic bishop. However, Pope Francis said he should and could be buried as a bishop... and so that put an end to that little bit of ecclesiastical nonsense![37]

When a Lutheran woman in 2016 asked Pope Francis if she could receive Communion in a Catholic Church, he again ignored canon law and told her to follow her "conscience." The woman posed the question to him at a Lutheran church in Rome. She said to him that her husband is Catholic and that they wished to "participate together in Communion" and that not doing so had caused "hurt." To the bewilderment of Catholics, Pope Francis at first said that answering her question is "not my competence" and then said, "I ask myself the same question."

He then told her an odd story about a bishop who "went a little wrong—48 years old, he married, [and then had] two children"—but who would attend Mass with them. "There are questions that only if one is sincere with oneself and the little theological light one has, must be responded to on one's own," he concluded, thoroughly confusing Catholics.[38] Later, a Vatican-approved Jesuit publication in Rome, *La Civiltà Cattolica*, edited by one of Pope Francis's advisers, published an article in favor of Communion for Lutherans.[39]

He also confused conservative Catholics by appearing in a photograph in which he received a blessing from the archbishop of Canterbury. He had adopted the practice of receiving blessings from Protestant pastors during his tenure as archbishop of Buenos Aires.

In one famous photo, he is kneeling as he receives a blessing from Evangelicals.[40]

"For many Roman Catholic traditionalists, this is one hell of an ecumenical mess, sending out confusing messages about the Faith, the (Roman) Catholic Church and the uniqueness of ministry of the Vicar of Christ," observed *Cranmer*, a popular Anglican blog in the United Kingdom. "Pope Francis is more Anglican than many believe, or would find it possible to admit."[41]

In 2016, the Vatican announced that it would make no attempts to evangelize members of Judaism. That statement, yet another historic first under Francis, appeared in a document released by the Vatican's Commission for Religious Relations with the Jews. "In concrete terms this means that the Catholic Church neither conducts nor supports any specific institutional mission work directed towards Jews," stated the document titled "The Gifts and Calling of God Are Irrevocable."[42]

Rabbi Abraham Skorka, one of the pope's close friends, has said that Francis's view of "evangelization" is aimed not at converting non-Christians but convincing Christians to embrace "social justice." "This is the idea of evangelization that Bergoglio is stressing— not to evangelize Jews," he said. "This he told me, on several opportunities."[43]

The upshot of his many speeches and writings on evangelization is that the Church shouldn't evangelize anyone but rather devote her energies to temporal political projects. Cardinal Walter Kasper, from whom Pope Francis takes many of this theological cues, has said that the Church's new understanding of evangelization is the exact opposite of how the word is used in common speech: "In strict theological language, evangelization is a very complex and overall term, and reality. It implies presence and witness, prayer and liturgy, proclamation and catechesis, dialogue and social work...which do not have the goal of increasing the number of Catholics. Thus evangelization, if understood in its proper and theological meaning, does not imply any attempt of proselytism whatsoever."[44]

Liberal politics, not the salvation of souls, preoccupies Francis's Vatican. In 2016, a reporter asked his secretary of state, Cardinal Pietro Parolin, "What are you most concerned about in today's world?" In his reply, he didn't mention a single spiritual issue. He talked instead about refugees, victims of exploitation and "war," "conflicts, violence, human rights violations, environmental degradation, extreme poverty, the trade and trafficking of arms, corruption and sinister commercial and financial plans."[45]

At a time of rampant loss of faith and morality, he gave an answer that could have been given by the head of the United Nations.

## Soft toward Everyone but Traditionalists

The only religious group whom Pope Francis dares to critique are fellow Catholics. They come in for frequent scoldings from him for their "rigidity." On numerous occasions, he has blasted them for adherence to the "law." In 2016, he even described them as "heretical" for not appreciating his loose interpretation of Catholicism. The essence of Catholicism, he said strangely, lies in accepting ambiguity:

> The Church never teaches us "or this or that." That is not Catholic. The Church says to us: "this and that," he said. "Strive for perfectionism: reconcile with your brother. Do not insult him. Love him. And if there is a problem, at the very least settle your differences so that war doesn't break out." This [is] the healthy realism of Catholicism. It is not Catholic [to say] "or this or nothing:" This is not Catholic, this is heretical. Jesus always knows how to accompany us, he gives us the ideal, he accompanies us towards the ideal, He frees us from the chains of the laws' rigidity and tells us: "But do that up to the point that you are capable." And he understands us very well. He is our Lord and this is what he teaches us.[46]

He has accused traditional Catholics of "self-absorbed pro-methean neopelagianism," without bothering to clarify the insult. Oozing contempt for traditionalist Catholics, he said they consid-ers themselves "superior to others because they observe certain rules or remain intransigently faithful to a particular Catholic style from the past" and that their "supposed soundness of doctrine or discipline leads instead to a narcissistic and authoritarian elitism, whereby instead of evangelizing, one analyzes and classifies others, and instead of opening the door to grace, one exhausts his or her energies in inspecting and verifying." (Bishop Fellay has said that Vatican officials tell him that these denunciations are directed pri-marily at "conservative Americans."[47])

Early in his papacy, Pope Francis was captured on videotape belittling an altar boy for holding his hands together piously. Were they stuck together, he asked the bewildered boy. Another time he mocked a Catholic group for sending him a note saying that its members had recited thousands of rosaries for him.

"It concerns me; when I was elected, I received a letter from one of these groups, and they said: 'Your Holiness, we offer you this spiri-tual treasure: 3,525 rosaries.' Why don't they say, 'we pray for you, we ask...,' but this thing of counting," he scoffed while talking to some fellow liberal priests and nuns. "And these groups return to practices and to disciplines that I lived through—not you, because you are not old—to disciplines, to things that in that moment took place, but not now, they do not exist today..."[48]

With a friend like this pope, orthodox Catholics don't need enemies.

# CHAPTER TEN

# The Permissive Pope

In the "ten tips to happiness" that he offered during a 2014 interview with the Argentinian weekly *Viva*, Pope Francis gave as the first tip: "live and let live."[1] That permissive spirit explains why the mainstream media often calls him the "cool" pope.[2]

Pope Francis belongs to a generation of priests who saw themselves as people pleasers keen to "understand the contemporary world." Pope Francis often makes it sound as if the Church's moral theology should be put up for a popular vote. "To find what the Lord asks of his Church today, we must lend an ear to the debates of our time and perceive the 'fragrance' of the men of this age," he has said.

Historians have established that bad popes of the past committed mortal sins. But Francis is the first pope to bless sins. He has become notorious for giving scandalous advice to Catholics in adulterous relationships. In April 2014, it came out that he had placed a call to an Argentinian woman who had written to him about her adulterous relationship. The woman, Jacquelina Lisbona, was ecstatic over receiving his phone call, in which he introduced himself as "Father Bergoglio" and informed her that she could receive Communion "without problems." When she told him that her local priest objected to her reception of Communion, Pope Francis replied, "There are some priests who are more papist than the Pope."[3]

The "cool" Pope was also a cool uncle, according to Francis's niece, María Inés Navaja, who told the press that when she entered a marriage without the blessing of the Church, her uncle congratulated her. She said, "He listens a lot, but doesn't judge, and never tells you what you have to do. I remember when I told him that I couldn't wait to [get married] in the Church, that I was a grownup now and I was going to get married in a civil marriage; he answered that 'it's the best news you've given me.'"[4]

According to Francis's close Argentinian friend, Oscar Crespo, who met with Francis in 2015, the pope made a similar comment to him about a mutual friend's adulterous relationship. When Crespo asked the pope if that friend could receive Communion, he replied, "Just tell her the Pope said that she can."[5]

## Liberalizing Annulment Procedures

In 2015, Pope Francis announced that he was liberalizing the Church's annulment procedures, pushing through permissive changes that canon lawyers have described as the most significant alteration to those procedures in four hundred years.

"It's a sweeping reform; it's a dramatic reform," said Chad Pecknold, a theologian at Catholic University. "It's a reform which essentially takes away the whole judicial process for deciding whether a marriage was null or not."[6]

Liberals inside and outside the Church cheered the changes, describing them as "pastoral" and a "Catholic version of no-fault Catholic divorce." But some bishops were astonished at the laxity of the changes, noting that they eliminate most of the safeguards in place to prevent the abuse of the annulment process.

Asked by a reporter at the cable channel EWTN if Pope Francis's changes could result in a rash of phony cases, Bishop Robert

Morlino of Wisconsin replied: "That could happen. That is the sort of thing that has been happening for 50 years in the United States and the tribunals. In the name of mercy, in the name of a kind of accommodation to people who can become very pushy and very insistent, the truth has been the casualty. If that kind of an abuse were to be prevalent as these new regulations go into effect, that would simply be a continuation of what has been the case for 50 years."[7]

"Relations between Pope Francis and the canonical-legal community are strained," says canon lawyer Michael Dunnigan in an interview for this book. "Most of the Holy Father's references to law and lawyers are negative, and he seems to see the law as almost the antithesis of mercy. Most canonists, by contrast, see the law itself as pastoral. Indeed, I would say that the Church of Christ is unintelligible without its juridic aspect. The reason is that, without law or a juridic principle in the Church, it would be difficult or impossible to speak coherently about the rights of the faithful or the constitution of the Church." For all of his talk of "collegiality," Pope Francis inserted these changes into canon law autocratically.

"The Holy Father engaged in very little consultation before promulgating his reform. For such a far-reaching revision of the law, one might have expected him to consult broadly with the Roman Curia, pontifical faculties of canon law, and professional associations of canonists. However, he did not do so," according to Dunnigan.

Another canon lawyer interviewed for this book says, "He is not winning points with canon lawyers, for sure." This priest recalled a conference of canon lawyers at which one stood up and asked, "Why does the pope hate us?" "There was a lot of anger among canon lawyers, with all of his unfounded novelties and his attacks on 'doctors of the law' and so forth," he continued.

Speaking to a group of priests and nuns at a pastoral conference in Rome in 2016, Pope Francis outraged Catholics by declaring that "the great majority" of Catholic marriages are invalid.[8] His inflammatory remark was apparently offered by way of explaining his permissive annulment practices. But the comment generated so much backlash—a columnist for the *Spectator* called it "disastrous," while a columnist for the *New York Times* called it "ridiculous" and "irresponsible"—that the Vatican decided, scandalously, to falsify the transcript of the meeting and change "great majority" to "a portion."[9]

The undoctored transcript, however, reveals his true thoughts. He had been saying for many years that a majority of Catholic marriages are invalid, according to Cardinal Walter Kasper: "I've spoken to the pope himself about this, and he said he believes that 50 percent of marriages are not valid," said Kasper in 2014.[10] (Catholic commentators dismissed this story at the time as wild "hearsay," but it turned out to be, if anything, an understatement.)

Pope Francis made other peculiar comments at that pastoral conference in Rome, indicative of his idiosyncratic take on Catholicism. He mused that as archbishop of Buenos Aires it was his practice to refuse to preside at "shotgun" weddings. He didn't make it clear why the desire of a couple to provide an illegitimate child with a married mother and father constituted an unworthy motive for marriage.

He added that he considers priests who don't baptize these illegitimate children to be "animals." It was an unusually harsh comment to make about priests who are simply following canon law, which instructs them to delay baptism until there is a "founded hope" the child will be raised by practicing Catholics. (In the first year of his pontificate, showing contempt for this provision of canon law, he baptized the child of an unmarried couple at the Sistine Chapel. He has said that he would even baptize "an expedition of Martians.")

The pope was also remarkably blasé about couples living together before marriage. He said the majority of couples in Buenos Aires taking marriage preparation courses were living together but that he didn't consider that too worrisome. He told the priests at the pastoral conference not to press such couples to marry. "They prefer to cohabitate, and this is a challenge, a task. Not to ask 'why don't you marry?' No, to accompany, to wait, and to help them to mature, help fidelity to mature," he said.

He even praised some of these premarital relationships and implied that it didn't matter whether these couples got married in the Church: "I've seen a lot of fidelity in these cohabitations, and I am sure that this is a real marriage, they have the grace of a real marriage because of their fidelity."

To orthodox Catholics, the juxtaposition of these remarks with his claim that most sacramental marriages are invalid was deeply unsettling. He appeared to be saying that premarital relationships can confer real grace upon couples while "most" sacramental marriages do not.

At the same pastoral conference, he said that traditional Catholics rely too much on "clarity of doctrine" and what "should be." "We want a doctrine that is as certain as mathematics—this doesn't exist," he said. They should instead be "welcoming, accompanying, integrating, discerning, without putting our noses in the 'moral life' of other people."

That last gibe seemed calculated to delight the media, as it often lectures the Church on "staying out of people's bedrooms."

His comments had a demoralizing effect on priests, some of whom complained that his denigrations were making it harder for them to fulfill their apostolates. "Please, Holy Father: Enough of these ad hoc, off-the-cuff, impromptu sessions, whether at thirty thousand feet or at ground level," wrote Monsignor Charles Pope from the archdiocese of Washington, DC. "Much harm through confusion has been caused by these latest remarks on marriage, cohabitation, baptism, confession, and pastoral practice . . . the impact hits priests hard, and I cannot deny a certain weariness and discouragement at this point."[11]

"I will be happy when this pontificate ends," says a priest interviewed for this book. "I have stopped paying attention to what he says. It is too painful."

Even as the pope demoralizes faithful priests, he makes a show of extending sympathy to lapsed ones. In 2016, the Vatican announced that he had made a special visit to priests who had broken their vows and started families, almost romanticizing their decision: "the young men in question took the difficult decision to leave the priesthood despite opposition in many cases from their fellow priests or their families after serving for several years in parishes where loneliness, misunderstanding, fatigue arising from their many responsibilities prompted them to rethink their choice." Opponents of a celibate priesthood greeted the announcement with enthusiasm.

## The Liberalizing Synod on the Family

The centerpiece of this permissive pontificate has been the pope's liberalizing Synod on the Family, which was a pretext to weaken the Church's sacramental discipline. Toward that end, he stacked the synod with proponents of situation ethics and dissenters from the pontificates of his predecessors.

A product of his team of ghostwriters and hand-picked delegates, the synod's preliminary report spoke of the "positive aspects" of premarital cohabitation and homosexual relationships. It praised the "precious support" homosexuals find in their relationships and condemned the Church for not turning "respectfully to those who participate in her life in an incomplete and imperfect way, appreciating the positive values they contain rather than their limitations and shortcomings."[12]

The pope's rattled aides scotched that draft after it generated significant backlash. But it remains a highly relevant document of this pontificate, as it reflected the unvarnished opinions of the pope and his advisers. The significance of the document was not lost on the left.

"For the LGBT Catholics in the United States and around the world, this new document is a light in the darkness—a dramatic new tone from a church hierarchy that has long denied the very existence of committed and loving gay and lesbian partnerships," said Chad Griffin, president of Human Rights Campaign, the largest LGBT rights organization in the United States, to the press after reading the document.[13]

"Reading this #Synod14 document, I don't know what to say. It feels like a whole new church, a whole new tone, a whole new posture. Wow," wrote Joshua McElwee, the Vatican correspondent for the *National Catholic Reporter*, on Twitter. Vatican reporter John Thavis called the statement a "pastoral earthquake" and reported that "at least one bishop asked what happened to the concept of sin."[14]

The controversial proposal at the heart of the synod—the granting of Communion to the divorced-and-remarried—was also shot down by the bishops. "Catholic bishops handed Pope Francis an embarrassing defeat Saturday by withholding support for one of his signature initiatives—a pathway for Catholics who have divorced and remarried to receive Communion—thus showing the strength of conservative resistance to the pope's liberalizing agenda," reported the *Wall Street Journal*.[15]

"We're not giving in to the secular agenda; we're not collapsing in a heap. We've got no intention of following those radical elements in all the Christian churches, according to the Catholic churches in one or two countries, and going out of business," explained Australian cardinal George Pell, who called the preliminary report "tendentious" and said "it didn't represent accurately the feelings of the synod fathers." He added, "In the immediate reaction to it, when there was an hour, an hour-and-a-half of discussion, three-quarters of those who spoke had some problems with the document." That document contained, he said, "a major absence," namely, a connection to "scriptural teaching" and "church tradition."[16]

These rebuffs from the synod fathers angered Pope Francis. At the end of the synod in 2015, he delivered a homily in which he excoriated traditionalists for their "blinkered viewpoints" and "closed hearts which frequently hide even behind the church's teachings, in order to sit in the chair of Moses and judge, sometimes with superiority and superficiality, difficult cases and wounded families."

Pope Francis gave Cardinal Kasper, the leading proponent for opening Communion up to Catholics in a state of adultery, a starring role at the synod. In a moment of indiscretion during it, Kasper denounced the conservative African cardinals as reactionaries who had no business influencing its outcome. "Africa is totally different from the West," he said, "especially about gays." The synod fathers, he said, should disregard their views: "they should not tell us too much what we have to do." Kasper at first denied making these remarks, saying, "I am appalled. I have never spoken this way about Africans and I never would." But an audiotape had captured them, and his denial disintegrated.[17]

Yet Kasper's proposal prevailed, shaping Pope Francis's post-synodal apostolic exhortation *Amoris Laetitia*. Using vague language, Pope Francis endorsed the proposal, writing that "divorced who have entered a new union, for example, can find themselves in a variety of situations, which should not be pigeonholed or fit into overly rigid classifications leaving no room for a suitable personal and pastoral discernment."

His advisers spelled out the meaning of the document more explicitly in interviews after its appearance. Jesuit father Antonio Spadaro, one of the pope's closest advisers, summed up the meaning of the document bluntly: "Francis has removed all the 'limits' of the past, even in the 'sacramental discipline' and for the so-called 'irregular' couples: and these couples 'become recipients of the Eucharist.'"[18]

To anyone who had listened closely to the pope's off-the-cuff interviews, the outcome of the synod was inevitable. In one interview, he had complained bitterly about the Church's prohibitions on adulterers: "they cannot be godfathers to any child being baptized, mass readings are not for divorcees, they cannot give communion, they cannot teach Sunday school, there are about seven things that they cannot do, I have the list over there. Come on!" He continued, "Thus, let us open the doors a bit more. Why can't they be godfathers and godmothers?"

## Criticism of *Amoris Laetitia*

The German philosopher Josef Seifert said that Jesus and Mary must be "weeping" over *Amoris Laetitia*. "Pope Francis, who does not even once mention the possibility of sacrilege or peril for the soul of a person who receives Communion unworthily, tells adulterers that in certain circumstances, which are to be considered individually, it is possible for those who live in adultery or in other 'irregular' unions to receive Holy Communion without changing their lives, and so to continue living as adulterers," he wrote.[19]

The effect of the pope's exhortation has been an unfolding disaster, said Bishop Athanasius Schneider. It "has unfortunately, within a very short time, led to very contradictory interpretations even among the episcopate," he notes.[20]

He argues that it has given aid and comfort to modernist dissenters within the Church, as bishops and priests "declare that AL represents a very clear opening-up to communion for the divorced and remarried, without requiring them to practice continence." It shocked him that "a president of a Bishops' Conference has stated, in a text published on the website of the same Bishops' Conference: 'This is a disposition of mercy, an openness of heart and of spirit that needs no law, awaits no guideline, nor bides on prompting. It can and should happen immediately.'"

A few bishops, twisting themselves into contortions, tried to present the document as consonant with Catholic tradition, arguing that it hadn't explicitly condoned Communion for adulterers. But even those straining efforts became unsustainable after Pope Francis sent a letter to bishops in the Buenos Aires region in September 2016. The letter praised their guidelines, based on *Amoris Laetitia*, that authorized Communion for adulterers in certain cases. "The document is very good," he wrote to them. "There are no other interpretations."[21] Around the same time, the diocese of Rome also issued guidelines permitting Communion for adulterers.

## Mixed Signals

The sending of mixed signals has been a hallmark of this pontificate. In 2016, Pope Francis called Emma Bonino one of Italy's "forgotten greats," odd praise given her status as one of the most radical pro-abortion activists in the country's history. After being arrested for performing illegal abortions, Bonino went on to become Italy's version of Margaret Sanger. "True," she has her critics, Pope Francis said. "But never mind," he continued before praising her activism in Africa.[22]

"Sometimes it seems as if Pope Francis is determined to purge all humor from the phrase 'more Catholic than the pope,'" said former Republican presidential candidate Alan Keyes, commenting on this episode. "Is Pope Francis blind to the fact that his praise for Bonino will be used to throw the lustrous vestments of the Papacy around the shoulders of the whole abortion movement, in order to enhance the glamour of evil?"[23]

Vatican correspondent Sandro Magister has reported that the pope is keeping his distance from the pro-life movement, illustrated by the minimal support that he has given the March for Life in Rome. "It remains to be understood why Pope Francis cherishes such a dislike, although he has condemned abortion on several occasions," said Magister. "In the US, the March for Life [near] the White House in Washington is already a classic. But in Rome at St. Peter's it's not. Pope Francis does not like to see it show up."[24]

According to Magister, the pope gives short shrift to pro-lifers, barely mentioning them in publications under his control and in his audiences. March for Life attendees are used to the secular media ignoring the event. But they were surprised to see in 2014 that the pope's own newspaper ignored it, too. "*L'Osservatore Romano* also practiced shunning the whole initiative, not even dedicating a single line to it," said Magister.

Magister suspects the reason for the pope's distance is that he prefers to oppose abortion on anti-capitalist grounds rather than traditionally moral ones: "It is in the context, of what he calls, throwaway culture. His real enemy within is not those that kill the young, innocent lives—they deserve mercy—but the international economic powers that have caused such killings out of idolatry and greed… outside of this vision of Jorge Mario Bergoglio, the March for Life becomes an obstacle to dialogue with postmodernism. Not a benefit to the image of the Church, but a burden."

Pope Francis has also kept his distance from Catholic activism opposed to gay marriage. In 2016, when the press asked him to comment on gay civil-unions legislation under consideration in Italy, he dodged the question, saying disingenuously that he couldn't answer it "because the pope is for everybody and he can't insert himself in the specific internal politics of a country."[25]

On issues like climate change, illegal immigration, gun control, and the death penalty, he has had no problem inserting himself into the internal politics of countries. During the vote over "Brexit" in

2016, he angered its supporters by opposing it. One of his aides said that a vote to depart would not lead to a "stronger Europe."[26] After the British voted to leave, Pope Francis continued to defend his opposition to Brexit, saying, "let's not throw the baby out with the bath water, let's try to jump-start things, to re-create."

To applause from the media, the Vatican has steered clear of culture-war debates in Europe. As debates over euthanasia and gay marriage heated up in Europe, the Vatican fell silent, according to the Religion News Service:

> Luigi Accattoli, a veteran Vatican analyst with Italy's Corriere della Sera newspaper, sees a "new way of being pope" in the former Cardinal Jorge Bergoglio: "Francis doesn't lash out against laws that violate 'non negotiable values,'" as the Vatican usually classifies issues like the protection of life or marriage. As French bishops organized mass rallies against a law that legalized gay marriage, Francis skirted any mention of it, even during a recent meeting with French lawmakers.[27]

In 2015, gay marriage became legal in Catholic Ireland. It passed in a referendum not in spite of the Church but in part because of it. Adopting Francis's "Who am I to judge?" stance, most Irish Catholic leaders sat on their hands.

"The Church's Decision Not to Lead the No Campaign Marks a New Reality," read one headline in the British press. According to press reports, a number of Irish priests voted for the initiative. One priest even penned an open op-ed in support of it, saying that "I am one of those clergy-persons who intends to vote yes, not to cock a snoot at the leadership of my church, or to jump on a popular bandwagon, but because I think it is the right thing to do...As a follower of Jesus, the à la carte Jew who recognized when certain laws had run their courses, I am convinced that now is the right time to have marriage equality."[28]

Dublin's archbishop, Diarmuid Martin, directed his rhetorical fire not at supporters of gay marriage but at the Church. Her teaching on marriage has been "harsh" and "dogmatic," he said. He made a weak and apologetic plea for a "pluralist society" in which "people of same-sex orientation have their rights and their loving and caring relationships recognized and cherished in a culture of difference, while respecting the uniqueness of the male-female relationship." A *Huffington Post* headline summed up the waffling character of the Church's stance during the debate: "Irish Bishop on Gay Marriage: 'I Would Hate for People to Vote No for Bigoted Reasons.'"[29]

In 2016, as Mexico debated gay marriage, Pope Francis's nuncio, Franco Coppola, said to the press that he "had no pope's order in the matter" and that "I could answer with the doctrine of the Church but that is not the answer I must give as a shepherd." This undercut earlier reports that Pope Francis supported Mexico's bishops in their opposition to gay marriage.

## *Rolling Stone*'s Pope

In 2015, *Rolling Stone* ran a cover story on the pope, titled "Pope Francis: The Times They Are A-Changin'," which praised him for "scolding" conservative Catholics and drawing attention to "income inequality." The article gloried in his utility to their hip causes. The libertine magazine also found much to approve in his past, such as the time he mocked Church leaders by saying they "want to stick the whole world inside a condom."[30]

Rock stars and celebrities, excited by the progressive and permissive direction of the papacy, now visit the Vatican in droves. In 2016, Pope Francis opened up the Sistine Chapel for the first time to a rock performer, David Evans, aka "The Edge," from the band U2.

"When they asked me if I wanted to become the first contemporary artist to play in the Sistine Chapel, I didn't know what to say because usually there's this other guy who sings," he said in reference to Bono. "Being Irish you learn very early that if you want to be asked to come back it's very important to thank the local parish priest for the loan of the hall," he said. He thanked Pope Francis "for allowing us to use the most beautiful parish hall in the world." "He's doing an amazing job and long may he continue," he added.[31]

An Italian Catholic organization was dismayed when Pope Francis invited the anti-Catholic singer Patti Smith to play a Vatican Christmas concert, calling the appearance "blasphemous," given that one of her most famous lines is "Jesus died for somebody's sins, but not mine." Smith responded to the controversy with defiance. "I will do what the f-ck I want," she said. "I like Pope Francis and I'm happy to sing for him. Anyone who would confine me to a line from 20 years ago is a fool!"[32]

In 2016, Pope Francis handed out awards to actors George Clooney, Richard Gere, and Salma Hayek for their promotion of the arts through a papal charity called Scholas Occurrentes. While he didn't mind receiving the help of these socially liberal celebrities, he drew the line at a donation from the government of the "center-right" president of Argentina, Mauricio Macri, who gave the organization $1.2 million. Pope Francis made a show of returning that donation. "Critics of the Macri administration said that the pope's rejection of the donation reflected his distaste for the president's introduction of austerity measures," reported the *Guardian*.[33]

In an effort to be hip, the Pontifical Council for Culture, under the leadership of Cardinal Gianfranco Ravasi, and the Vatican newspaper *L'Osservatore Romano* have taken to eulogizing pop stars. As Fr. George Rutler wrote, "when David Bowie died, *L'Osservatore Romano*, aching to be the Church of What's Happening Now, eulogized the genius of Bowie, excusing his 'ambiguous image' as one of his 'excesses' but then remarking his 'personal sobriety, even in his dry, almost thread-like body.'"

Rutler also recalled the "extravagant tribute that the editor of

*L'Osservatore Romano* paid to the crooner Michael Jackson when he died of acute Propofol and Benzodiazepine intoxication." The headline over that story asked breathlessly, "But will he actually be dead?" and said "Jackson's transgenderizing surgeries were 'a process of self definition that was beyond race,'" reported Rutler. As for the charges of pedophilia against Jackson, *L'Osservatore Romano* opined: "Everybody knows his problems with the law after the pedophilia accusations. But no accusation, however serious or shameful, is enough to tarnish his myth among his millions of fans throughout the entire world."[34]

Desperate to appear in sync with pop culture, Ravasi made use of Italian actress Nancy Brilli in a video promoting his council's #LifeofWomen campaign. In the video, the saucy actress asks, "What do you think about yourself, your strengths, your difficulties, your body, and your spiritual life?" "The video was the brainchild of 15 professional women—all but one of them Italian—chosen by Cardinal Gianfranco Ravasi to advise him on the agenda for 'Women's Cultures: Equality and Difference,'" reported the *New York Daily News*.[35] After the video generated widespread complaints, Ravasi pulled it.

## The "Cool Pope" and Feminism

The "cool" pope often pays homage to modern feminism and criticizes his predecessors for their alleged sexism. He has said "that the feminine presence in the Church has not fully emerged because the temptation of machismo has not left space to make visible the role women are entitled to within the community." He has also said that "women in the Church are more important than bishops and priests."[36]

In 2016, the Vatican launched a magazine called *Women-Church-World*, which had begun as a supplement in *L'Osservatore Romano*, to provide feminists with a platform to criticize the Church. In its first edition, the magazine editorialized that the Church had "largely ignored" the contribution of women to the Church's life. In its previous supplemental form, it had run an article in favor of women preaching at Masses, which canon law forbids.[37]

In a bow to feminist pressures, Vatican officials have said that it is "theoretically possible" for women to be cardinals and to hold such positions as the Holy See's secretary of state. In 2016, Pope Francis announced that he would consider ordaining women deacons. He authorized the formation of a commission to study the issue. That decision was made in a typically haphazard form, after women religious had asked him at a Vatican meeting: "Why not construct an official commission that might study the question?" He replied, "Constituting an official commission that might study the question? I believe yes. It would do good for the church to clarify this point. I am in agreement. I will speak to do something like this."[38]

This caused consternation among many Catholics, as Pope John Paul II and Pope Benedict XVI had resisted such talk. The consternation grew when Pope Francis officially established the commission in August 2016 and placed on it a supporter of female priests.[39]

Nor did Francis's predecessors ever warm to the subject of a married priesthood, another subject on which Pope Francis has sent mixed signals. He has spoken of the value of a celibate priesthood, but said that that "could change" and that the subject of married priests "is on his agenda."

According to several bishops, he is open to reconsidering that discipline. Bishop Hans-Jochen Jaschke of Hamburg said Francis "made no sign of refusal" after the German bishops raised the issue with him. Brazilian bishop Erwin Kräutler, one of his close advisers, said that Pope Francis urged him to make "bold, daring proposals" after he broached the subject with him and that Francis was leaning toward letting national conferences decide the issue.[40] His childhood friend Oscar Crespo told the press that during a visit to the Vatican Francis described a celibate priesthood as "archaic." In 2016, papal biographer Austen Ivereigh wrote a piece saying that the next synod is "likely" to address the issue of ordaining married men.[41] But it has since been announced that the 2018 synod's theme will be "Youth, Faith, and Vocational Discernment." According to Vatican correspondent Edward Pentin, Pope Francis was "keen" to discuss married priests, but "that proposal was understood to have been voted down by the majority of members on the XIV Ordinary Council of the Synod of Bishops, the body charged with drawing up the theme of the next synod."[42]

## "The Meeting Is the Message"

The leftist press also admires the audiences that he grants to avant-garde activists. For a pope who likes to say that the "meeting is the message," these encounters clearly hold subversive value to him. For example, in 2015, he granted the transgender activist Diego Lejarraga an audience after Lejarraga complained in a letter that the Church had "marginalized" him. According to Lejarraga, Pope Francis phoned him twice after receiving his letter and then invited him to the Vatican. Lejarraga told the Spanish press that Francis reassured him that God loves all his children "as they are" and the "Church loves you and accepts you as you are."

From time to time, Pope Francis has appeared to reaffirm the Church's opposition to gender theories, but his meeting with Lejarraga sent a different message. Lejarraga brought his fiancée with him to the meeting with the pope, which culminated in an embrace. The press burbled over the meeting for days, declaring that "the unexpected overture marks an important gesture of acceptance of lesbian, gay, bisexual or transgender Catholics."[43] The Vatican offered no clarification on the meaning of the meeting. Indeed, Pope Francis boasted about the meeting in 2016, recalling warmly that he had invited the "he that was her but is he" to the Vatican. His comments indicated that he approved of his transgenderism and his gay marriage: "I received them and they were happy...Life is life and you must take things as they come."[44]

Yet when it leaked out during his visit to America that Pope Francis had met Kim Davis, the Kentucky clerk imprisoned briefly for declining to issue gay-marriage licenses, the liberal elite expressed disappointment in the cool pope. But he moved quickly to win back their affection. He authorized his press secretary to spin the meeting as a meaningless gesture, akin to a random rope line greeting.[45]

"The Pope did not enter into the details of the situation of Mrs. Davis and his meeting with her should not be considered a form of support of her position in all of its particular and complex aspects," said his press secretary. "Such brief greetings occur on all papal visits and are due to the Pope's characteristic kindness and availability. The only real audience granted by the Pope at the Nunciature was with one of his former students and his family."

That former student turned out to be a homosexual caterer with his boyfriend in tow, prompting such excited reports from the liberal media as "Vatican distances Pope Francis from Kentucky clerk Kim Davis. Meanwhile, the Vatican confirmed that Francis met with a gay friend and his partner a day earlier."

Once liberals heard these reports, he returned to their good graces. As one liberal pundit put it to his colleagues, only half-facetiously, "You Can Like the Pope Again! Vatican Distances Pope from Kim Davis."[46] A grateful cast on NBC's *Saturday Night Live* depicted Pope Francis in a skit untangling himself from Kim Davis's embrace.

His former student Yayo Grassi rushed to the press to inform them that he and his boyfriend, Iwan, had received a papal blessing and that Francis, in a previous exchange, had assured him that "I want you to know that in my work there is absolutely no place for homophobia."[47]

While offering a "clarification" on the Kim Davis meeting, the Vatican didn't bother to clarify that papal remark to Grassi. It was content to let the Church's critics think that it no longer takes its own moral teachings seriously anymore.

Such meetings have always appealed to Bergoglio. During his tenure as archbishop of Buenos Aires, he made a point of keeping in touch with disgraced clerics, such as Jerónimo José Podestá, a Catholic bishop whose radicalism led to his removal from office. "Bergoglio visited the ostracised bishop on his deathbed and gave him the last rites. He then ensured that the man's widow, Clelia Luro, and her children were provided for—even though she was a feminist as radical as was imaginable on the Catholic spectrum, who used to celebrate mass with her husband," writes author Paul Vallely.[48]

## The Church Muddled

St. Ignatius established the Jesuit order to advance the "Church militant." But Pope Francis, in a bid to be popular with the liberal elite, prefers a Church muddled. He is chipping away at Church teachings as he plays to the anti-conservative prejudices of the powerful. Francis doesn't fear losing the good opinion of "fundamentalists," whom he regularly caricatures as out of step with the modern zeitgeist. But he is afraid of losing the good opinion of the liberal elite.

St. Paul wrote his letters to "fools for Christ" to confirm them in their faith. Pope Francis writes letters to opponents of Christian teaching to confirm them in their errors. Italian atheist Eugenio Scalfari felt so confirmed in his unbelief and relativism after his epistolary exchanges with Francis that he gushed, "an openness to modern and secular culture of this breadth, such a profound vision between conscience and its autonomy, has never before been heard from the chair of St. Peter."[49]

His pontificate has proceeded almost like an apology tour,

designed to allay the anxieties of the liberal elite. On his way back from Armenia in 2016, he insulted Catholics by offering a series of gratuitous apologies tailored to left-wing sensibilities: "I think that the Church not only should apologize...to a gay person whom it offended but it must also apologize to the poor as well, to the women who have been exploited, to children who have been exploited (by being forced to) work. It must apologize for having blessed so many weapons." He bemoaned the "closed Catholic culture" of the past and celebrated the supposed enlightenment of modern times: "The culture has changed—and thank God."[50]

After this extravagant apology, the liberal Jesuit Fr. Thomas Reese marveled on Twitter, "Pope Francis is speaking about gays and lesbians in ways that would have gotten anyone else disciplined, censured, or silenced ten years ago."

# CHAPTER ELEVEN

# How Francis Is Undoing the Legacy of Pope John Paul II and Pope Benedict XVI

In a veiled swipe at his two predecessors, Pope Francis told an interviewer that Vatican II had encouraged openness to "modern culture" and "dialogue with non-believers" but that after it "very little was done in that direction" in the Church. He promised to correct this shortcoming: "I have the humility and ambition to want to do something."[1]

Close advisers to Pope Francis, such as Cardinal Kasper, have acknowledged the lack of continuity between this pontificate and past ones. The program of Pope Francis is "not to preserve everything as it has been of old," according to Kasper.[2]

The liberal aides of Pope Francis speak of him as a revolutionary pope steadily working to liberalize the Church after a period of conservative retrenchment. To progressives concerned that the changes haven't been quick enough, Archbishop Victor Fernández, one of the pope's ghostwriters, offered words of reassurance: "The pope goes slow because he wants to be sure that the changes have a deep impact. The slow pace is necessary to ensure the effectiveness of the changes. He knows there are those hoping that the next pope will turn everything back around."[3]

By laying the groundwork for change so methodically, "it's more difficult to turn things back," said Fernández. The pope is aiming for "irreversible" change and that even if some cardinals have "regrets" about electing him that "doesn't change anything," said Fernández.

It is now taken for granted in the press that Francis's pontificate is a repudiation of the restorationist priorities of Pope John Paul II and Pope Benedict XVI. As the *Wall Street Journal* put it, Pope Francis is presiding over a "new Rome," in which he "has effectively reversed course."[4]

Where Pope John Paul II and Pope Benedict XVI tried to counteract the influence of liberal theology, Pope Francis is seeking to spread it, noted the *Journal*.

"Pope Francis' immediate predecessors, John Paul II and Benedict XVI, devoted much of their pontificates to correcting what they deemed unjustified deviations from tradition in the name of Vatican II," wrote Vatican correspondent Francis X. Rocca, while Francis "In word and deed...has argued that the church's troubles reflect not recklessness but timidity in interpreting and applying the principles of Vatican II, especially the council's call for the church to open itself to the modern world."[5]

"Popes John Paul and Benedict, who had played key roles at Vatican II, concluded that the church had gone too fast and too far in innovations ranging from the abandonment of religious garb to the acceptance of liberal ideas on sexual morality," Rocca continued. "In response, they issued the first universal catechism since the 16th century, systematically laying out the church's fundamental teachings; they censured dissent among theologians and within religious orders; and they reversed moves to expand the role of bishops in the development of church teaching and practice."[6]

Francis's predecessors worried about liturgical looseness, but he shrugs at it. They resisted calls for reopening discussion on issues such as married priests and female deacons, but he signals an open-ness to it. At a time of rampant religious relativism, they revived a distinctive Catholic identity, but he downplays it. They acknowl-edged differences between Islam and Christianity; he blurs them. They upheld moral absolutes; he "discerns" exceptions to them.

Some apologists for the pope and his "mercy-over-morals priori-ties," as the press has put it, have tried to pass off these and other differences as a mere change of style. But they go well beyond it, as manifest in his support for changing the Church's sacramental discipline for the divorced-and-remarried. If anything, the changes of style are at the service of changes in substance. His deliberately "pastoral" style is tied to a progressive theology.

In 2011, Pope Benedict XVI delivered a speech to the Tribunal of the Roman Rota about the dangers of "pseudo-pastoral claims." In retrospect, the speech reads like a warning of his successor's pontifi-cate, which has been nothing if not pseudo-pastoral. In the name of false pastoralism, Pope Francis pits canon law and doctrine against mercy and the Gospel. In this speech, Pope Benedict XIV takes direct aim at that distortion, arguing that canon law is not contrary to mercy but a safeguard of it:

> Canon law is at times undervalued, as if it were a mere techni-cal instrument at the service of any given subjective interest, even one that is not founded on truth. Instead, canon law must always be considered in its essential relationship with justice, in the recognition that, in the Church, the goal of juridical activ-ity is the salvation of souls...It is necessary to note the wide-spread and deeply rooted, though not always evident, tendency to place justice and charity in opposition to one another, as if the two were mutually exclusive...One must avoid pseudo-pastoral claims that would situate questions on a purely hori-zontal plane.

Quoting Pope John Paul II, Pope Benedict described this "misplaced compassion" as a counterfeit of charity, "sentimentality, pastoral only in appearance." He called churchmen to courage, which becomes "more relevant the more injustice appears to be the easiest approach to take, insofar as it implies accommodating the desires and expectations of the parties or even the conditioning of the social context."

The self-consciously "pastoral" Catholicism to which Pope Benedict XVI referred is now on daily display under Pope Francis. A streak of antinomianism, the heresy that drives a wedge between divine law and mercy, runs through many of his speeches and serves as the subtext of his criticism of conservative Catholics.

"Among Catholics there are many, not a few, many, who believe to hold the absolute truth," Pope Francis has said. "They go ahead by harming others with slander and defamation, and they do great harm...And it must be combated."[7]

Pope John Paul II and Pope Benedict XVI exhorted Catholics to seek the truth, but Pope Francis makes them feel guilty for pursuing it. In his view, the crisis in the Church is due not to a betrayal of orthodoxy but to an emphasis on it. He rarely misses an opportunity to portray orthodox Catholics as unmerciful and unhinged. "It is amazing to see the denunciations for lack of orthodoxy that come to Rome," he has said dismissively of Catholics worried about unsound catechesis in their dioceses.[8]

To the extent that Francis's Vatican condemns anyone, it is conservatives. Stop objecting to heterodoxy, he has lectured them: "If the Christian is a restorationist, a legalist, if he wants everything clear and safe, then he will find nothing. Those who today always look for disciplinarian solutions, those who long for an exaggerated doctrinal 'security,' those who stubbornly try to recover a past that no longer exists—they have a static and inward-directed view of things. In this way, faith becomes an ideology among other ideologies."[9]

By condemning these Catholics, Pope Francis is implicitly condemning his predecessors, who urged the faithful to cleave to orthodoxy and value Catholic tradition and doctrinal fidelity.

In a homily that almost perfectly anticipates Pope Francis's caricaturing of orthodox Catholics as fundamentalists, Pope Benedict XVI said, "Today, having a clear faith based on the Creed of the Church is often labeled as fundamentalism. Whereas relativism, that is, letting oneself be 'tossed here and there, carried about by every wind of doctrine,' seems the only attitude that can cope with modern times. We are building a dictatorship of relativism that does not recognize anything as definitive and whose ultimate goal consists solely of one's own ego and desires."

The St. Gallen group, the cabal of liberal cardinals who were instrumental in Bergoglio's election as pope, had long groused about the "fundamentalist" views of Pope John Paul II and Pope Benedict XVI. They bristled when Pope John Paul II wrote in his encyclical *Veritatis Splendor* that situation ethics reinforces the moral relativism widespread in society. Said Pope John Paul II: "An attitude of this sort corrupts the morality of society as a whole, since it encourages doubt about the objectivity of the moral law in general and a rejection of the absoluteness of moral prohibitions regarding specific human acts, and it ends up by confusing all judgments about values." References to that document have been conspicuously absent from Pope Francis's writings.

Through Pope Francis, the St. Gallen group got its revenge in *Amoris Laetitia*, where the pope implicitly challenges *Veritatis Splendor* by stating that the avoidance of adultery is a mere "ideal," which a Catholic can violate if he "discerns" that his circumstances and conscience justify it. "Hence it can no longer simply be said that all those in any 'irregular' situations are living in a state of mortal sin and are deprived of sanctifying grace," Pope Francis wrote.

## Opposition to the Latin Mass

At the beginning of Francis's pontificate, an unnamed Vatican diplomat was quoted in the *National Catholic Reporter* as saying, "The traditional Latin Mass brigade is finished."[10] The remark wasn't far off. Unlike his predecessors, Pope Francis has shown no particular attachment to the Church's liturgical traditions—his indifference to rubrics are visible during his papal masses—and views liturgical conservatives with contempt.

Under his pontificate, religious dedicated to the Church's liturgical traditions have had to run for cover. One of Pope Francis's first moves was to harass a growing traditionalist order in Italy called the Franciscan Friars of the Immaculate, which had enthusiastically embraced *Summorum Pontificum*, Pope Benedict's XVI order authorizing wider use of the traditional Latin Mass. Dismayed by the conservative direction of the order, Pope Francis authorized Vatican officials to meddle in the order's affairs.

These Vatican officials decreed: "the Holy Father Francis has directed that every religious of the congregation of the Franciscan Friars of the Immaculate is required to celebrate the liturgy according to the ordinary rite and that, if the occasion should arise, the use of the extraordinary form (Vetus Ordo) must be explicitly authorized by the competent authorities, for every religious and/or community that makes the request."[11]

According to the Vatican correspondent Sandro Magister, this harassment of the order displeased Pope Benedict XVI. Magister reported that the "ban imposed by pope Bergoglio on the congregation of the Franciscan Friars of the Immaculate against celebrating the Mass in the ancient rite has been an effective restriction of that freedom of celebrating in this rite which Benedict XVI had guaranteed for all" and that "It emerges from conversations with his visitors that Ratzinger himself has seen in this restriction a 'vulnus' [or wound] on his 2007 motu proprio *Summorum Pontificum*."[12]

"What Pope Francis did to the Franciscan Friars of the Immaculate is disgusting," said a monsignor interviewed for this book. Another high-ranking Church official interviewed for this book said that the pope's treatment of orders like the Franciscan Friars of the Immaculate has "emboldened" liberal bishops to harass conservatives in their dioceses. "Liberal bishops know they have the upper hand now," he said.

"Nobody wants to end up like the Franciscan Friars of the Immaculate," said a priest interviewed for this book. "Now is the time to lie low."

In various interviews and speeches, Pope Francis has made it clear that it wouldn't bother him if the traditional Latin Mass movement died. He has mischaracterized Benedict's rationale for authorizing wider use of it as a "prudential decision motivated by the desire to help people who have this sensitivity." In fact, Benedict had authorized wider use of the traditional Latin Mass both for the sake of older Catholics and for the sake of future generations of Catholics, whom he feared wouldn't have access to the liturgical riches of the Catholic patrimony.

Pope Benedict XVI repeatedly spoke of the need to tighten up the liturgy after a period of liberalization in Vatican II's wake. He called for a "reform of the reform." Pope Francis is on record calling that movement "mistaken."[13]

He doesn't want a reform of the reform. He supports all of the changes made to the Mass in the 1960s. After a Mass in 2015 commemorating Pope Paul VI's decision to replace the traditional Latin Mass with the vernacular mass, Pope Francis commented, "Let us give thanks to the Lord for what he has done in his church in these 50 years of liturgical reform. It was really a courageous move by the church to get closer to the people of God so that they could understand well what it does, and this is important for us: to follow Mass like this."[14]

In his view, the interest among young Catholics in pre–Vatican II liturgical traditions constitutes empty nostalgia.

"When we were discussing those who are fond of the ancient liturgy and wish to return to it, it was evident that the Pope speaks with great affection, attention, and sensitivity for all in order not to hurt anyone," Czech archbishop Jan Graubner said to Vatican Radio. "However, he made a quite strong statement when he said that he understands when the old generation returns to what it experienced, but that he cannot understand the younger generation wishing to return to it."

Graubner quoted Pope Francis as saying, "When I search more thoroughly, I find that it is rather a kind of fashion. And if it is a fashion, therefore it is a matter that does not need that much attention. It is just necessary to show some patience and kindness to people who are addicted to a certain fashion."[15]

This dismissive view contrasts sharply with the view of Pope Benedict XVI, who interpreted youth interest as a sign of spiritual health. "Young persons too have discovered this liturgical form, felt its attraction, and found in it a form of encounter with the Mystery of the Most Holy Sacrifice particularly suited to them," he wrote in *Summorum Pontificum*. "What earlier generations held as sacred, remains sacred for us too."

In 2016, Pope Francis gave an interview in which he reiterated his dim view of youth interest in the ancient liturgy, casting it as sinister: "I ask myself about this. For example, I always try to understand what's behind the people who are too young to have lived the pre-conciliar liturgy but who want it. Sometimes I've found myself in front of people who are too strict, who have a rigid attitude. And I wonder: How come such a rigidity? Dig, dig, this rigidity always hides something: insecurity, sometimes even more..."[16]

Even when members of the current Curia give voice to the

liturgical concerns of the previous pope, Pope Francis makes sure to undercut their comments. Consider the humiliation that Cardinal Robert Sarah, who is prefect of the Congregation for Divine Worship and the Discipline of the Sacraments, suffered after he endorsed the liturgical views of Pope Benedict XVI. He received a widely publicized rebuke from the pope after merely suggesting at a conference in 2016 that "It is very important that we return as soon as possible to a common orientation, of priests and the faithful turned together in the same direction—eastwards, or at least towards the apse—to the Lord who comes."

Sarah's statement set off a panic among the liturgical liberals around Pope Francis, and within days Sarah had been called on the carpet. Francis-friendly bishops, such as Cardinal Vincent Nichols of the United Kingdom, instructed their priests to disregard Sarah's suggestion. Nichols sent them a letter saying that this is no time to "exercise personal preference or taste." That was followed up by a Vatican "clarification," which indicated obliquely that Sarah had been confronted by Pope Francis over the matter. Sarah was in effect told to knock off his talk of a "reform of the reform." According to the pope's spokesmen, that phrase is no longer to be used, as it is the "source of misunderstandings."[17]

According to the *Tablet*, a liberal Catholic weekly in the United Kingdom, "It is highly unusual for the Vatican to publicly slap down a Prince of the Church, yet not entirely surprising given how Cardinal Sarah has operated since his appointment to lead the Holy See's liturgy department. There have been a series of incidents that reveal the cardinal is part of a faction making life difficult for this Pope: take, for example, the fact it took Cardinal Sarah's department more than a year to implement Francis' simple request that women should be included in the Holy Thursday foot-washing ritual."[18]

In October 2016, Cardinal Sarah received a fresh snub: Pope Francis dropped all twenty-seven of his department's members and replaced them with a roster of liturgical liberals, including Piero

Marini, a prominent opponent of traditionalists and an advocate of liturgical dance.

"This almost total clean-out of an entire Congregation's voting members in a single hit—unprecedented in Vatican history, so it seems—is also in effect a sharp rebuff to Pope Emeritus Benedict XVI, the centerpiece of whose pontifical legacy was a restoration of tradition, dignity, and Latin in the Sacred Liturgy," wrote Fr. Brian Harrison on the day it happened. "One is filled with a deep sense of foreboding as to what changes to the way we are expected to worship, and what possible undermining of Benedict's liberation of the Traditional Latin Rite, are portended by today's breathtaking papal purge."[19]

## Freezing Out Conservatives, Promoting Liberals

According to the prominent German philosopher Robert Spaemann, churchmen connected to Pope John Paul II and Pope Benedict XVI have been rendered irrelevant by this pontificate. "He has excluded the Institute John Paul II for Studies on the Family from the pre-Synod consultations," he said. "I wonder why he throws so many people out of the Vatican who had been called in by Benedict."[20] (In 2016, Pope Francis changed the leadership of the John Paul II Institute, telling its new leader to broaden the "life" agenda to include environmentalism.[21])

"He has frozen out Benedict's appointments," says a Church insider, who asked to remain anonymous, in an interview for this book. "To the extent that they are still around, they are just figureheads at this point." Indeed, Vatican observers speak of a "de-Ratzingerization" of the Curia, evident in Francis's sacking of Benedict-friendly bishops from the crucially important Congregation of Bishops.

"Soon after his election, Francis removed two Americans—Cardinal Justin Rigali and Cardinal Raymond Burke—from the congregation. Both men were major players in constituting the American episcopacy during the papacy of Benedict XVI. Rigali also previously served as secretary of the congregation," reported the *National Catholic Reporter.* "Many of the bishops appointed during that era formed the core of 'culture warrior' bishops who kept such issues as opposing same-sex marriage, the contraception mandate of the Affordable Care Act, as well as religious liberty foremost on the agenda of the U.S. Conference of Catholic Bishops. The tone of the conference in recent years has become heavily legalistic both in terms of pastoral approach within the church and in battling in court over civil matters."[22]

Pope Francis is stacking the Curia with determined progressives and giving plum assignments to dissenters who had been sidelined during Benedict's pontificate. In 2015, Pope Francis made Fr. Timothy Radcliffe, one of the Dominican Order's most flagrant liberals, a consultor to the Pontifical Council for Justice and Peace. Radcliffe had visited Bergoglio during his tenure as archbishop of Buenos Aires and then had a "long conversation" with him after he became pope. Radcliffe was pleased at his promotion "out of the blue."[23]

Radcliffe is a perfect representative of the progressive ideology that Pope Francis seeks to normalize in the Church. Radcliffe is known for his open promotion of gay-rights ideology, his support for Communion for the divorced-and-remarried, and his insistence that the Church embrace female deacons and "loosen" its opposition to female priests and other feminist innovations. He has said that gay sex is "expressive of Christ's self-gift." He is heartened by the increasing support for gay civil unions under Pope Francis, and has urged Catholics to watch *Brokeback Mountain* and read "gay novels." Catholics, he said, must "belong to each other across every theological boundary." Gay priests, he argues, are among the "most impressive and dedicated" priests in the Church today and applauds Francis for appreciating their "gifts."[24]

Many churchmen who hold the same views as Radcliffe have gone from the margins to the mainstream under Pope Francis.

"The liberals are in charge," says a Church official interviewed for this book. Pope Francis is "like a low-level Argentinian pol" who surrounds himself with liberal cronies and refuses to brook dissent, he says.

"Discussions during the Synod on the Family revealed the determination with which a group of pastors and theologians do not hesitate to undermine the Church's doctrinal cohesion. This group functions in the manner of a powerful, international, well-heeled, organized and disciplined party," according to Monsignor Michel Schooyans. "The active members of this party have ready access to the media; they frequently appear unmasked. They operate with backing from some of the highest authorities in the Church. The main target of these activists is Christian morality, criticized for having a severity incompatible with the 'values' of our time. We must find ways which lead the Church to please, by reconciling its moral teaching with human passions."[25]

"He has loosened the awful intellectual clamp imposed by John Paul II and Benedict XVI where people were afraid of being silenced," Mary McAleese, the former president of Ireland, has said.[26]

That appears painfully true to conservative Catholics. In a sign of the free-wheeling atmosphere under Pope Francis, Johan Bonny, the bishop of Antwerp, explicitly citing the pope's liberalism, has said that the Church should embrace gay relationships. "There should be recognition of a diversity of forms," he said. "We have to look inside the church for a formal recognition of the kind of interpersonal relationship that is also present in many gay couples. Just as there are a variety of legal frameworks for partners in civil society, one must arrive at a diversity of forms in the church."

Under previous popes, such a baldly heterodox claim would have generated a Vatican reprimand. In Bonny's case, he not only escaped a reprimand but received a promotion. After his comments, he was given by the Vatican a position at the Synod on the Family. "Do not underestimate the significance of this," said Professor Rik Torfs, a canon law expert and rector of the Catholic University of Leuven. "Bonny advocates a change from principles long held as unshakable, something no bishop could have done under the dogmatic pontificates of Pope John Paul II and Pope Benedict XVI."[27]

In 2016, Pope Francis entrusted the Pontifical Academy for Life to a social liberal, Archbishop Vincenzo Paglia, whose praise for the propagandistic television show *Modern Family* has confused Catholics.[28] Under the direction of such worldly progressives, the Vatican has received criticism for its unreliable documents. Conservative Catholics, for example, protested the risqué and misleading content in sexual education materials that the Vatican distributed at World Youth Day in Poland in 2016.[29] The materials encouraged the use of sexually explicit films as occasions for discussion and neglected to highlight Church teaching. "It's bad enough when Planned Parenthood pushes perverse forms of sex education into our schools. For the Vatican to jump on that bandwagon is a nightmare scenario," said Judie Brown, president of the American Life League.[30]

Pope Francis's post-synodal apostolic exhortation *Amoris Laetitia* marked a theological reversal from Pope John Paul II's *Familiaris Consortio*, which he wrote in 1981. That reversal may go down as one of the most historically significant moments of his papacy and is likely to reverberate through the Church for years to come.

In *Familiaris Consortio*, Pope John Paul II had explicitly rejected access to Communion for the divorced and remarried and reaffirmed moral absolutes against the objections of situation ethicists. *Amoris Laetitia* strikes at the roots of his work by encouraging the "help of the sacraments" for the divorced-and-remarried, by emphasizing conscience over magisterial teaching, and by obscuring the distinction between mortal and venial sin.

Cardinals who were close to Pope John Paul II have been dismayed by *Amoris Laetitia*. Cardinal Carlo Caffarra, the former archbishop of Bologna, has described the document as "objectively unclear" and bemoans that it has given rise to a "conflict of interpretations ignited even among bishops."[31]

"What has been certain before has become problematic," wrote Jude Dougherty, the former head of Catholic University's philosophy department. "Pope Francis' ambiguous teaching on marriage and the family as well as on other matters lends itself to interpretation by a secular media all too willing to promote a progressive interpretation of any document, indicating that the Church has changed its former teaching."[32]

It is commonly said by the media that Francis's pontificate is one of "mercy." But in fact he is teaching Catholics that they don't need mercy, for they haven't sinned. Pope John Paul II had anticipated this problem when he wrote in *Veritatis Splendor*, "It is quite human for the sinner to acknowledge his weakness and to ask mercy for his failings; what is unacceptable is the attitude of one who makes his own weakness the criterion of the truth about the good, so that he can feel self-justified, without even the need to have recourse to God and his mercy."

In other words, if living in a state of adultery doesn't constitute "mortal sin" and doesn't deprive one of "sanctifying grace," as Pope Francis says in *Amoris Laetitia*, why would anyone need mercy?

## Cardinal Martini's Dream Realized

"Proselytism is solemn nonsense," Pope Francis said to the Italian atheist Eugenio Scalfari after reassuring him that he didn't want him to convert to Catholicism. Pope Francis's opposition to Catholic evangelization is impossible to square with the message of *Dominus Iesus*, the 2000 document issued by Joseph Ratzinger and approved by Pope John Paul II, which said "If it is true that the followers of other religions can receive divine grace, it is also certain that objectively speaking they are in a gravely deficient situation in comparison with those who, in the Church, have the fullness of the means of salvation." That document also sought to "rule out, in a radical way…a religious relativism which leads to the belief that 'one religion is as good as another.'"

The members of the St. Gallen group disdained that document and pushed for the election of Bergoglio in the hopes of neutralizing it. Cardinal Walter Kasper openly criticized that document, calling it an "unfortunate affirmation."[33] Kasper now celebrates that under Francis the Church enjoys a diversity of belief and practice suppressed by previous popes and that Catholic evangelization no longer occurs. "So 'the door is open' for admission of the divorced and remarried to the sacraments," Kasper has said. "There is also some freedom for the individual bishops and bishops' conferences. Not all Catholics think the way we Germans think. Here [in Germany] something can be permissible which is forbidden in Africa. Therefore, the pope gives freedom for different situations and future developments."[34]

Pope Francis's decision in 2013 to establish a special Council of Cardinals to advise him was an implicit rebuke to his predecessors, who had been criticized by the Catholic left for "centralizing" the Church. Pope Francis found the idea for this council of cardinals in the work of the Milanese cardinal Carlo Maria Martini, who was one the chief critics of Pope John Paul II and Pope Benedict XVI.

Martini was a loud supporter of "democratizing" the Church and proposed to further it by making the Church more "synodal." Martini claimed that the Church was "200 years out of date" and that it should adjust its teachings to the philosophy and culture of the post-Enlightenment West.

Giving credit to Martini for the idea behind the Council of Cardinals, Pope Francis made a revealing comment about its significance: "This is the beginning of a Church whose organization is not only vertical but also horizontal. When Cardinal Martini spoke about this and emphasized the role of the Councils and Synods, he knew only too well how long and difficult the road ahead in that direction would be."

Marco Garzonio, who is a biographer of Martini, has written that the liberal Church of Pope Francis represents the realization of Martini's dream for a more temporally minded church:

> Martini believed in and never gave up on the "dream," which Bergoglio is now trying to get onto its feet so that it can be turned into reality.
>
> In the interview of August 8, 2012, published in "Corriere della Sera" on September 1, the day after his death, Martini, with the grave tone of the testamentary bequest and the prophetic admonition, also indicated the practical means: the pope should surround himself with twelve bishops and cardinals if he wants the barque of Peter not to be submerged by internal waves and by a society that no longer believes in it, two hundred years behind as it is on issues like the family, the young, the role of women (this being a topic on which Pope Francis has promised to speak more).

Garzonio added that one of the pope's comments—that God is not "Catholic"—comes straight from Martini's work: "In 2007 Martini said in the book-interview 'Nighttime conversations in Jerusalem': 'You cannot make God Catholic. God is beyond the limits and definitions that we establish.' Many there were who tore their garments. In the Catholic world this seemed to some almost a blasphemy."[35]

## Supporting Liberal Nuns

Pope Benedict XVI attempted to address the problem of politically and theologically liberal nuns in the United States. It has been an open secret for decades that American nunneries operate as centers of left-wing dissent. To take just one example, Sister Carol Keehan, who makes more than a million dollars a year as a health care lobbyist, helped Barack Obama pass Obamacare with its contraceptive mandate. Pope Benedict XVI had sent a team of Vatican officials to conduct a doctrinal investigation of the Leadership Conference of Women Religious. The expectation was that that investigation would result in a serious orthodox reform of the organization.

No such reforms ever took place. In 2015, Pope Francis pulled the plug on the investigation and let it be known through his aides that he had no intention of arresting the liberalization of U.S. nuns. Churchmen around Pope Francis indicated their displeasure at the investigation, with Boston cardinal Seán O'Malley going so far as to call Benedict's investigation a "disaster."

The liberal media was thrilled by this turn of events. The *New York Times* ran a story in 2015 titled "Vatican Ends Battle with US Catholic Nuns' Group," with a picture of the nuns, bereft of habits, meeting with Pope Francis. The story noted that Francis had "abruptly" ended Benedict's investigation.

"Under the previous pope, Benedict XVI, the Vatican's doctrinal office had appointed three bishops in 2012 to overhaul the nuns' group, the Leadership Conference of Women Religious, out of concerns that it had hosted speakers and published materials that strayed from Catholic doctrine on such matters as the all-male priesthood, birth control and sexuality, and the centrality of Jesus to the faith," it reported. "But Francis has shown in his two-year papacy that he is less interested in having the church police doctrinal boundaries than in demonstrating mercy and love for the poor and vulnerable— the very work that most of the women's religious orders under investigation have long been engaged in."

"He met with them himself for almost an hour, and that's an extravagant amount of papal time," Eileen Burke-Sullivan, a feminist theologian at Creighton University said to the *Times*. "It's about as close to an apology, I would think, as the Catholic Church is officially going to render."[36]

"Radical Nuns Okayed by Pope Francis" was among the headlines Francis's whitewash of the group had produced. Officials under Pope Benedict XVI had spoken about the "doctrinal errors" and "secular mentality" of U.S. nuns. But the final report on them produced by Francis's Vatican muted these criticisms and ended up praising their political liberalism, likening it to Francis's. U.S. nuns, according to the report, "resonate with Pope Francis' insistence that 'none of us can think we are exempt from concern for the poor and for social justice.'"[37]

It is no accident that Pope Francis in 2016 made a critic of Benedict's investigation of U.S. nuns, Archbishop Joseph Tobin, a cardinal, a promotion not lost on the liberal Catholic press, which warmly recalled Tobin's role in protecting the nuns.

"Tobin is a former superior general of the worldwide Redemptorist religious order, who served from 2010 to 2012 as the number two official at the Vatican's Congregation for Institutes of Consecrated Life and Societies of Apostolic Life, better known as the 'Congregation for Religious,' during the time when the Vatican was conducting two separate investigations of American nuns," wrote John Allen. "Tobin was publicly critical of those probes, suggesting they had been launched without dialogue or consultation with the women religious, and behind the scenes that didn't always sit well with some of the prelates who had pushed for them in the first place. Many observers believed at the time his 2012 transfer to Indianapolis, before the usual five-year term in a Vatican office was up, reflected some unhappiness with his more conciliatory line."[38]

A Church insider interviewed for this book called the Tobin promotion "a direct poke in the eye to Burke," a reference to Cardinal Raymond Burke, who had disagreed with Tobin's opposition to the investigation.

While keeping his hands off orders of politically liberal nuns, he is seeking to "reform" orders of contemplative nuns. In 2016, he issued a binding document governing their orders. Conservatives balked at it, seeing it as an attempt to force traditional houses of contemplative nuns to conform to the liberal regime of Francis.[39] "This is a scary document. It could kill off the lifeblood of the church," said a priest interviewed for this book.

Pope Francis appointed the liberal Brazilian João Braz de Aviz to head up the Vatican's congregation for religious life. Oblivious to the fact that liberal religious orders are dying, Braz de Aviz has lectured formation directors obtusely, "Do not distance yourself from the great lines of the Second Vatican Council." He holds that "those that are distancing themselves from the council to make another path are killing themselves—sooner or later, they will die. They will not have sense. They will be outside the church. We need to build, using the Gospel and the council as a departure point."[40] In fact, the religious orders most suspicious of the liberal interpretation of Vatican II favored by Pope Francis and his aides are flourishing.

On matters both doctrinal and political, Pope Francis is breaking with the direction of his predecessors. In the area of diplomacy, Pope Francis is pursuing policies of pacifism and appeasement, which represent a significant departure from the policies of the John Paul II era. As Pope John Paul II biographer George Weigel has written, "the contemporary Vatican seems to have forgotten some crucial lessons from the teaching and diplomacy of the saint who came to Rome from Cracow and became the most consequential pope of the second half of the second millennium." Francis's Vatican, wrote Weigel, has embraced the appeasement policies of Cardinal Agostino Casaroli, who served as a leading diplomat during the Cold War and favored "détente" with the Soviet Union:

> Those guiding the Holy See's interface with politics today were born and bred in the Casaroli School. And they are busily replicating Casaroli's accommodationist (or, if you prefer, less confrontational) formula. This seems clear, if unfortunately clear, in the Vatican's diplomacy with Vladimir Putin's Russia, and in the Holy See's refusal to describe what is afoot in Ukraine as a gross violation of international law: an armed aggression by one state against another. It seems evident in the welcome that was afforded Raúl Castro in the Vatican several months ago. Now, to judge from the just-concluded papal visit to Ecuador, Bolivia, and Paraguay, Casaroli 2.0 seems to be informing the Vatican's approach to the new authoritarians of continental Latin America.[41]

Even Pope Francis's canonization of Pope John Paul II, a movement which began under Pope Benedict XVI, was seen as "manipulative," according to German philosopher Robert Spaemann, insofar as Francis combined it with the canonization of Pope John XXIII in an attempt to pacify liberals in the Church.

"It was already apparent that Francis views his predecessor Pope John Paul II from a critical distance when he canonized him together with John XXIII, even though a second required miracle was not attributed to the latter," Spaemann has said. "It seemed as if the Pope wanted to relativize the importance of John Paul II."[42]

The Polish Church remains upset about Francis's slighting treatment of John Paul II. "It is spoken about openly in private, but rarely in public," writes Fr. Raymond de Souza. "If ever there was a contemporary Cause that deserved, as it were, a solo canonisation, it was that of John Paul, perhaps the most consequential historical figure of our time. Had Providence brought the two Causes to maturity at the same time, that would have been one thing, but it was altogether different to waive the requirements for John XXIII in order, it appeared, to diminish or to balance out the attention given to John Paul."

At the actual canonization ceremony, Pope Francis appeared indifferent. "It was conducted in such an understated fashion as to come off rather flat, despite the enormous number of bishops who came from all over the world. Pope Francis said next to nothing about John Paul, and nothing about Poland at all, despite the immense number of Poles in Rome," according to de Souza.[43]

## A Worldly Vatican

Respect for worldly opinion and secular prestige have also figured far more into this pontificate than the two previous ones. Pope Francis has accelerated canonization movements his predecessors stalled while blocking politically incorrect causes they supported. Croatian Catholics, for example, were disappointed to learn that the canonization cause of Cardinal Aloysius Stepinac has been suspended by Pope Francis out of fear of offending the Serbian orthodox. The victim of a Soviet disinformation campaign, Stepinac has long been the subject of smears. Pope John Paul II and Pope Benedict XVI rejected this communist-inspired propaganda. But Pope Francis is taking it seriously, telling Orthodox clerics that he is no "rush" to canonize Stepinac.[44]

Meanwhile, his support for the canonization of Óscar Romero continues to win him points from the liberal elite. In El Salvador, supporters of Che Guevara call Romero the "saint of America," but many conservatives feel ambivalence toward the pope's drive to make him a saint.[45]

Pope Francis is also winning praise for his "modernizing" of Vatican operations. Reporters walking around the Vatican have spoken of the rise of "God's consultants," a worldly group of advisers that Francis has hired. Vatican correspondent John Allen says Francis's reliance on these advisers "represents a clear break with the Vatican's traditional ambivalence about relying on secular expertise, on the grounds that secular values are inevitably part of the package... In the past the Vatican [showed]...an instinctive distrust of claims to specialized expertise from people who don't share the moral and metaphysical worldview of Catholicism. They fear that while they might build a better mousetrap, they also might smuggle alien values and ways of doing business into the Church."[46]

The reliance on these experts backfired in the case of Francesca Chaouqui, a public relations consultant whom the Italian press dubbed "pope's lobbyist" after Pope Francis handpicked her to work on a Vatican financial commission. In 2015, she was arrested by Vatican authorities after she was accused of leaking, in violation of Holy See laws, financial details to the Italian press.

Traditionalists had protested her appointment, pointing to her lewd Facebook selfies and outré tweets. Francis, in "who am I to judge?" mode, ignored these complaints, and Vatican officials extolled "her authoritative leadership based on strong relational and communicative endowments."

Previous popes weren't so easily impressed by the "communicative endowments" of a prospective Vatican employee. They were more interested in orthodoxy. But that is now the last, not the first, consideration at the Vatican. In the course of her Vatican trial, she was accused of trying to seduce a Vatican monsignor, a charge that she has vehemently denied.[47]

In 2015, the Vatican hired PricewaterhouseCoopers to help reform its finances, but then mysteriously pulled its contract the following year, leading some to wonder if the talk of reform under Francis had been overblown. After some bad press, the contract was later renewed.[48]

Some Vatican employees have complained about the unfair labor practices of a "social justice" pope. He tends to romanticize the sufferings of the proletariat, whom he calls the "pueblo." "The word 'people' is not a logical category, it is a mystical category," he has said. But as *Crux* reported, "some of the Vatican's own lay employees would like to ask him, 'What about us?'"

"Most lay workers in the Vatican who spoke to *Crux* did so on background, because they're not authorized to give interviews and also for fear of consequences on the job," it was reported. "'If it was up to Pope Francis, we'd all work for free,' one Vatican employee said."[49]

On matters both large and small, Pope Francis has deviated from the path of his predecessors. His program has been not to complete their projects but to derail them and pursue his own. Like many priests of his generation, he had chafed under the conservative remnants in the post–Vatican II Church. As pope, he saw his chance to wipe them out. Whether he will succeed remains an open question. "While Pope Francis has had a great acceptance in milieus which otherwise have little to do with the Church, there exists a polarization within the Church," allows Cardinal Christoph Schönborn.[50]

# CHAPTER TWELVE

# Will Paul Correct Peter?

In his Letter to the Galatians, St. Paul wrote that he corrected the first pope, St. Peter, "to his face because he clearly was wrong." St. Paul objected to St. Peter's imposition of obsolete Jewish customs on the Gentiles, saying to him, "If you, though, a Jew, are living like a Gentile and not like a Jew, how can you compel the Gentiles to live like Jews?"

St. Thomas Aquinas cited that confrontation as an example of how "prelates must be questioned, even publicly, by their subjects" for the good of the Catholic faith. St. Augustine, noting St. Peter's acceptance of St. Paul's rebuke, commented that "St. Peter himself gave the example to those who govern so that if sometimes they stray from the right way, they will not reject a correction as unworthy even if it comes from their subjects."

As the current pontificate fosters more and more confusion and error, Catholics, both lay and clerical, find themselves playing St. Paul to Francis's St. Peter. Occasioning much of the criticism is the pope's elastic view of the Church's moral teachings, particularly its teaching on divorce.

Before the second part of the Synod on the Family in 2015, a group of conservative cardinals wrote an anxious letter to Pope Francis, complaining in effect that the synod was in danger of turning into a debacle of theological relativism, manipulation, and phony collegiality.[1]

"As the Synod on the Family begins, and with a desire to see it fruitfully serve the Church and your ministry, we respectfully ask you to consider a number of concerns we have heard from other synod fathers, and which we share," they wrote. In diplomatic language, they essentially accused him and his advisers of running a fixed synod for the sake of undermining Church teaching.

The rules of the synod were designed to shut the conservative bishops out, they wrote: "The absence of propositions and their related discussions and voting seems to discourage open debate and to confine discussion to small groups; thus it seems urgent to us that the crafting of propositions to be voted on by the entire synod should be restored. Voting on a final document comes too late in the process for a full review and serious adjustment of the text."

"A number of fathers feel the new process seems designed to facilitate predetermined results on important disputed questions," they continued. Beyond process questions, they worried, the synod was flirting with ideological novelties that would end up hurting the family and weakening the Church:

> Finally and perhaps most urgently, various fathers have expressed concern that a synod designed to address a vital pastoral matter—reinforcing the dignity of marriage and family— may become dominated by the theological/doctrinal issue of Communion for the divorced and civilly remarried. If so, this will inevitably raise even more fundamental issues about how the Church, going forward, should interpret and apply the Word of God, her doctrines and her disciplines to changes in culture. The collapse of liberal Protestant churches in the modern era, accelerated by their abandonment of key elements of Christian belief and practice in the name of pastoral adaptation, warrants great caution in our own synodal discussions.

In Britain, 461 priests signed a letter petitioning Pope Francis and the synod fathers to remain true to the Church's perennial teaching on marriage:

> We wish, as Catholic priests, to re-state our unwavering fidelity to the traditional doctrines regarding marriage and the true meaning of human sexuality, founded on the Word of God and taught by the Church's Magisterium for two millennia... We affirm the importance of upholding the Church's traditional discipline regarding the reception of the sacraments, and that doctrine and practice remain firmly and inseparably in harmony.[2]

According to the *Catholic Herald*, "One signatory, who asked to remain anonymous, claimed there 'has been a certain amount of pressure not to sign the letter and indeed a degree of intimidation from some senior Churchmen.'"

Pope Francis ignored these letters. He accused the conservative bishops of surrendering to the "hermeneutic of conspiracy."[3] But there was nothing paranoid about their concerns. What they suspected would happen did: Pope Francis used the synod as a pretext to push a conclusion he had reached before it even began.

## A Church Divided

"The Pope during the Synod will show whose side he is on," said Archbishop Jan Paweł Lenga. "If he accepts the statement of those who want to distribute Holy Communion to the divorced, there would be a heresy in the Church, and if he does not accept, there could be a schism in the Church." He added, "Either we are on the side of Christ, or on the side of the devil. There is no third option. The common people are sometimes closer to Christ than priests."[4]

"I wonder if he realizes how much confusion he is causing," said an unnamed conservative cardinal to Reuters in 2016. Another high-ranking cleric said that this pontificate is alarming "not only tradition-minded priests but even liberal priests who have complained to me that people are challenging them on issues that are very straight-forward, saying 'the pope would let me do this' why don't you?'"[5]

A Catholic psychiatrist told the *Washington Post* that one of his patients quit therapy, saying, "I'm much more of a Pope Francis–Nancy Pelosi Catholic, and you're an old-school, Pope John Paul II Catholic."[6]

"We have a serious issue right now, a very alarming situation where Catholic priests and bishops are saying and doing things that are against what the church teaches, talking about same-sex unions, about Communion for those who are living in adultery," a church official said to the *Washington Post*. "And yet the pope does nothing to silence them. So the inference is that this is what the pope wants."

Providence Bishop Thomas Tobin commented, "In trying to accommodate the needs of the age, as Pope Francis suggests, the Church risks the danger of losing its courageous, countercultural, prophetic voice, one that the world needs to hear."[7]

Chaos erupted after the release of *Amoris Laetitia*, with bishops and national conferences dividing over its meaning and application. Some bishops are using it as a justification for loosening up their policies; others are ignoring it and maintaining traditional policies. In the United States, divorced-and-remarried Catholics can receive Communion in such cities as San Diego and Chicago but not in Philadelphia.

"Priests are divided from one another, priests from bishops, bishops among themselves. There's a tremendous division that has set in in the Church, and that is not the way of the Church. That is why we settle on these fundamental moral questions which unify us," according to Cardinal Raymond Burke.[8]

This chaos is not contrary to the pope's program for the Church but a deliberate component of it.

"What Francis has done in effect is give local bishops permission and space to try innovations that are more flexible, merciful, and pastoral," said Lisa Cahill, a liberal theologian at Boston University. "Hence individual bishops or dioceses can come up with their own policies."[9]

According to Archbishop André-Joseph Léonard, former primate of Belgium, the pope and his advisers crafted intentionally fuzzy documents at the Synod on the Family as a form of heterodox misdirection: "I was a bit disappointed by the fact that they cultivated ambiguity around the most sensitive issues. Some bishops told me the texts were deliberately formulated in an ambiguous way, in order to leave them open to interpretation in different directions."[10]

Bishop Thomas Tobin has written sardonically, "The good news is, that because of this ambiguity, people can do just about whatever they want. The bad news is, that because of this ambiguity, people can do just about whatever they want. Go figure!"[11]

In Europe, liberal national conferences have embraced the ambiguity. "The door is open," said Cardinal Kasper. "There is also some freedom for the individual bishops and bishops' conferences... things are not any more so abstract and permeated with suspicion, as it was the case in earlier times."[12] Cardinal Lehmann has said, "Francis wants us to explore new paths. Sometimes you don't have to wait until the large tanker begins to move."[13]

## Resisting the Revolution

"The people who traditionally have been defenders of papal authority for the last 50 years suddenly find themselves out of step with the pope, and that's a very strange situation," Fr. Gerald Murray said to the *Wall Street Journal*. "This is an exploding land mine and I regret that it's going to be a continual fight until it's changed back to the old discipline. The unity of the church's pastoral ministry is affected severely when you have contrasting practices in different places...There may not be a schism in the sense of a rejection of papal authority, but there is going to be a debate in the church about the directions in which the pope is taking the church and whether we should go along or we should resist."[14]

Some bishops, such as Cardinal Burke, have made it clear that they will not submit to Francis's revolution. "I shall resist," Cardinal Burke has said. "I can do nothing else. There is no doubt that it is a difficult time; this is clear, this is clear."[15]

"In Amoris Laetitia [308] the Holy Father Francis writes: 'I understand those who prefer a more rigorous pastoral care which leaves no room for confusion.' I infer from these words that His Holiness realizes that the teachings of the Exhortation could give rise to confusion in the Church," said Cardinal Caffarra. "Personally, I wish—and that is how so many of my brothers in Christ (cardinals, bishops, and the lay faithful alike) also think—that the confusion should be removed, but not because I prefer a more rigorous pastoral care, but because, rather, I simply prefer a clearer and less ambiguous pastoral care."[16]

Under Pope Francis, the Church is moving down the same ruinous path as liberal Protestantism. In the 1960s, the British journalist Malcolm Muggeridge wrote that the Catholic Church was joining the "army of progress just when it is in total disarray." Muggeridge found it mystifying that the Church, "having witnessed the ruinous consequences to its Protestant rivals of compounding with contemporary trends, should now seem set upon following a like course." "Just when the Reformation appears to be finally fizzling out, another, it seems, is incubating in Rome," Muggeridge wrote. "Luther escapes from John Osborne's hands into—of all places—the Vatican."[17]

Fifty years later, the condition of the Church appears just as bleak, as Pope Francis tries to revive that failed formula of trendy political liberalism and fashionable heterodoxy. Indeed, Muggeridge's metaphor has materialized in the Catholic celebrations of Martin Luther's Reformation led by Pope Francis.

Ross Douthat of the *New York Times* wonders what the "Francis effect" on the Church will be and proposes that sociologists of religion study dioceses that "are conducting clearer Francis-blessed experiments than others."[18] One simple place to start is the floundering archdiocese of Buenos Aires. According to the Latin American press, even the "Francis effect" in Argentina has been embarrassingly negligible, with the Buenos Aires seminary producing only three priestly ordinations in 2016.[19]

Fr. Julio Miranda, rector of the seminary in Buenos Aires, told *Clarin* that the Pope "has had no impact" on vocations. As the paper put it, the "appointment of an Argentine pope, precisely from the Archdiocese of Buenos Aires, with the idea of the 'Church of the peripheries,' 'missionary' (church) that will convey 'the joy of the Gospel,' could not mitigate the fall in consecrated vocations."[20]

German cardinal Walter Brandmüller sees no evidence that the Francis effect has strengthened the Church. "It is superficial. Were this a religious movement, the churches would be full," he has said. A "laissez-faire" Catholicism, he said, "would mean watching passively the devastation of the Church from within."[21] Even Cardinal Kurt Koch, who is sympathetic to the pope's liberal spin on Catholicism, has acknowledged that the glowing talk around this pontificate is largely empty: "There is a lot of excitement about him, but as one can certainly see, in the people leaving the church in many countries, you can't really detect a Francis effect."[22]

# Francis Fatigue

Pope Benedict XVI has spoken of a "two-sided, deep crisis" in the Church since Vatican II, which was triggered by a modernist theology that rejected the centrality of Catholicism to the salvation of souls:

If it is true that the great missionaries of the 16th century were still convinced that those who are not baptized are forever lost—and this explains their missionary commitment—in the Catholic Church after the Second Vatican Council that conviction was finally abandoned.

From this came a deep double crisis. On the one hand this seems to remove any motivation for a future missionary commitment. Why should one try to convince the people to accept the Christian faith when they can be saved even without it? But also for Christians an issue emerged: the obligatory nature of the faith and its way of life began to seem uncertain and problematic. If there are those who can save themselves in other ways, it is not clear, in the final analysis, why the Christian himself is bound by the requirements of the Christian faith and its morals. If faith and salvation are no longer interdependent, faith itself becomes unmotivated.[23]

That crisis has only deepened under Pope Francis, as its identity becomes increasingly politicized and non-theological.

"Right up to this day, many people have been trying to determine Francis' true intentions. If you ask cardinals and bishops, or the pope's advisors and colleagues, or veteran Vatican observers about his possible strategy these days—the Pope's overarching plan—they seem to agree on one point: The man who sits on the Chair of St. Peter is a notorious troublemaker," says *Der Spiegel*.[24]

Out of this chaos has come a measure of Francis fatigue.

According to *Politico*, "Francis has not proved to be a magnet for people converting to Catholicism or attending Sunday mass, according to data. In Italy, attendance at places of worship decreased in 2014 to 28.8 percent of the population compared to more than 30 percent during the years of Ratzinger, according to Istat, the Italian statistics bureau." At the same time, it continued, "the Union of Rational Atheists and Agnostics in Italy reported last week that online applications to download a form allowing people to 'de-baptize' themselves, meaning to formally request to be taken off the Church's rolls as a member, reached an all-time high in 2015 of 47,726."[25]

Catholics feel that his popularity with the liberal elite comes "at the expense of the Church," and that his "snazzy sayings" mean nothing, said German novelist Martin Mosebach. "What is concerning about Pope Francis is the atmosphere he creates—as though an entirely new Church has been created which has never existed before in this way," said Mosebach. "As though Francis is correcting centuries of abnormal development and is creating a new type of Church without dogma, without mysticism. A Church which finds itself in compliance with the current social consensus."[26]

Supporters, such as the Jesuit Antonio Spadaro, concede that his pontificate is perplexing. "I don't believe that Francis seriously expects that he will be able to complete the processes that he has initiated," he said. As to where he is directing the Church, he said, "It's very possible that he himself doesn't even know."[27]

The late Chicago cardinal Francis George, who was an early supporter of the pope, nevertheless found the pope's ambiguity irritating.

> Why doesn't he himself clarify these things? Why is it necessary that apologists have to bear that burden of trying to put the best possible face on it? Does he not realize the consequences of some of his statements, or even some of his actions? Does he not realize the repercussions? Perhaps he doesn't. I don't know whether he's conscious of all the consequences of some of the things he's said and done that raise these doubts in people's minds.
>
> That's one of the things I'd like to have the chance to ask him, if I ever get over there. Do you realize what has happened, just by that very phrase "Who am I to judge?" How it's been

used and misused? It's very misused, because he was talking about someone who has already asked for mercy and been given absolution whom he knows well. That's entirely different than talking to somebody who demands acceptance rather than asking for forgiveness. It's constantly misused.[28]

The pope appears unfazed by these criticisms. Asked during a 2016 interview about the complaints of conservative Catholics, he replied defiantly: "They say no to everything. I go ahead, without looking over my shoulder."[29]

Under Pope John Paul II and Pope Benedict XVI, the Church stood as a rock in a rising sea of secularism, and many conservatives swam toward it. But that appeal is rapidly diminishing under Pope Francis.

Writing in *Time* magazine, journalist Rod Dreher spoke for many conservatives when he wrote, "I'm an ex-Catholic whose decision to leave the Catholic Church is not challenged by Francis' words but rather confirmed." Pope Francis, he continued, "makes me realize that the good, if incomplete, work that John Paul II and Benedict XVI did to restore the Church after the violence of the [liberal] revolution stands to be undone. The 'spirit of Pope Francis' will replace the 'spirit of Vatican II' as the rationalization people will use to ignore the difficult teachings of the faith."[30]

Shocked by the pope's speech to the U.S. Congress in 2015, Albert Mohler, president of the Southern Baptist Theological Seminary, commented to *LifeSiteNews* that "it must send a very clear signal to conservative Catholics that they have faced exactly what they feared, a Pope who is not only leaning left, but is going to take the Roman Catholic Church to the left with him."[31]

"Morale is low," says a priest in an interview for this book. "We reached a moment of hope after the last two popes. That hope has been replaced by fear and trembling. Francis is the worst pope in centuries."

"We were spoiled with the last two popes," says another priest interviewed for this book. "Now we are on Code Red Alert."

In 2016, forty-five scholars sent a letter to the Church's cardinals, asking them to seek clarification from the pope on *Amoris Laetitia*. The group, which included such prominent theologians as Fr. Aidan Nichols, identified nineteen statements in the pope's exhortation that lend themselves to "heretical" interpretation.

> As Catholic theologians and philosophers, church historians and pastors of souls, we are writing to you in your capacity as Dean of the College of Cardinals to request that the College of Cardinals and the Patriarchs of the Catholic Church take collective action to respond to the dangers to Catholic faith and morals posed by the apostolic exhortation Amoris laetitia issued by Pope Francis on March 19th 2016. This apostolic exhortation contains a number of statements that can be understood in a sense that is contrary to Catholic faith and morals. We have specified the nature and degree of the errors that could be attributed to Amoris laetitia in the accompanying document. We request that the Cardinals and Patriarchs petition the Holy Father to condemn the errors listed in the document in a definitive and final manner, and to authoritatively state that Amoris laetitia does not require any of them to be believed or considered as possibly true.

"Just as it is lawful to resist the pope that attacks the body," argued St. Robert Bellarmine, the celebrated sixteenth-century Jesuit, "it is also lawful to resist the one who attacks souls or who disturbs civil order, or, above all, who attempts to destroy the Church. I say that it is lawful to resist him by not doing what he orders and preventing his will from being executed."

"Bellarmine envisioned the possibility of a pope who held heretical views occupying the papacy," says a Jesuit scholar interviewed for this book. "One of the scenarios he wrote about was that the college of cardinals could resist such a pope." But this priest added, without any apparent irony, that he didn't think the crisis would reach that point, because "God will strike Francis dead before he destroys the Church."

In November 2016, four cardinals, frustrated by the pope's refusal to clarify his heterodox statements about marriage and conscience, released to the public a letter they had written to him. They explained that they released it after he declined to answer it for almost two months. Signed by three European cardinals (Cardinals Walter Brandmüller, Carlo Caffarra, and Joachim Meisner) and an American cardinal (Raymond Burke), the letter urged Pope Francis to dispel the "grave disorientation and great confusion of many faithful regarding extremely important matters for the life of the Church."[32]

It is difficult to find a parallel in Church history to such a challenge. (One pope, Honorius I, was condemned by the Church for his "impious doctrines," but the condemnation came after his death.) In the letter, the cardinals are in effect asking the pope if he supports basic tenets of Catholic moral theology. Cardinal Burke has said that the cardinals will make a "formal act of correction of a serious error" if he continues to ignore the letter.

So far he has. One of his advisers tweeted out (then deleted the tweet) an image comparing the cardinals to a "worm" while the pope dismissed them as mental defectives who see life "in black and white."[33] Though said to be "boiling with rage" about the challenge, he has affected a pose of indifference, saying that his critics are "not making me lose any sleep."[34]

But Catholics in the pews are. Increasingly bewildered by this pontificate, they wonder: How did it come to this? How did the papacy go from safeguarding doctrinal unity to shattering it? How did it go from fighting a sinful world to joining it? How did it go from a spiritual bastion to a partner of the United Nations and a pagan political order?

A professor of theology, who directs dissertations that touch on the subject of bad popes, just shook his head when asked about the state of this pontificate. "My students now have more material," he said with a grim chuckle.

The crisis created by this pontificate's toxic combination of political liberalism and doctrinal relativism is a historically singular one, which gives its unfolding a disconcerting drama: How will it end? What if he succeeds? The left is already anticipating that the next pope will be a Francis clone. A hopeful *New York Times* reports on "Pope Francis' Race against Time to Reshape the Church." By the end of 2016, he had named forty-four cardinals, a third of the college of cardinals and perhaps enough, the *Times* implied, "to ensure that his vision of the Church" outlasts him.[35]

Dismayed by that prospect, Catholics find consolation in the words of Jesus Christ, that the "gates of hell will not prevail" against the Church. They also find consolation in the long and resilient history of the Church, which has faced countless challenges, both external and internal, and survived. Yet with a measure of dread they also know that for the Church to survive they must undertake the most peculiar of duties. Where their ancestors defended the pope from enemies of the faith, they now must defend the faith from a pope who aligns with her enemies.

# Acknowledgments

Finding a publisher for a book, let alone a politically incorrect book like this one, is a tricky task. Thanks to the large-mindedness of Kate Hartson at Hachette Book Group, I found one. I am grateful to her for enthusiastically supporting the presentation of a point of view that receives little coverage in the media. I also thank Matt Latimer and Keith Urbahn at the literary agency Javelin for their effective representation and advice.

While writing the book, I received research assistance or encouragement from the following people, to whom I owe thanks: Roger McCaffrey, Daniel Allott, Wladyslaw Pleszczynski, R. Emmett Tyrrell Jr., Scott Daily, Steve Tallman, Michele Diatta, James Bendell, Anne Braden, and Mary Neumayr.

Thanks also to my entire family, with special mention of my parents, John and Bridget Neumayr. It is through them that I received the Roman Catholic faith—the spark from which this book came and to which it is intended to pay truthful service.

# Notes

## Chapter One: The Pope They Have Been Waiting For

1. Alan Riding. "Pope Says Taking Sides in Nicaragua Is Peril to Church." *New York Times*, March 5, 1983. http://www.nytimes.com/1983/03/05/world/pope-says-taking-sides-in-nicaragua-is-peril-to-church.html.
2. "Stasi Files Implicate KGB in Pope Shooting." *Deutsche Welle*, January 4, 2005. http://www.dw.com/en/stasi-files-implicate-kgb-in-pope-shooting/a-1538173-0.
3. "Former Soviet Spy: We Created Liberation Theology," Catholic News Agency, May 1, 2015. http://www.catholicnewsagency.com/news/former-soviet-spy-we-created-liberation-theology-83634.
4. Michael Hichborn. "The Marxist Core of the Catholic Campaign for Human Development." Lepanto Institute, November 11, 2015. http://www.lepantoinstitute.org/cchd/the-marxist-core-of-the-catholic-campaign-for-human-development.
5. "Former Soviet Spy: We Created Liberation Theology," Catholic News Agency, May 1, 2015. http://www.catholicnewsagency.com/news/former-soviet-spy-we-created-liberation-theology-83634.
6. Larry Rohter. "As Pope Heads to Brazil, Rival Theology Persists." *New York Times*, May 7, 2007. http://www.nytimes.com/2007/05/07/world/americas/07iht-07theology.5593324.html.
7. Nicole Winfield. "Liberation Theology Rehabilitation Continues at Vatican." Associated Press, May 7, 2015. http://www.usnews.com/news/world/articles/2015/05/07/liberation-theology-rehabilitation-continues-at-vatican.
8. "The Pope: How the Church Will Change." *La Repubblica*, October 1, 2013. http://www.repubblica.it/cultura/2013/10/01/news/pope_s_conversation_with_scalfari_english-67643118.
9. James Fitzpatrick. "Catholic Newspeak?" Catholic Exchange, March 18, 2003. http://catholicexchange.com/catholic-newspeak.

10. Joshua J. McElwee. "Pope Meets with Liberation Theology Pioneer." *National Catholic Reporter*, September 25, 2013. https://www.ncronline .org/news/theology/pope-meets-liberation-theology-pioneer.

11. Kaya Oakes. "Immigration and the Francis Effect." *Foreign Policy*, September 24, 2015. http://foreignpolicy.com/2015/09/24/pope-francis -congress-catholic-washington-immigration.

12. Cindy Wooden. "Pope Lifts Suspension of Father D'Escoto, Former Sandinista Official," Catholic News Service, August 4, 2014. https://www.ncronline.org/ news/global/pope-lifts-suspension-father-descoto-former-sandinista -official.

13. "In New Declarations, Priest Pardoned by Pope Francis Says, 'The Holy Spirit Sends Us Jesus' Message through Fidel Castro.'" *Rorate Caeli*, August 6, 2014. http://rorate-caeli.blogspot.com/2014/08/in-new-declara tions-priest-pardoned-by.html.

14. Atila Sinke Guimaraes. "Bird's Eye View of the News," Tradition in Action, July 31, 2013. http://www.traditioninaction.org/bev/158bev07_31_2013.htm.

15. "Vatican: Gay Partnerships and Cohabitation Can Be Positive." Associated Press, October 13, 2014. http://www.nydailynews.com/news/world/vatican -gay-partnerships-cohabitation-positive-article-1.1972754.

16. Josephine McKenna. "Burke: Church under Francis Is a 'Ship without a Rudder.'" *National Catholic Reporter*, October 13, 2014. https://www.ncr online.org/news/vatican/burke-church-under-francis-ship-without-rudder.

17. Bishop Athanasius Schneider. "Bishop Athanasius Schneider Replies to *The Remnant*'s Open Letter on *Amoris Laetitia*." *Remnant*, June 2, 2016. http://remnantnewspaper.com/web/index.php/articles/item/2558 -bishop-athanasius-schneider-replies-to-the-remnant-s-open-letter-on -amoris-laetitia.

18. "Under Bergoglio, Christianity Matters Less." *Rorate Caeli*, November 13, 2014. http://rorate-caeli.blogspot.com/2014/11/under-bergoglio-christia nity-matters.html.

19. Damian Thompson. "Is the Pope Catholic? Here's Why Many of His Flock Aren't Sure." Heat Street, June 6, 2016. http://heatst.com/uk/ is-the-pope-catholic-heres-why-many-of-pope-francis-flock-arent-sure.

20. Maike Hickson. "Famed German Philosopher Makes Waves for Criticizing Pope Francis' 'Autocratic' Style." *LifeSiteNews*, April 27, 2015. https:// www.lifesitenews.com/news/famed-german-catholic-philosopher-makes -waves-for-criticizing-pope-francis.

21. "Rebel Pope Urges Catholics to Shake Up Dioceses." Associated Press, July 25, 2013. http://www.huffingtonpost.com/huff-wires/20130725/lt-brazil-pope.

22. Michael Chapman. "Catholic Bishop: 'Pope Francis Is Fond of Creating a Mess: Mission Accomplished.'" CNS, October 22, 2014. http://www.cns news.com/news/article/michael-w-chapman.

23. Josh Feldman. "Pope Francis Addresses 'Ultraconservatives (and Limbaugh?) Calling Him a Marxist." *Mediaite*, December 14, 2013. http://www.mediaite .com/online/pope-francis-addresses-ultraconservatives-and-limbaugh -calling-him-a-marxist.

24. Javier Cámara and Sebastián Pfaffen. *Understanding Pope Francis.* (N.p.: Create Space Independent Publishing Platform, 2015), 37.

25. James Carroll. "Who Am I to Judge?" *New Yorker*, December 23, 2013. http://www.newyorker.com/magazine/2013/12/23/who-am-i-to-judge.

26. John Allen. "Why Francis Won't Let Women Become Priests." *Time*, March 6, 2015. http://time.com/3729904/francis-women.

27. "Pope Says Communists Are Closet Christians." Reuters, June 29, 2014. http://www.reuters.com/article/us-pope-communism-idUSKBN0F 40L020140629.

28. Billy Hallowell. "What Is the Root of All Social Evil? The Pope Weighs In . . ." *Blaze*. http://www.theblaze.com/stories/2014/04/28/what-is-the-root-of -all-social-evil-the-pope-weighs-in.

29. Paul Kengor. "The Hillary-Alinsky-Lucifer Connection." *American Spectator*, July 26, 2016. http://spectator.org/the-hillary-alinsky-lucifer-connection.

30. Cindy Wooden. "Hammer-Sickle Crucifix Raises Eyebrows during Pope Francis' Visit to Bolivia." Catholic News Service, July 9, 2015. https:// www.ncronline.org/news/global/hammer-sickle-crucifix-raises-eyebrows -during-pope-francis-visit-bolivia.

31. Frank Bajak. "Morales Calls Pope's Teachings 'Socialist.'" Associated Press, July 10, 2015. https://www.yahoo.com/news/morales-calls-pope-francis -teachings-socialist-190527293.html.

32. Mark Binelli. "Pope Francis: The Times They Are A-Changin'," *Rolling Stone*, January 28, 2014. http://www.rollingstone.com/culture/news/pope-francis -the-times-they-are-a-changin-20140128.

## Chapter Two: "Who Am I to Judge?"

1. Francis X. Rocca. "As Pope, Benedict Worked to Promote Understanding of Vatican II." Catholic News Service, February 20, 2013. http://www.catholic news.com/services/englishnews/2013/as-pope-benedict-worked-to-pro mote-understanding-of-vatican-ii.cfm.

2. Bill Keller. "Is the Pope Catholic?" *New York Times*, May 4, 2002. http:// www.nytimes.com/2002/05/04/opinion/04KELL.html.

3. Cindy Wooden. "Pope Francis Explains Why He Chose St. Francis of Assisi's Name." Catholic News Service, March 18, 2013. http://www.thecatholic telegraph.com/pope-francis-explains-why-he-chose-st-francis-of-assisis -name/13243.

4. Anthony Faiola. "Champion of Workers and the Poor." *Washington Post*, April 3, 2005. http://www.washingtonpost.com/wp-dyn/articles/A22031-2005Apr2.html.

5. "From the IOR to the Gay Lobby: Pope Francis Tells All on Flight from Rio to Rome." *La Stampa*, July 29, 2013. http://www.lastampa.it/2013/07/29/vaticaninsider/eng/the-vatican/from-the-ior-to-the-gay-lobby-pope-francis-tells-all-on-flight-from-rio-to-rome-DquIgXJyjqKfIeuwSEz8jP/pagina.html.

6. Thomas C. Fox. "Quinn to Priest Group: Church Poised at a Moment of Far-Reaching Consequences." *National Catholic Reporter*, July 27, 2014.

7. Jason Horowitz. "What Does a Pope Like to Wear? Francis Keeps It Simple." *Washington Post*, March 18, 2013. https://www.washingtonpost.com/world/what-does-a-pope-like-to-wear-francis-keeps-it-simple/2013/03/18/d43d2bc4-8ffd-11e2-9cfd-36d6c9b5d7ad_story.html.

8. Ernesto Cardenal. "How Pope Francis Is Carrying Out a Revolution." *Huffington Post*, March 30, 2015. http://www.huffingtonpost.com/rev-ernesto-cardenal/how-pope-francis-is-carry_b_6550002.html.

9. Sean Smith. "Fr. Hans Kung Says Pope Has Responded to His Call for Discussion on Infallibility Dogma." *Tablet*, April 27, 2016. http://www.thetablet.co.uk/news/5482/0/fr-hans-kung-says-pope-has-responded-to-his-call-for-discussion-on-infallibility-dogma-.

10. Emily Schmall and Larry Rohter. "A Conservative with a Common Touch." *New York Times*, March 13, 2013. http://www.nytimes.com/2013/03/14/world/europe/new-pope-theologically-conservative-but-with-a-common-touch.html.

11. John Vennari. "Pastoral Discernment and Dead Members 'Alive.'" Catholic Family News, June 4, 2016. http://www.cfnews.org/page88/files/4eeba581b9fe9b063f35d6a76ea39a42-559.html.

12. David Gibson. "Cardinal Kasper Is the Pope's Theologian." Religion News Service, June 3, 2014. https://www.ncronline.org/news/vatican/cardinal-kasper-popes-theologian.

13. Carol Glatz. "Church Must Not Be Self-Centered, Pope Francis Told Cardinals." *Catholic Herald*, March 28, 2013. http://www.catholicherald.co.uk/news/2013/03/28/church-must-not-be-self-centred-pope-francis-told-cardinals.

14. Paul Elie. "How Pope Francis Became the People's Pontiff." *Vanity Fair*, September 14, 2015. http://www.vanityfair.com/news/2015/09/pope-francis-usa-tour.

15. Gerard O'Connell. "Cardinal Kasper: Some Fear a Domino Effect at the Synod on the Family." *America*, September 29, 2014. http://americamagazine.org/content/all-things/cardinal-kasper-some-fear-domino-effect-synod-family.

16. Christine Niles. "Cardinal Donald Wuerl: A New Bishop of Bling." *Church*

*Militant*, November 9, 2015. http://www.churchmilitant.com/news/article/cdl.-wuerl.

17. Jim Yardley and Jason Horowitz. "Pope Replaces Conservative U.S. Cardinal on Influential Vatican Committee." *New York Times*, December 16, 2013. http://www.nytimes.com/2013/12/17/world/europe/pope-replaces-conservative-us-cardinal-on-influential-vatican-committee.html.

18. John Allen. "Meet the Prototype for a 'Pope Francis Bishop.'" *Crux*, May 11, 2016. https://cruxnow.com/church/2016/05/11/meet-the-prototype-for-a-pope-francis-bishop.

19. Patrick Downes. "Cardinal-designate Mafi of Tonga Called a 'Simple, Humble' Man." Catholic News Service, February 12, 2015. https://www.ncronline.org/news/cardinal-designate-mafi-tonga-called-simple-humble-man.

20. John Allen. "Pope's New Cardinal in Papua New Guinea Checks All the Boxes." *Crux*, October 1, 2016. https://cruxnow.com/analysis/2016/10/17/popes-new-cardinal-papua-new-guinea-ticks-boxes.

21. Nicole Winfield. "Pope Sends US Church Message with Cardinal Choices." Associated Press, October 9, 2016. http://bigstory.ap.org/article/a56968a860d0416db7861b47237a5ab6/francis-names-17-cardinals-13-whom-electors-3-usa.

22. Ines San Martin. "Pope Vows He Won't Be Slowed Down by 'Ultra-Conservatives.'" *Crux*, July 3, 2016. https://cruxnow.com/vatican/2016/07/03/pope-says-hes-not-looking-shoulder-ultra-conservatives.

23. Philip Pullela. "Pope Francis Includes Women, Muslims for First Time in Holy Thursday Rite." Reuters, March 29, 2013. http://blogs.reuters.com/faithworld/2013/03/29/pope-francis-includes-women-muslims-for-first-time-in-holy-thursday-rite.

24. Elie, "How Pope Francis Became the People's Pontiff."

25. John-Henry Westen. " 'Pope Will Show Whose Side He Is On' during Synod, Says Archbishop." *LifeSiteNews*, September 10, 2015. https://www.lifesitenews.com/news/explosive-video-pope-will-show-whose-side-hes-on-during-synod-says-archbish.

26. John Allen. "Comeback of Honduran 'Vice Pope' Symbolizes Pope Francis Era." *Crux*, May 12, 2015. https://cruxnow.com/church/2015/05/12/comeback-of-honduran-vice-pope-symbolizes-pope-francis-era.

27. "Maradiaga Says Müller Needs to 'Be a Bit More Flexible.'" *La Stampa*, January 21, 2014. http://www.lastampa.it/2014/01/21/vaticaninsider/eng/news/maradiaga-says-muller-needs-to-be-a-bit-more-flexible-vZdAXTfW8PCqOqYloLM4oM/pagina.html.

28. Nicholas Boyle. "Either One Thing or the Other." *Tablet*, January 30, 2014. http://www.thetablet.co.uk/features/2/1415/other/give-the-tablet-for-easter.

29. Sandro Magister. "The German Option of the Argentine Pope." *Chiesa*, April 28, 2016. http://chiesa.espresso.repubblica.it/articolo/1351283?eng=y.

30. Maike Hickson. "In a Series of Strategic Moves, Pope Marginalizes Orthodox Prelates." 1P5, April 23, 2016. http://www.onepeterfive.com/in-a-series-of-strategic-moves-pope-marginalizes-orthodox-prelates.

31. Joseph Pelletier. "Bombay Cardinal Pushes Gay Rights in India." *Church Militant*, February 3, 2016. http://www.churchmilitant.com/news/article/india-supreme-court-to-reconsider-gay-rights.

32. "Build Civilization of Love in Response to Bombings, Cardinal Urges." Catholic News Service, April 22, 2013. http://www.catholicnews.com/services/englishnews/2013/build-civilization-of-love-in-response-to-bombings-cardinal-urges-cns-1301796.cfm.

33. Sandro Magister. "The Pope Is Not Infallible: Here Are Eight Proofs." *Chiesa*, June 13, 2016. http://chiesa.espresso.repubblica.it/articolo/1351315?eng=y.

34. Thomas C. Fox. "Francis to Religious: Don't Sweat Too Much the CDF." *National Catholic Reporter*, June 11, 2013. https://www.ncronline.org/blogs/ncr-today/francis-religious-dont-sweat-too-much-cdf.

35. "Celebrities Who Support Pope Francis." *Hollywood Reporter*, September 26, 2015. http://www.hollywoodreporter.com/news/celebrities-who-support-pope-francis-827021.

36. "Salma Hayek: 'I Think Pope Francis Is the Best Pope That Has Ever Existed.'" Rome Reports, May 30, 2016.

37. "The Pope and Liberation Theology." Tom Hayden, The Peace and Resource Center, December 24, 2013. http://tomhayden.com/home/the-pope-liberation-theology.html.

38. Stoyan Zaimov. "Atheist Bill Maher Asks Catholic Rick Santorum: 'How Am I on the Pope's Side and You Are Not?'" *Christian Post*, August 31, 2015. http://www.christianpost.com/news/atheist-bill-maher-asks-catholic-rick-santorum-how-am-i-on-the-popes-side-and-youre-not-144118.

39. Ross Douthat. "Will Pope Francis Break the Church?" *Atlantic*, May 2015. http://www.theatlantic.com/magazine/archive/2015/05/will-pope-francis-break-the-church/389516.

40. Laurie Goodstein and Elisabetta Poveldo. "Pope Sets Down Goals for an Inclusive Church, Reaching Out 'on the Streets.'" *New York Times*, November 26, 2013. http://www.nytimes.com/2013/11/27/world/europe/in-major-document-pope-francis-present-his-vision.html.

41. Laurie Goodstein. "Pope Says Church Is 'Obsessed' with Gays, Abortion and Birth Control." *New York Times*, September 19, 2013. http://www.nytimes.com/2013/09/20/world/europe/pope-bluntly-faults-churchs-focus-on-gays-and-abortion.html.

42. Francis X. Rocca. "Pope Francis and the New Rome." *Wall Street Journal*, April 3, 2015. http://www.wsj.com/articles/pope-francis-and-the-new-rome-1428075101.

43. James Taranto. "When the Archbishop Met the President." *Wall Street Journal*, March 31, 2012. http://www.wsj.com/articles/SB100014240527 02303816504577311800821270184.

44. "And Now the Mueller Interview." Fr. Ray Blake's Blog, October 3, 2013. http://marymagdalen.blogspot.com/2013/10/and-now-mueller-interview .html.

45. George Varga. "Elton Praises Pope." *San Diego Union-Tribune*, October 29, 2014. http://www.sandiegouniontribune.com/news/2014/oct/29/ phil-collins-remembers-alamo-elton-cheers-the-pope.

46. John Allen. "Pope on Homosexuals: 'Who Am I to Judge?' " *National Catholic Reporter*, July 29, 2013. https://www.ncronline.org/blogs/ncr-today/ pope-homosexuals-who-am-i-judge.

47. Nick Squires. "Pope's 'Eyes and Ears' in Vatican Bank 'Had String of Homosexual Affairs." *Telegraph*, July 19, 2013. http://www.telegraph.co.uk/ news/worldnews/europe/vaticancityandholysee/10191600/Popes-eyes -and-ears-in-Vatican-bank-had-string-of-homosexual-affairs.html.

48. Sandro Magister. "The Prelate of the Gay Lobby." *Chiesa*, July 18, 2013. http://chiesa.espresso.repubblica.it/articolo/1350561?eng=y.

49. Fr. Michael P. Orsi. "Do the Pope's Remarks Undermine Celibacy?" Catholic Exchange, August 2, 2013. http://catholicexchange.com/do-the-popes -remarks-undermine-celibacy.

50. Thomas D. Williams. "Vatican Radio Posts, Then Removes Photo of Lesbian Kiss." Breitbart, July 8, 2015. http://www.breitbart.com/national-security/ 2015/07/08/vatican-radio-posts-then-removes-photo-of-lesbian-kiss.

51. "A Gay Lobby at the Vatican?" Catholic News Agency, January 13, 2016. http://www.catholicnewsagency.com/news/a-gay-lobby-at-the-vatican -one-cardinal-says-its-real-and-pope-francis-is-responding-15439.

52. Carol Kuruvilla. "Secret Gay Society Poses Security Threat for Pope Francis: Ex-Swiss Guard." *New York Daily News*, January 21, 2014. http://www .nydailynews.com/news/world/secret-gay-society-vatican-poses-security -threat-ex-swiss-guard-article-1.1586607.

53. Philip Pullella. "Vatican Sacks Priest after He Comes Out as Gay." Reuters, October 3, 2015. http://www.reuters.com/article/vatican-preist-gay-id USL5N12307H20151003.

54. Lucas Grindley. "The Advocate's Person of the Year: Pope Francis." *Advocate*, December 16, 2013. http://www.advocate.com/year-review/2013/12/16/ advocates-person-year-pope-francis.

55. Pat Buchanan. "US and Catholicism in Crisis." Creators Syndicate, September 22, 2015. https://www.creators.com/read/pat-buchanan/09/15/us-and -catholicism-in-crisis.

56. Marcelo González. "The Horror!" *Rorate Caeli*, March 13, 2013. http:// rorate-caeli.blogspot.com/2013/03/the-horror-buenos-aires-journalist.html.

57. "Open Letter to Papa Francesco from Lucrecia Rego de Planas." Triregnum, October 12, 2013. http://triregnum.blogspot.com/2013/10/open-letter-to -papa-francesco-from.html.

58. Paul Vallely. "Where Pope Francis Learned Humility." *Atlantic*, August 23, 2015. http://www.theatlantic.com/international/archive/2015/08/pope -francis-cordoba-exile-humble/402032.

59. "Is Pope Francis Leaving Vatican at Night to Minister to Homelss?" *Huffington Post*, December 3, 2013. http://www.huffingtonpost.com/2013/12/ 02/pope-francis-homeless_n_4373884.html.

60. "Obama Is Fan of Pope Francis: 'Hugely Impressed.'" *Huffington Post*, October 3, 2013. http://www.huffingtonpost.com/2013/10/03/obama -pope-francis_n_4036329.html.

61. Mark Hensch. "Obama Praises Church for Honoring Archbishop Romero." *Hill*, May 23, 2015. http://thehill.com/blogs/blog-briefing-room/ 243021-obama-praises-church-for-honoring-archbishop-romero.

62. Howard Chua-Eoan and Elizabeth Dias. "Pope Francis, the People's Pope." *Time*, December 11, 2013. http://poy.time.com/2013/12/11/ person-of-the-year-pope-francis-the-peoples-pope.

63. John Allen. "Right Wing 'Generally Not Happy' with Francis, Chaput Says." *National Catholic Reporter*, July 23, 2013. https://www.ncronline .org/blogs/ncr-today/right-wing-generally-not-happy-francis-chaput-says.

64. Alana Massey. "Take What You Need and Leave the Rest." *Guardian*, September 23, 2015. https://www.theguardian.com/world/2015/sep/23/ non-catholics-who-love-pope-francis.

65. Timothy Egan. "Lapsed, but Listening." *New York Times*, October 10, 2013. http://opinionator.blogs.nytimes.com/2013/10/10/lapsed-but-listening.

66. "Under Bergoglio, Christianity Matters Less." *Rorate Caeli*, November 13, 2014. http://rorate-caeli.blogspot.com/2014/11/under-bergoglio-christ ianity-matters.html.

67. Doug Erickson. "Bishop Robert Morlino: Pope Francis Has Made Me a Stronger Culture Warrior." *Wisconsin State Journal*, March 10, 2014. http:// host.madison.com/wsj/news/local/bishop-robert-morlino-pope-francis-has -made-me-a-stronger/article_a7e5def6-33d1-5b57-ab29-1f300cd6347b.html.

68. Claire Gecewicz. "Most U.S. Catholics Rely Heavily on Their Own Conscience for Moral Guidance." PewResearchCenter, April 19, 2016. http://www.pewresearch.org/fact-tank/2016/04/19/most-catholics-rely -heavily-on-their-own-conscience-for-moral-guidance.

69. David Kaufman. "Pope Francis' Star Is Fading Back Home—And Here's Why It Matters." *New York Post*, July 4, 2016. http://nypost.com/2016/07/04/ pope-francis-star-is-fading-back-home-and-heres-why-it-matters.

70. Jacopo Barigazzi. "Pope Alienates Base, Sees Numbers Drop." *Politico*, January 12, 2016. http://www.politico.eu/article/a-pope-flop.

71. Carol Zimmerman. "Pope Francis' Appeal Not Measurable Yet in Church Attendance." Catholic News Service, March 13, 2014. https://www.ncronline .org/news/vatican/pope-francis-appeal-not-measurable-yet-church -attendance.
72. Joshua McElwee. "Catholicism Can and Must Change, Francis Forcefully Tells Italian Church Gathering." *National Catholic Reporter*, November 10, 2015. https://www.ncronline.org/news/vatican/catholicism-can-and -must-change-francis-forcefully-tells-italian-church-gathering.

## Chapter Three: The Left's Long March to the Papacy

1. Russell Shaw. "Vatican II and the Culture of Dissent." *Crisis*, February 1, 2006. http://www.crisismagazine.com/2006/vatican-ii-and-the-culture-of-dis sent-2.
2. Edward Pentin. "Cardinal Daneels Admits to Being Part of 'Mafia Club' Opposed to Benedict XVI." *National Catholic Register*, September 24, 2015. http://www.ncregister.com/blog/edward-pentin/cardinal-danneels- part-of-mafia-club-opposed-to-benedict-xvi.
3. "Belgium Cardinal Tried to Keep Abuse Victim Quiet." *National Catholic Reporter*, August 301, 2010. https://www.ncronline.org/news/account ability/belgium-cardinal-tried-keep-abuse-victim-quiet.
4. Sandro Magister. "Six More Votes for Gay Unions." *Chiesa*, June 10, 2013. http://chiesa.espresso.repubblica.it/articolo/1350534?eng=y.
5. Jeanne Smits. "Cardinal Danneels Admits Being Part of Clerical 'Mafia' That Plotted Francis' Election." *LifeSiteNews*, September 25, 2015. https://www .lifesitenews.com/news/cardinal-danneels-admits-being-part-of-clerical -mafia-that-plotted-francis.
6. Jan Bentz. "Cardinal to German Bishops: Push for Change While We Have Francis as Pope." *LifeSiteNews*, November 14, 2016. https://www .lifesitenews.com/news/german-cardinal-push-for-change-while-francis-is -leading-church.
7. Jeanne Smits. "Cardinal Danneels Admits Being Part of Clerical 'Mafia' That Plotted Francis' Election." *LifeSiteNews*, September 25, 2015. https:// www.lifesitenews.com/news/cardinal-danneels-admits-being-part-of -clerical-mafia-that-plotted-francis.
8. Maike Hickson. "Swiss Bishops Confirm Existence of Cardinal Danneels' 'Mafia' against Benedict XVI." *LifeSiteNews*, September 29, 2015. https:// www.lifesitenews.com/opinion/swiss-bishops-confirm-existence-of -cardinal-danneels-mafia-against-benedict.
9. Nick Hallett. "Ultra-Liberal Pro-Gay Marriage Cardinal 'Tried to Cover Up Sexual Abuse.'" Breitbart, October 11, 2015. http://www.breitbart

.com/london/2015/10/11/ultra-liberal-pro-gay-marriage-cardinal
-tried-to-cover-up-sex-abuse.

10. John Allen. "New Belgian Cardinal Poised to Be Key Papal Ally in Europe." *Crux*, October 11, 2016. https://cruxnow.com/global-church/2016/10 /11/new-belgian-cardinal-poised-key-papal-ally-europe.

11. John Allen. "New Pope, Jesuit Bergoglio, Was Runner-Up in 2005 Conclave." *National Catholic Reporter*, March 3, 2013. https://www.ncronline.org/ blogs/ncr-today/papabile-day-men-who-could-be-pope-13.

12. "Libero Quotidiano: 'Islam: When Bergoglio Attacked Ratzinger.'" *Rorate Caeli*, August 22, 2014. http://rorate-caeli.blogspot.com/2014/08/libero -quotidiano-when-bergoglio.html.

13. Ines San Martin. "Benedict XVI Says He Dismantled Vatican's 'Gay Lobby.'" *Crux*, July 1, 2016. https://cruxnow.com/vatican/2016/07/01/ benedict-xvi-says-dismantled-vaticans-gay-lobby.

14. David Gibson. "Secret 'Catacombs Pact' Emerges after 50 Years, and Pope Francis Gives It New Life." Religion News Service, November 3, 2015. http://religionnews.com/2015/11/03/the-catacombs-pact-emerges-after -50-years-and-pope-francis-gives-it-new-life.

15. Ibid.

16. Cindy Wooden. "Back to the Catacombs: New Emphasis Placed on Bishops' Simplicity Pact." Catholic News Service, November 13, 2015. http://www .catholicnews.com/services/englishnews/2015/back-to-the-catacombs -new-emphasis-placed-on-bishops-simplicity-pact.cfm.

17. Roberto de Mattei. "The So-Called 'Poor Church': From Vatican II to Francis." *Rorate Caeli*, June 15, 2015. http://rorate-caeli.blogspot.com/ 2016/06/the-so-called-poor-church-from-vatican.html.

18. "Entrevistas Históricas: Orianna Fallaci Entrevista Dom Hélder Câmara." Socialist Morena. http://www.socialistamorena.com.br/entrevistas-historicas -oriana-fallaci-entrevista-dom-helder-camara.

19. Gerard O'Connell. "Call Him a Saint?" *America*, April 27, 2015. http:// www.americamagazine.org/issue/call-him-saint.

20. Michael Hichborn. "The Marxist Core of the Catholic Campaign for Human Development." Lepanto Institute, November 18, 2015. http://www .lepantoinstitute.org/cchd/the-marxist-core-of-the-catholic-campaign-for -human-development.

21. Jim Yardley and William Neuman. "In Bolivia, Pope Francis Apologizes for Church's 'Grave Sins.'" *New York Times*, July 9, 2015. http://www.nytimes .com/2015/07/10/world/americas/pope-francis-bolivia-catholic-church -apology.html.

22. "Pope Francis: Speech at World Meeting of Popular Movements." Vatican Radio, October 7, 2015. http://en.radiovaticana.va/news/2015/07/10/ pope_francis_speech_at_world_meeting_of_popular_movements/1157291.

23. Jim Yardley and Paulina Villegas. "At Mass, Pope Francis Embraces 'Misunderstood' of Mexico." *New York Times*, February 15, 2016.

24. "Church Magazine in Mexico City Questions Pope's Rebuke of Bishops." Catholic News Service, March 9, 2016. http://www.catholicherald.co.uk/news/2016/03/09/church-magazine-in-mexico-city-questions-popes-rebuke-of-bishops.

25. Laurie Goodstein. "Ex-Archbishop Speaks about Catholic Church and Homosexuality." *New York Times*, May 14, 2009. http://www.nytimes.com/2009/05/15/us/15weakland.html.

26. Simon Caldwell. "Pope Benedict Wanted to Be a Librarian." *Telegraph*, August 5, 2010. http://www.telegraph.co.uk/news/worldnews/the-pope/7928493/Pope-Benedict-wanted-to-be-a-librarian.html.

27. "Liberals Dying or Hiding?" *National Catholic Reporter*, February 18, 2010. https://www.ncronline.org/news/liberals-dying-or-hiding.

28. David Gibson. "Fox News Columnist Rips Pope Francis, Loses Catholic News Service Gig." Religion News Service, December 4, 2013. http://religionnews.com/2013/12/06/fox-news-columnist-ripped-pope-francis-loses-catholic-news-service-gig.

29. Jim McDermott. "Catholic Theologians Condemn Ross Douthat's Recent Piece on the Pope." *America*, October 27, 2015. http://americamagazine.org/content/dispatches/catholic-theologians-condemn-ross-douthats-recent-piece-pope.

30. Ines San Martin. "Priest Who Does Vatican PR Says He Won't Sue Conservative Blogger." *Crux*, March 4, 2015. https://cruxnow.com/church/2015/03/04/priest-who-does-vatican-pr-says-he-wont-sue-conservative-blogger.

31. Allison Walter. "Fr. Charles Curran: Pope Francis' Reforms Are 'More Than Just Style.'" *National Catholic Reporter*, April 15, 2016. https://www.ncronline.org/news/people/fr-charles-curran-pope-francis-reforms-are-more-just-style.

32. Jeannine Gramick. "Where Are the Priests of Vatican II?" *National Catholic Reporter*, August 3, 2016. https://www.ncronline.org/blogs/ncr-today/where-are-priests-vatican-ii.

33. Gibson, "Secret 'Catacombs Pact.'"

## Chapter Four: The Liberal Jesuit from Latin America

1. Fr. Antonio Spadaro. "A Big Heart Open to God." *America*, September 30, 2013. http://americamagazine.org/pope-interview.

2. Chencho Alas. "Liberation Theology and Pope Francis I." Alas, February 14, 2015. http://discover-peace.org/blog/english-version/liberation-theology-and-pope-francis-i.

3. Ibid.

4. Philip Pullella. "Pope Expected to Rein in Liberal Jesuits." UPI, February 23, 1982. http://www.upi.com/Archives/1982/02/23/Pope-expected-to-rein -in-liberal-Jesuits/4731383288400.

5. Mario Aguilar. *Pope Francis: His Life and Thought* (Cambridge: Lutterworth Press, 2014), 46.

6. Spadaro, "A Big Heart Open to God."

7. Peter Hebblethwaite. "Don Pedro in History." *America*, February 16, 1991. http://americamagazine.org/issue/100/don-pedro-history-2.

8. Jon Anderson. "How Francis Can Save the Jesuits." *Catholic Herald*, November 12, 2015.

9. Austen Ivereigh. *The Great Reformer* (New York: Henry Holt, 2014), 119–120.

10. Ibid.

11. Spadaro, "A Big Heart Open to God."

12. James Carroll. "Who Am I to Judge?" *New Yorker*, December 23, 2013. http://www.newyorker.com/magazine/2013/12/23/who-am-i-to-judge.

13. Spadaro, "A Big Heart Open to God."

14. Jim O'Grady. "Pope Francis Wasn't Always So Humble." WNYC News, September 18, 2015. http://www.wnyc.org/story/pope-francis-wasnt-always -so-humble.

15. Paulo Prada and Helen Popper. "Behind the Charm, a Political Pope." Reuters, March 27, 2013. http://www.reuters.com/article/us-pope-profile -specialreport-idUSBRE92Q09P20130327.

16. David Gibson. "Who Are the Jesuits?" Religion News Service, September 18, 2015. http://religionnews.com/2015/09/18/jesuits-understand-pope -francis-need-know-saint-ignatius.

17. "An Argentine Prosecutor Speaks about Jorge Mario Bergoglio." From Rome, February 12, 2015. https://fromrome.wordpress.com/2015/02/12/an -argentine-prosecutor-speaks-about-bergoglio.

18. Wen Stephenson. "How Pope Francis Came to Embrace Not Just Climate Justice but Liberation Theology." *Nation*, September 19, 2015. https:// www.thenation.com/article/how-pope-francis-came-to-embrace-not-just -climate-justice-but-liberation-theology.

19. "New Marxist Phase of the Jesuits." Tradition in Action, October 23, 2016. http://traditioninaction.org/RevolutionPhotos/A701-Sosa.htm.

20. "Killing in the Name of God Is an Aberration, but Insulting Religions Is Wrong." *La Stampa*, January 15, 2015. http://www.lastampa.it/2015/ 01/15/vaticaninsider/eng/world-news/killing-in-the-name-of-god-is-an -aberration-but-insulting-religions-is-wrong-35zozqAwZvDy7u6bQX jhLP/pagina.html.

21. Jorge Mario Bergoglio and Rabbi Abraham Skorka. *On Heaven and Earth* (New York: Image, 2010), 93.

22. Bull of Indiction of the Jubilee of Mercy. http://www.iubilaeummisericor diae.va/content/gdm/en/giubileo/bolla.html.

23. Garry Wills. "Jesuits in Disarray." *New York Review of Books*, March 28, 2002. http://www.nybooks.com/articles/2002/03/28/jesuits-in-disarray.

24. Francis Rocca. "Pope Francis and the New Rome." *Wall Street Journal*, April 3, 2015. http://www.wsj.com/articles/pope-francis-and-the-new -rome-1428075101.

25. "Jesuit University and High School Alumni in Congress." Ignatian Solidarity Network. http://ignatiansolidarity.net/jesuit-university-high-school-alumni -congress.

26. Paul Shaughnessy. "Are the Jesuits Catholic?" *Weekly Standard*, June 3, 2002. http://www.weeklystandard.com/are-the-jesuits-catholic/article/2586.

27. John Allen. "Who Francis May Be Based on Who Bergoglio Was." *National Catholic Reporter*, April 5, 2013. https://www.ncronline.org/ blogs/all-things-catholic/who-francis-may-be-based-who-bergoglio-was.

28. Spadaro, "A Big Heart Open to God."

29. Anian Christoph Wimmer. "Interview with Robert Spaemann on Amoris Laetitia." Catholic News Agency, April 29, 2016. http://www.catholicnews agency.com/news/full-text-interview-with-robert-spaemann-on-amoris -laetitia-10088.

30. John Vennari. "Situation Ethics Enshrined." Catholic Family News, April 20, 2016. http://www.cfnews.org/page88/files/88cd932e0fb30da936d5 47131dbddacf-571.html.

31. "We Overcame Their Traditions, We Overcame Their Faith." *Latin Mass*, January–February 1994, https://www.ewtn.com/library/priests/coulson.txt.

32. Carol Glatz. "Pope: Priests Lacking Mercy Shouldn't Hear Confession; Get Desk Job." Catholic News Service, September 10, 2015. http://www.catholic news.com/services/englishnews/2015/pope-says-priests-lacking-mercy -should-have-desk-job.cfm.

33. Spadaro, "A Big Heart Open to God."

34. Joshua McElwee. "Francis Asks Priests to Learn That Life Isn't Black and White, but Shades of Grey." *National Catholic Reporter*, August 25, 2016. https:// www.ncronline.org/news/vatican/francis-asks-seminaries-teach-life -isnt-black-and-white-shades-grey.

35. Steve Skojec. "Forte: Pope Did Not Want to Speak 'Plainly' of Communion for Remarried." 1P5, May 7, 2016. http://www.onepeterfive.com/pope -speaking-plainly-communion-divorced-messy.

36. Carly Holman. "No, Michael Moore, Hillary Will Never Be 'America's Pope Francis." Conservative Review, October 28, 2016. https://www.conser

vativereview.com/commentary/2016/10/michael-moore-hillary-will
-never-be-americas-pope-francis.

37. Damon Linker. "Pope Francis' Machiavellian Strategy to Liberalize the Catholic Church." *Week*, October 15, 2014. http://theweek.com/articles/443083/pope
-francis-machiavellian-strategy-liberalize-catholic-church.

38. Elisabetta Piqué. *Pope Francis: Life and Revolution*. (Chicago: Loyola Press, 2014).

39. Sandro Magister. "'Amoris Laetitia' Has a Ghostwriter: His Name Is Victor Manuel Fernández." *Chiesa*, May 25, 2016. http://chiesa.espresso.
repubblica.it/articolo/1351303?eng=y.

40. Maike Hickson. "CDF Prefect Characterizes Statement Made by Papal Adviser as 'Heretical.'" 1P5, June 8, 2016. http://www.onepeterfive.com/
cdf-prefect-characterizes-statement-made-by-papal-adviser-as-heretical.

41. "Bergoglio's Sister Reveals." Novus Ordo Watch, March 19, 2013. http://
www.novusordowatch.org/wire/bergoglio-nephew-swearwords.htm.

42. Sandro Magister. "Francis' Patient Revolution." *Chiesa*, October 24, 2014.
http://chiesa.espresso.repubblica.it/articolo/1350910?eng=y.

43. "For the Record: Boff Speaks on the New Pope." *Rorate Caeli*, April 8, 2013.
http://rorate-caeli.blogspot.com/2013/04/for-record-boff-speaks-on
-new-pope.html.

44. "Pope Francis and Clergy Sexual Abuse in Argentina." BishopAccountability
.org. http://www.bishop-accountability.org/Argentina.

45. John Allen. "New Hire Is Good News for Pope Francis on Anti-Abuse Effort."
*Crux*, April 1, 2016. https://cruxnow.com/church/2016/04/01/new-hire-is
-good-news-for-pope-francis-on-anti-abuse-effort.

46. Marcelo González. "The Horror!" Rorate Caeli, http://rorate-caeli.blog
spot.com/2013/03/the-horror-buenos-aires-journalist.html.

47. Michael Cromartie. "John L. Allen, Jr. and Paul Vallely at the March 2014 Faith Angle Forum." EPPC, March 24, 2014. https://eppc.org/
publications/john-l-allen-jr-paul-vallely-march-2014-faith-angle-forum.

## Chapter Five: The Unholy Alliance

1. Dawn Hu. "GU Faculty among Highest Donors to Obama Campaign."
*Hoya*, November 21, 2008. http://www.thehoya.com/gu-faculty-among
-highest-donors-to-obama-campaign.

2. Phyllis Schlafly and George Neumayr. *No Higher Power: Obama's War on Religious Freedom* (Washington, DC: Regnery Publishing, 2012), 79–80.

3. Kevin Dolak. "Voter Fraud Nun Resigns as Dean." ABC News, March 12, 2013. http://abcnews.go.com/US/ohio-nun-accused-voter-fraud-resigns-job
-college/story?id=18711636.

4. Michael Bastach. "Al Gore: 'I Could Become Catholic' because of Pope's Global Warming Stance." *Daily Caller*, May 5, 2015. http://dailycaller .com/2015/05/05/al-gore-i-could-become-a-catholic-because-of-popes -global-warming-stance.

5. Joshua McElwee. "Organizers, Union Leaders Seek to Influence Francis' US Visit through Vatican Meetings." *National Catholic Reporter*, June 9, 2015. https://www.ncronline.org/news/faith-parish/organizers-union-leaders -seek-influence-francis-us-visit-through-vatican-meetings.

6. Thomas Williams. "Pro-Abort Dems Tell Pope What to Say to U.S. Congress." Breitbart, September 8, 2015. http://www.breitbart.com/big-government/ 2015/09/08/pro-abort-dems-tell-pope-what-to-say-to-u-s-congress.

7. John-Henry Westen. "Leaked E-Mails Show George Soros Paid $650K to Influence Bishops During Pope's U.S. Visit." *LifeSiteNews*, August 23, 2016. https://www.lifesitenews.com/news/breaking-leaked-e-mails-show -george-soros-paid-to-influence-bishops-during.

8. Elizabeth Yore. "Behind the Bronze Doors: Soros Radicals Collude with Vatican." Remnant, October 24, 2016. http://remnantnewspaper.com/web /index.php/articles/item/2830-behind-the-bronze-doors-soros-radicals -collude-with-vatican.

9. Edmund Kozak. "WikiLeaks: Podesta and Left-Wing Activist Plot 'Catholic Spring.'" *LifeZette*, October 12, 2016. http://www.lifezette.com/polizette/ wikileaks-podesta-left-wing-activist-plot-catholic-spring.

10. Jonah Bennett. "Leaked E-Mails: Hillary Campaign Staffer Worried That 'Amen' Might Be Too Offensive." Daily Caller, October 20, 2016. http:// dailycaller.com/2016/10/20/leaked-emails-hillary-campaign-staffer -worried-that-amen-might-be-too-offensive.

11. Brent Budowsky. "Bernie Sanders, Hillary Clinton, and Pope Francis." *Observer*, July 16, 2015. http://observer.com/2015/07/bernie-sanders -hillary-clinton-and-pope-francis.

12. "Pope Discusses Literacy, Dignity with Widow of Paulo Freire." *Catholic News Herald*, April 27, 2015. http://catholicnewsherald.com/features/ vatican/195-news/roknewspager-vatican/7679-pope-discusses-literacy -dignity-with-widow-of-paulo-freire.

13. Ben Max. "In Pope Francis, De Blasio Finds Ultimate Validator." *Gotham Gazette*, September 24, 2015. http://www.gothamgazette.com/index.php/ government/5903-in-pope-francis-de-blasio-finds-ultimate-validator.

14. Thomas Williams. "Bernie Sanders Calls Pope Francis a 'Socialist' Like Himself." Breitbart, February 24, 2016. http://www.breitbart.com/big-govern ment/2016/02/24/bernie-sanders-calls-pope-francis-a-socialist-like -himself.

15. Jason Horowitz. "As Bernie Sanders Heads to Vatican, a Visit with Pope

Francis Seems in Doubt." *New York Times*, April 15, 2016. http://www.ny
times.com/2016/04/16/us/politics/bernie-sanders-vatican.html.

16. Jim Yardley. "Pope Francis Suggests Donald Trump Is 'Not Christian.'" *New
York Times*, February 18, 2016. http://www.nytimes.com/2016/02/19/
world/americas/pope-francis-donald-trump-christian.html.

17. "A Revolution of Tenderness." March 17, 2016. https://popefrancis16.com.

18. "Pelosi Statement on Pope Francis' Address to Congress." Office of Nancy
Pelosi, September 24, 2015. https://pelosi.house.gov/news/press-releases/
pelosi-statement-on-pope-francis-address-to-congress.

19. Hanna Trudo. "Biden: Pope Francis Wouldn't Endorse Sanders' Policies."
*Politico*, April 15, 2016. http://www.politico.com/story/2016/04/joe-biden
-pope-bernie-sanders-222040.

20. Gardiner Harris. "Joe Biden Speaks about Faith and Curing Cancer at the
Vatican." *New York Times*, April 29, 2016. http://www.nytimes.com/
2016/04/30/world/europe/joe-biden-speaks-about-faith-and-curing-cancer
-at-the-vatican.html.

21. Claire Chretien. "Pro-Abortion VP Joe Biden Speaks at Vatican Event on Adult
Stem Cells." *LifeSiteNews*, April 29, 2016. https://www.lifesitenews.com/
news/pro-abortion-vp-joe-biden-speaks-at-vatican-event-on-adult-stem-cells.

22. Monique Garcia and Ray Long. "Illinois Lawmakers Approve Gay Marriage
in Historic Vote." *Chicago Tribune*, November 6, 2013. http://articles
.chicagotribune.com/2013-11-06/news/ct-met-gay-marriage-illinois-1106
-20131106_1_illinois-senate-gay-marriage-gay-lawmakers.

23. Dan Riehl. "Nancy Pelosi Paints Marco Rubio as a Bad Catholic." Breitbart,
May 29, 2015. http://www.breitbart.com/big-government/2015/05/29/
nancy-pelosi-paints-mark-rubio-as-a-bad-catholic.

24. Michael Lindenberger. "Kentucky's Attorney General Explains Why He
Won't Defend Gay Marriage Ban." *Time*, March 4, 2014. http://time.com/
12568/kentucky-gay-marriage-jack-conway.

25. Christopher Hale. "What Tim Kaine, Donald Trump, and Pope Francis
Have in Common." *Time*, July 23, 2016. http://time.com/4420430/tim
-kaine-catholic-abortion.

26. Betsy Woodruff. "Tim Kaine's Time With a Marxist Priest." *Daily Beast*,
October 3, 2016. http://www.thedailybeast.com/articles/2016/10/03/tim
-kaine-s-time-with-a-marxist-priest.html.

27. "San Jose Bishop Blasts Trump." California Catholic, October 25, 2016.
http://cal-catholic.com/?p=26133.

28. Daniel Politi. "It Sure Sounds like Pope Francis Doesn't Think Americans
Should Vote for Trump." *Slate*, November 6, 2016. http://www.slate.com/
blogs/the_slatest/2016/11/06/pope_francis_speaks_up_against_walls
_days_before_the_election.html.

29. Edward Pentin. "How the Vatican Views Trump's Presidential Victory."

*National Catholic Register*, November 15, 2016. http://www.ncregister .com/daily-news/how-the-vatican-views-trumps-presidential-victory.

30. Emma Green. "Hillary Clinton Ties Herself to Francis on Climate Change." *Atlantic*, September 25, 2015. http://www.theatlantic.com/politics/archive/ 2015/09/hillary-clinton-fangirl-francis-climate-change/407362.

31. David Weigel. "The Pope Name-Dropped a Radical Catholic Activist, and Bernie Sanders Couldn't Be Happier." *Washington Post*, September 24, 2015. https://www.washingtonpost.com/news/post-politics/wp/2015/09/24/ the-pope-name-dropped-a-radical-catholic-activist-and-bernie-sanders -couldnt-be-happier.

32. Peter Dreier. "Did Pope Francis Just Endorse Socialist Pacifist Dorothy Day for Sainthood?" *Huffington Post*, September 25, 2015. http://www.huffing tonpost.com/peter-dreier/did-pope-francis-endorse-pacifist-dorothy-day _b_8194354.html.

33. Daniel Burke. "Book on Monk Thomas Merton's Love Affair Stirs Debate." Religion News Service, December 22, 2009. http://usatoday30.usatoday .com/news/religion/2009-12-23-Merton23_st_N.htm.

34. Rose Marie Berger. "Why the Pope's Mention of Thomas Merton Was More Controversial Than You Think." Religion News Service, October 3, 2015. http://www.huffingtonpost.com/entry/thomas-merton-pope-francis_us _560af93be4b0af3706de5881.

35. Simone Campbell. "Pope Francis' Impact on the Catholic Vote in 2016." Philly. com, May 5, 2016. http://articles.philly.com/2016-05-05/news/72835386 _1_pope-francis-catholic-vote-mea-culpa.

36. John Allen. "Dolan: Francis Should Call Out Moderate Muslims." *Crux*, September 4, 2014. https://cruxnow.com/church/2014/09/04/pope-francis -should-call-out-moderate-muslims-ny-cardinal-says.

37. Phyllis Bennis and Manuel Perez Rocha. "Standing before Congress, Pope Francis Calls Out the 'Industry of Death.'" Common Dreams, September 24, 2015. http://www.commondreams.org/views/2015/09/24/standing -congress-pope-francis-calls-out-industry-death.

38. Paul Gosar. "Why I Am Boycotting Pope Francis' Address to Congress." Townhall, September 17, 2015. http://townhall.com/columnists/congress manpaulgosar/2015/09/17/why-i-am-boycotting-pope-francis-address-to -congress-n2053596.

39. "Pope Francis Never Mentioned Jesus in His Speech to Congress." *Federalist*, September 24, 2015. http://thefederalist.com/2015/09/24/ pope-francis-never-mentioned-jesus-in-his-speech-to-congress.

40. Evan Lips. "Obama Snubs Former Vatican Envoys Flynn, Glendon in Party Planned for Pope Francis." NewBostonPost, September 21, 2015. http:// newbostonpost.com/2015/09/21/obama-snubs-former-vatican-envoys -flynn-glendon-in-party-planned-for-pope-francis.

41. Michael Hichborn. "Marxists in the Pontifical Academy of Social Sciences." Lepanto Institute, December 21, 2015. http://www.lepantoinstitute.org/faith-and-life/marxists-in-the-pontifical-academy-of-social-sciences.

42. Brian Roewe. "Vatican Official Rebuts Pro-Life Concerns with Recent Climate Conference." *National Catholic Reporter*, May 21, 2015. https://www.ncronline.org/blogs/eco-catholic/vatican-official-rebuts-pro-life-concerns-recent-climate-conference.

43. Michael O'Loughlin. "New Chicago Archbishop Blase Cupich: A Moderate Voice." Crux, September 19, 2014. https://cruxnow.com/church/2014/09/19/new-chicago-archbishop-appears-to-be-cupich.

44. Blase Cupich. "Planned Parenthood and the Muted Humanity of the Unborn Child." *Chicago Tribune*, August 3, 2015. http://www.chicagotribune.com/news/opinion/commentary/ct-blase-cupich-abortion-planned-parenthood-perspec-0804-20150803-story.html.

45. Manya Brachear Pashman. "Cupich Supports Dialogue over Divorced, Remarried Catholics Receiving Communion." *Chicago Tribune*, October 16, 2015. http://www.chicagotribune.com/news/ct-cupich-communion-divorced-remarried-catholics-20151016-story.html.

46. Susan Berry. "Chicago Archbishop Encourages Communion for Pro-Abortion Catholics, Vague on Gay Marriage." Breitbart, December 1, 2014. http://www.breitbart.com/big-government/2014/12/01/chicago-archbishop-encourages-pro-abortion-catholics-to-receive-communion-vague-on-gay-marriage.

47. Jane Michaels. "Durbin, Cupich Urge Supporters of Immigration Reform to Speak Out, Vote." *Chicago Tribune*, May 4, 2015. http://www.chicagotribune.com/suburbs/winnetka/news/ct-wtk-immigration-panel-tl-0507-20150504-story.html.

48. Brian Roewe. "Cupich to Chicago Laborers: 'Pope Francis Is with You; I Am with You.'" *National Catholic Reporter*, September 18, 2015. https://www.ncronline.org/news/faith-parish/cupich-chicago-laborers-pope-francis-you-i-am-you.

49. "Pope Taps Cupich for Key Bishops-Making Panel." *Crux*, July 7, 2016. https://cruxnow.com/church-in-the-usa/2016/07/07/pope-positions-cupich-influence-bishops-appointments.

50. Manya Brachear Pashman and Ted Gregory. "Chicago Archbishop Cupich to Be Elevated to Rank of Cardinal." *Chicago Tribune*, October 9, 2016.

51. Michael O'Loughlin. "Pope Francis Sends 'Social Justice' Bishop to San Diego." *Crux*, March 2, 2015. https://cruxnow.com/church/2015/03/02/pope-francis-to-send-social-justice-bishop-to-san-diego.

52. Peter Rowe. "Bishop Has Long Christmas Wish List for Diocese." *San Diego Union-Tribune*, December 23, 2015. http://www.sandiegouniontribune.com/news/2015/dec/23/bishop-has-long-christmas-wish-list-for-diocese.

53. Molly Ball. "Pope Francis Sounds like a Democrat." *Atlantic*, September 24, 2015. http://www.theatlantic.com/politics/archive/2015/09/why-pope -francis-sounds-like-a-democrat/407023.
54. David Gibson. "Globe-Trotting Cardinal Theodore McCarrick Is Almost 84 and Working Harder Than Ever." Religion News Service, June 21, 2014. https:// www.ncronline.org/news/people/globe-trotting-cardinal-theodore -mccarrick-almost-84-and-working-harder-ever.
55. Maike Hickson. "Cardinal Kasper Defends Ireland's Gay Marriage Decision." *LifeSiteNews*, May 29, 2015. https://www.lifesitenews.com/ news/gay-unions-now-central-to-synod-agenda-after-irish-vote-cardinal -kasper.
56. Thomas Sowell. "The Left Has Its Pope." Creators Syndicate, September 22, 2015. https://www.creators.com/read/thomas-sowell/09/15/the-left-has -its-pope.
57. Robert Tracinski. "Marxifix Maximus: Pope Francis and the Surrender of the Church." *Federalist*, July 16, 2015. http://thefederalist.com/2015/07/16/ marxifix-maximus-pope-francis-and-the-surrender-of-the-church.
58. Stanley Kurtz. "The Truth About Obama's 'Catholic Roots.'" National Review Online, March 23, 2014. http://www.nationalreview.com/corner/ 373994.

## Chapter Six: The First Radical Green Pope

1. Wen Stephenson. "How Pope Francis Came to Embrace Not Just Climate Justice but Liberation Theology." *Nation*, September 19, 2015. https:// www.thenation.com/article/how-pope-francis-came-to-embrace-not-just -climate-justice-but-liberation-theology.
2. "Pope Francis Hopes for Global and Transformational Agreement on Climate Change." CNSnews.com, November 29, 2015. http://www.cnsnews.com/ news/article/cnsnewscom-staff/pope-hopes-global-and-transformational -agreement-climate-change.
3. "Pope Calls for More Courage on Climate Change." Agence France-Presse, January 15, 2015. http://news.abs-cbn.com/global-filipino/world/01/15/ 15/pope-calls-more-courage-climate-change.
4. Edward Pentin. "Vatican Light Show Aims to Push Climate Change Agreement." *National Catholic Register*, December 7, 2015. https://www.nc register.com/blog/edward-pentin/vatican-light-show-to-focus-on-climate -change/blank.htm.
5. "Archbishop Fisichella's Remarks on Jubilee Year of Mercy at Press Con-ference." Zenit, December 4, 2015. https://zenit.org/articles/archbishop -fisichella-s-remarks-on-jubilee-year-of-mercy-at-press-conference.

6. Austin Ruse. "Pope Francis Appoints Population Control Extremist to Vatican Post." Breitbart, June 17, 2015. http://www.breitbart.com/big-government/2015/06/17/pope-francis-appoints-population-control-extremist-to-vatican-post.

7. Naomi Klein. "A Radical Vatican?" *New Yorker*, July 10, 2015. http://www.newyorker.com/news/news-desk/a-visit-to-the-vatican.

8. Steffano Gennarini. "Who Is Jeffrey Sachs and Why Was He at the Vatican?" *LifeSiteNews*, March 14, 2015. https://www.lifesitenews.com/opinion/who-is-jeffrey-sachs-and-why-was-he-at-the-vatican.

9. Ines San Martin. "Everything You Need to Know about Sanders' Vatican Visit." *Crux*, April 14, 2016. https://cruxnow.com/church/2016/04/14/everything-you-need-to-know-about-sanders-vatican-visit.

10. Atila Sinke Guimaraes. "Who Is Inspiring Francis on Ecology?" Tradition in Action, May 29, 2015. http://www.traditioninaction.org/bev/178bev05_29_2015.htm.

11. Coral Davenport and Laurie Goodstein. "Pope Francis Steps Up Campaign on Climate Change, to Conservatives' Alarm." *New York Times*, April 27, 2015. http://www.nytimes.com/2015/04/28/world/europe/pope-francis-steps-up-campaign-on-climate-change-to-conservatives-alarm.html.

12. Joshua McElwee. "EPA Chief at Vatican: Obama 'Aligned With Pope Francis' on Climate Change." *National Catholic Reporter*, January 30, 2015. https://www.ncronline.org/blogs/eco-catholic/epa-chief-vatican-obama-aligned-francis-climate-change.

13. Ibid.

14. Ines San Martin. "The Pope and Leo DiCaprio Chat about the Environment." *Crux*, January 28, 2016. https://cruxnow.com/life/2016/01/28/the-pope-and-leo-dicaprio-chat-about-the-environment.

15. James Delingpole. "Vatican Heavies Silence Climate Heretics at UN Papal Summit." Breitbart, April 28, 2015. http://www.breitbart.com/big-government/2015/04/28/vatican-heavies-silence-climate-heretics-at-un-papal-summit.

16. "Michael Löwy Discusses Pope Francis's Recent Encyclical Laudato Si', Ecosocialism, and Left Unity in Europe Today." *Links*, February 19, 2016. http://links.org.au/node/4623.

17. "The Pope's Divisions." *Economist*, June 20, 2014. http://www.economist.com/blogs/erasmus/2014/06/francis-capitalism-and-war.

18. Thomas Williams. "Pope Francis Confesses He Knows Little about the Economy." Breitbart, July 14, 2015. http://www.breitbart.com/big-government/2015/07/14/pope-francis-confesses-he-knows-little-about-the-economy.

19. Stephen Moore. "Vatican's Left Turn Would Leave the Poor Even Poorer." *Washington Times*, January 4, 2015. http://www.washingtontimes.com/news/2015/jan/4/stephen-moore-pope-francis-misguided-policies-hurt.

20. Steven Malanga. "Brother Glum, Mother Earth." *City Journal*, June 19, 2015. http://www.city-journal.org/html/brother-glum-mother-earth-11600.html.

21. David Barrett. "Vatican Calls for Global Government to Oversee Markets." *Catholic Herald*, October 28, 2011. http://www.catholicherald.co.uk/news/2011/10/28/vatican-calls-for-global-government-to-oversee-markets.

22. Claire Chretien. "Cardinal Turkson to Head New Vatican Dicastery for Justice, Peace, 'Care of Creation.'" *LifeSiteNews*, August 31, 2016. https://www.lifesitenews.com/news/cardinal-turkson-to-head-new-vatican-dicastery-promoting-justice-peace-care.

23. Thomas Williams. "Vatican Basilica Switches Lights off for 'Earth Hour' to Protest Climate Change." Breitbart, March 19, 2016. http://www.breitbart.com/national-security/2016/03/19/vatican-basilica-switches-lights-off-for-earth-hour-to-protest-climate-change.

24. Marie Venner. "Philippines Archdiocese, Concerned by Coal, Joins Campaign to 'Break Free' from Fossil Fuels." *National Catholic Reporter*, May 10, 2016. https://www.ncronline.org/blogs/eco-catholic/philippines-archdiocese-concerned-by-coal-joins-campaign-break-free-fossil-fuels.

25. Lisa Palmieri-Billig. "New Curriculum for Seminarians, Inspired by Pope Francis." *La Stampa*, May 30, 2016. http://www.lastampa.it/2016/05/30/vaticaninsider/eng/news/new-curriculum-for-seminarians-inspired-by-pope-francis-VlqAuTBrGXjE91Qixo3eKM/pagina.html.

26. Michael O'Loughlin. "Live-Blogging the U.S. Bishops' Fall Meeting." *America*, November 14, 2016. http://www.americamagazine.org/content/dispatches/live-blogging-us-bishops-fall-meeting.

27. Kristan Hawkins. "Al Gore Pushes Population Control as Environmental Solution." LifeNews.com, June 24, 2011. http://www.lifenews.com/2011/06/24/al-gore-pushes-populaton-control-as-environmental-solution.

28. William Welch. "Pope: Catholics Need Not Breed Like 'Rabbits.'" *USA Today*, January 19, 2015. http://www.usatoday.com/story/news/2015/01/19/pope-birth-control-comments/22017365.

29. David Gibson. "Don't Breed 'Like Rabbits.'" Religion News Service, January 20, 2015. https://www.washingtonpost.com/national/religion/dont-breed-like-rabbits-was-pope-francis-breaking-new-ground-on-birth-control/2015/01/20/7c7f302e-a0e7-11e4-91fc-7dff95a14458_story.html.

30. Heather Saul. "Pope Francis Insists Catholics Do Not Need to Breed 'Like Rabbits' and Criticizes Woman for 'Tempting God' With Eighth Pregnancy." *Independent*, January 20, 2015. http://www.independent.co.uk/news/people/pope-francis-insists-catholics-do-not-need-to-breed-like-rabbits-and-criticises-woman-for-tempting-9989382.html.

31. Lindsey Bever. "Pope Says 3 Children per Family Is about Right: Catholics Don't Need to Breed 'Like Rabbits.'" *Washington Post*, January 20, 2015. https://www.washingtonpost.com/news/morning-mix/wp/2015/01/

20/pope-says-3-children-per-family-is-about-right-catholics-dont-need-to
-breed-like-rabbits.

32. "Holy See Rep 'Welcomes' UN Target for 'Universal Access to Sexual and Reproductive Health.' " Voice of the Family, June 3, 2016. http://voiceofthe family.com/holy-see-rep-welcomes-un-target-for-universal-access-to-sexual -and-reproductive-health.

33. Sarah Pulliam Bailey and Michelle Boorstein. "Pope Francis Suggests Contraception Could Be Permissible in Zika Fight." *Washington Post*, February 18, 2016. https://www.washingtonpost.com/news/acts-of-faith/ wp/2016/02/17/mexico-confirms-zika-virus-cases-in-pregnant-women -as-pope-francis-exits-the-country.

34. E. Christian Brugger. "Pope Francis and Contraception: A Troubling Scenario." *National Catholic Register*, February 24, 2016. http://www.ncregister .com/daily-news/pope-francis-and-contraception-a-troubling-scenario.

35. James F. Davis. "The Evolution Debate Begins." Accuracy in Academia, April 6, 2011. http://www.academia.org/the-evolution-debate-begins.

36. Daniel Berger. "Pope Francis: God is not 'a magician with a magic wand.' " MSNBC, October 29, 2014. http://www.msnbc.com/msnbc/pope-francis -god-not-magician-magic-wand#50899.

37. Father X. "Does Pope Francis Really Believe the Gospels?" *Remnant*, August 18, 2015. http://remnantnewspaper.com/web/index.php/articles/ item/1943-does-pope-francis-really-believe-the-gospels.

38. John-Henry Westen. "Vatican Bishop: Pope's View on Global Warming Is as Authoritative as the Condemnation of Abortion." *LifeSiteNews*, December 18, 2015. https://www.lifesitenews.com/news/vatican-bishop-popes -view-on-global-warming-is-as-authoritative-as-the-cond.

39. "On Evolution, Theology and Thomism: An Interview with Michael Chaberek." Evangelical Philosophical Society, July 26, 2015. http://blog .epsociety.org/2015/07/on-evolution-theology-and-thomism.html.

40. Christopher Ferrara. "Laudato Si: The Teilhard Connection." Fatima Network Perspectives, August 18, 2015. http://fatima.org/perspectives/sv/ perspective764.asp.

41. Colin Schultz. "The Pope Would Like You to Accept Evolution and the Big Bang." Smithsonian.com, October 28, 2014. http://www.smithsonianmag .com/smart-news/pope-would-you-accept-evolution-and-big-bang -180953166.

42. Chris White. "Pope's Climate Change Isn't Resonating among Conservatives, Study Finds." *Daily Caller*, http://dailycaller.com/2016/10/25/popes -climate-message-isnt-resonating-among-conservatives-study-finds.

43. Rosie Scammell. "Cardinal George Pell Takes a Swing at Pope Francis' Environmental Encyclical." Religion News Service, July 17, 2015. https://www.wash ingtonpost.com/national/religion/cardinal-george-pell-takes-a-swing-at

-pope-francis-environmental-encyclical/2015/07/17/ecc04ef8-2cbb-11e5
-960f-22c4ba982ed4_story.html.

## Chapter Seven: The Open-Borders Pope

1. Jim Yardley and Azam Ahmed. "Pope Francis Wades into U.S. Immigration Morass with Border Trip." *New York Times*, February 17, 2016.

2. Jim Yardley. "Pope Francis Suggests Donald Trump Is Not Christian." *New York Times*, February 18, 2016. http://www.nytimes.com/2016/02/19/world/americas/pope-francis-donald-trump-christian.html.

3. "Huckabee: Unprecedented for a Pope to Weigh in on Election." Fox News, February 18, 2016. http://www.foxnews.com/transcript/2016/02/18/huckabee-unprecedented-for-pope-to-weigh-in-on-election.

4. Michael O'Loughlin. "Trump v. Clinton Matchup Has Catholic Leaders Scrambling." *Crux*, May 9, 2016. https://cruxnow.com/church/2016/05/09/trump-v-clinton-matchup-has-catholic-leaders-scrambling.

5. Pam Key. "Mary Matalin: Pope Francis Just Gave Donald Trump 'a Big, Fat Wet Kiss.'" Breitbart, February 18, 2016. http://www.breitbart.com/video/2016/02/18/mary-matalin-pope-francis-just-gave-donald-trump-a-big-fat-wet-kiss.

6. "Pope Invites Refugees to Join Him on Stage for Audience." Associated Press, June 22, 2016. https://cruxnow.com/ap/2016/06/22/pope-invites-refugees-join-stage-audience.

7. "Francis: Refugees Are the Tip of the Iceberg, Europe Must Welcome Them." *La Stampa*, September 14, 2015. http://www.lastampa.it/2015/09/14/vaticaninsider/eng/the-vatican/francis-refugees-are-the-tip-of-the-iceberg-europe-must-welcome-them-Z588xG5rurwqC8oz6YFaJL/pagina.html.

8. Jim Yardley and William Neuman. "In Bolivia, Pope Francis Apologizes for Church's 'Grave Sins.'" *New York Times*, July 9, 2015. http://www.nytimes.com/2015/07/10/world/americas/pope-francis-bolivia-catholic-church-apology.html.

9. Jerry Bowyer. "Scholar Who Taught John Paul II to Appreciate Capitalism Worries about Pope Francis." *Forbes*, June 3, 2014. http://www.forbes.com/sites/jerrybowyer/2014/06/03/scholar-who-taught-john-paul-ii-to-appreciate-capitalism-worries-about-pope-francis-2/#18afb6203891.

10. Michelle Caruso-Cabrera. "Pope's Sharp Words Make a Wealthy Donor Hesitate." CNBC, December 30, 2013. http://www.cnbc.com/2013/12/30/pope-francis-wealthy-catholic-donors-upset-at-popes-rhetoric-about-rich.html.

11. Uri Friedman. "Refugees and the 'Globalization of Indifference.'" *Atlantic*, April 16, 2016. http://www.theatlantic.com/international/archive/2016/04/refugees-pope-francis-lesbos/477870.

12. Tom Kington. "Pope Francis Criticizes Indifference toward Immigrants' Plight." *Los Angeles Times*, July 8, 2013. http://articles.latimes.com/2013/jul/08/world/la-fg-wn-pope-immigration-20130708.

13. Daniel Politi. "Pope Calls on European Parishes to Take in Refugees." *Slate*, September 6, 2015. http://www.slate.com/blogs/the_slatest/2015/09/06/pope_calls_on_european_parishes_to_take_in_refugees.html.

14. Virginia Hale. "Christians Told to 'Pray in Silence...Don't Disturb the Migrants.'" Breitbart, June 6, 2016. http://www.breitbart.com/london/2016/06/06/parishioners-told-pray-silence-migrants.

15. Griff Witte. "Hungarian Bishop Says Pope Is Wrong about Refugees." *Washington Post*, September 7, 2015.

16. "Poland's Catholics Ambiguous over Pope Francis' Call for Parishes to Take in Muslim Refugees." Associated Press, September 12, 2015. http://www.foxnews.com/world/2015/09/12/poland-catholics-ambiguous-over-pope-francis-call-for-parishes-to-take-in.html.

17. "Interview: Pope Francis." *Croix*, May 17, 2016. http://www.la-croix.com/Religion/Pape/INTERVIEW-Pope-Francis-2016-05-17-1200760633.

18. Robert Mackey. "Hungarian Leader Rebuked for Saying Muslim Migrants Must Be Blocked 'to Keep Europe Christian.'" *New York Times*, September 3, 2015. http://www.nytimes.com/2015/09/04/world/europe/hungarian-leader-rebuked-for-saying-muslim-migrants-must-be-blocked-to-keep-europe-christian.html.

19. Thomas Williams. "Pope's Origins Skew His Views on Migrant Crisis, Cardinal Asserts." Breitbart, May 9, 2016. http://www.breitbart.com/london/2016/05/09/popes-origins-skew-views-migrant-crisis-cardinal-asserts.

20. "Charlemagne Prize: Pope Francis' Full Speech." Rome Reports, May 6, 2016. http://www.romereports.com/2016/05/08/charlemagne-prize-pope-francis-full-speech.

21. "Interview: Pope Francis." *Croix*, May 17, 2016. http://www.la-croix.com/Religion/Pape/INTERVIEW-Pope-Francis-2016-05-17-1200760633.

22. Yaron Steinbuch. "Pope Francis Reneges on Offer to Take in Christian Refugees." *New York Post*, April 22, 2016. http://nypost.com/2016/04/22/pope-francis-reneges-on-offer-to-take-in-christian-refugees.

23. "Interview: Pope Francis." *Croix*, May 17, 2016. http://www.la-croix.com/Religion/Pape/INTERVIEW-Pope-Francis-2016-05-17-1200760633.

24. Frances D'Emilio. "Pope to Young on Poland Trip: Believe 'in a New Humanity.'" *Washington Post*, July 31, 2016. https://www.washingtonpost.com/world/europe/faithful-fill-meadow-ahead-of-popes-last-mass-in-poland/2016/07/31/648fd23e-56e9-11e6-b652-315ae5d4d4dd_story.html.

25. Joseph Pelletier. "Italian Bishop Rejects 'Peaceful Muslims' Rhetoric." *Church Militant*, August 4, 2016. http://www.churchmilitant.com/news/article/italian-bishop-rejects-peaceful-muslims-rhetoric.

26. Damian Thompson. "Why Bishops Love the EU." *Catholic Herald*, May 12, 2016. http://www.catholicherald.co.uk/issues/may-13th-2016/why-bi shops-love-the-eu.

27. "USCCB Migration Committee Chairman Reacts to Supreme Court Decision on Immigration." United States Conference of Catholic Bishops, June 23, 2016. http://www.usccb.org/news/2016/16-078.cfm.

28. Michael O'Loughlin. "Defying the Governor, Indianapolis Archbishop Takes in Syrian Refugees." *Crux*, December 8, 2015. https://cruxnow.com/church/2015/12/08/defying-the-governor-indianapolis-archbishop-takes-in-syrian-refugees.

29. Susan Berry. "U.S. Catholic Bishops Celebrate National Migration Week: 'Welcome the Stranger among Us.'" Breitbart, January 3, 2016. http://www.breitbart.com/big-government/2016/01/03/u-s-catholic-bishops-celebrate-national-migration-week-welcome-stranger-among-us.

30. Denis Grasska. "California Bishop Urges Catholics to Combat Anti-Islamic Bigotry." Catholic News Service, February 23, 2016. http://www.america magazine.org/issue/california-bishop-urges-catholics-combat-anti-islamic-bigotry.

31. Nancy Wiechec. "Nuncio at Border Mass Prays for an End to Barriers That Separate People." Catholic News Service, October 24, 2016. http://www.catholicnews.com/services/englishnews/2016/nuncio-at-border-mass-prays-for-an-end-to-barriers-that-separate-people.cfm.

32. Thomas Reese. "In Response to Trump, Vatican Official Says Church Should Be Prophetic." *National Catholic Reporter*, November 12, 2016. https://www.ncronline.org/news/politics/response-trump-vatican-official-says-church-should-be-prophetic#.WCebKFf54J8.twitter.

33. "In-Flight Press Conference of His Holiness Pope Francis from Santiago de Cuba to Washington, D.C." Vatican, September 22, 2015. http://w2.vatican.va/content/francesco/en/speeches/2015/september/documents/papa-francesco_20150922_intervista-santiago-washington.html.

## Chapter Eight: The Pacifist Pope

1. Umberto Bacchi. "Pope Francis Lashes Out at Death Penalty 'Torture' Quoting Dostoyevsky." International Business Times, March 20, 2015. http://www.ibtimes.co.uk/pope-francis-lashes-out-death-penalty-torture-quoting-dostoyevsky-1492890.

2. "In the Silence of the Cross, Uproar of Weapons Ceases." *National Catholic Register*, August 7, 2013. http://www.ncregister.com/blog/edward-pentin/pope-in-the-silence-of-the-cross-uproar-of-weapons-ceases.

3. Francis X. Rocca. "Pope Francis Calls for Abolishing Death Penalty and Lifetime Imprisonment." Catholic News Service, October 13, 2014. https://

www.ncronline.org/blogs/francis-chronicles/pope-francis-calls-abolish
ing-death-penalty-and-life-imprisonment.

4. "Statement by His Holiness Pope Francis to the 'Judges, Summit on
Human Trafficking and Organized Crime." Vatican, June 3, 3016. https://
w2.vatican.va/content/francesco/en/speeches/2016/june/documents/
papa-francesco_20160603_summit-giudici.html.

5. Elise Harris. "Prisoners to Be Pope Francis' Special Guests at Mass in
St. Peter's." Catholic News Agency, November 3, 2016. http://www.catholic
newsagency.com/news/prisoners-to-be-pope-francis-special-guests-at-mass
-in-st-peters-36170.

6. "Pope Francis Holds Special Mass for Prisoners: 'We Can All Make Mistakes.'"
Associated Press, November 6, 2016. http://www.cbsnews.com/news/pope
-francis-holds-special-mass-for-prisoners-we-can-all-make-mistakes.

7. Thomas Williams. "Pope Francis Amps Up Opposition to Death Penalty."
Breitbart, June 22, 2016. http://www.breitbart.com/big-government/2016/
06/22/pope-francis-amps-opposition-death-penalty.

8. Avery Cardinal Dulles. "Catholicism & Capital Punishment." *First Things*,
April 2001. http://www.firstthings.com/article/2001/04/catholicism-amp
-capital-punishment.

9. Francis X. Rocca. "Pope Francis Calls for Abolishing Death Penalty and
Lifetime Imprisonment." Catholic News Service, October 13, 2014. https://
www.ncronline.org/blogs/francis-chronicles/pope-francis-calls-abolishing
-death-penalty-and-life-imprisonment.

10. Jeff Jacoby. "No, Pope Francis, It Is Not Hypocritical for the Good to
Make Weapons." *Boston Globe*, June 24, 2015. https://www.bostonglobe
.com/opinion/2015/06/24/pope-francis-not-hypocritical-for-good-make
-weapons/Q8fWS8QVNeEfNwoQE7RUNI/story.html.

11. Cassandra Vinograd. "Orlando Massacre: Pope Francis Lashes Out over
Access to Arms." NBC News, June 13, 2016. http://www.nbcnews.com/
storyline/orlando-nightclub-massacre/orlando-massacre-pope-francis
-lashes-out-over-access-arms-n590886.

12. "Fox's Greg Gutfeld Lashes Out at the Pope for 'Lecturing on Guns' after
Orlando." Media Matters, June 13, 2016. https://www.mediamatters.org/
video/2016/06/13/fox-s-greg-gutfeld-lashes-out-pope-lecturing-guns
-after-orlando/210912.

13. Michael O'Loughlin. "US Bishops Throw Support to Obama's Gun Control
Proposal." *Crux*, January 6, 2016. https://cruxnow.com/church/2016
/01/06/us-bishops-throw-support-to-obamas-gun-control-proposal.

14. Joshua McElwee. "Landmark Vatican Conference Rejects Just War Theory, Asks
for Encyclical on Nonviolence." *National Catholic Reporter*, April 14, 2016.
https://www.ncronline.org/news/vatican/landmark-vatican-conference
-rejects-just-war-theory-asks-encyclical-nonviolence.

15. Mary Anastasia O'Grady. "Behind the Pope's Embrace of Castro." *Wall Street Journal*, May 17, 2015. http://www.wsj.com/articles/behind-the-popes -embrace-of-castro-1431898937.

16. "Pope Francis Appeases the Castros in Repressive Cuba." *Washington Post*, September 21, 2015. https://www.washingtonpost.com/opinions/ deferring-to-the-castros/2015/09/21/30001198-6075-11e5-8e9e-dce8a 2a2a679_story.html?utm_term=.ceed2b19430e.

17. Gerard O'Connell. "Cuba's Raul Castro Tells Pope Francis: 'I Could Become a Catholic Again.'" *America*, May 10, 2015. http://americamagazine.org/ content/dispatches/cubas-raul-castro-tells-pope-francis-i-could-become -catholic-again.

18. Mary Anastasia O'Grady. "Ecuador's Correa Wants to Co-Opt Pope Francis." *Wall Street Journal*, July 5, 2015. http://www.wsj.com/articles/ SB11301772451238044816904581086313392621434.

19. Uki Goni. "The Peronist Roots of Pope Francis' Politics." *New York Times*, August 12, 2015. http://www.nytimes.com/2015/08/13/opinion/uki-goni -peronist-roots-of-pope-francis-politics.html.

20. "Pope Calls Abbas 'Angel of Peace' during Visit." Associated Press, May 16, 2015. http://www.usatoday.com/story/news/world/2015/05/16/pope-calls -palestinian-leader-angel-of-peace-during-visit/27441533.

21. Alan Dershowitz. "Will a Notorious Anti-Semite Become the Pope?" Gatestone Institute, February 19, 2013. https://www.gatestoneinstitute .org/3594/cardinal-andres-rodriguez-maradiaga.

22. "Pope Declines Dalai Lama Meeting in Rome." BBC, December 12, 2014. http://www.bbc.com/news/world-europe-30455187.

23. Cardinal Joseph Zen. "What Will 2016 Bring the Church in China?" AsiaNews, January 9, 2016. http://www.asianews.it/news-en/What-will -2016-bring-the-Church-in-China-36349.html.

24. Paddy Agnew. "Churchman Gave Chinese Agents False Documents about Pope's Health, Trial Told." *Irish Times*, March 18, 2016. http://www.irish times.com/news/social-affairs/religion-and-beliefs/churchman-gave -chinese-agents-false-documents-about-pope-s-health-trial-told-1.2578935.

25. George Weigel. "Only Francis Can Go to China?" *First Things*, June 1, 2016. http://www.firstthings.com/web-exclusives/2016/06/only-francis-can -go-to-china.

26. Lisa Jucca, Benjamin Kang Lim, and Greg Torode. "After Decades of Mistrust, Pope Pushes for Diplomatic Breakthrough with China." Reuters, July 14, 2016. http://www.reuters.com/investigates/special-report/china-vatican.

27. Hilary White. "Cardinal Zen in his own words: 'In our acceptance of the provisions from Rome there is a limit, the limit of conscience.'" What's Up with the Synod?, October 28, 2016. http://whatisupwiththesynod .com/index.php/2016/10/28/cardinal-zen-in-his-own-words-in-our

-acceptance-of-the-provisions-from-rome-there-is-a-limit-the
-limit-of-conscience.

28. David Feith. "The Vatican's Illusions about Chinese Communism." *Wall Street Journal*, November 3, 2016. http://www.wsj.com/articles/the-vati cans-illusions-about-chinese-communism-1478215875.

## Chapter Nine: "I Don't Want to Convert You"

1. "Under Bergoglio, Christianity Matters Less." *Rorate Caeli*, November 13, 2014. http://rorate-caeli.blogspot.com/2014/11/under-bergoglio-christianity -matters.html.

2. Jonathan Merritt. "Is Francis the First Protestant Pope?" Religion News Service, April 10, 2013. http://religionnews.com/2013/04/10/is-francis-the -first-protestant-pope.

3. "Francis to Refugees: Christian or Muslim, the Faith Your Parents Instilled in You Will Help You Move On." Rome Reports, January 20, 2014. http:// www.romereports.com/2014/01/20/francis-to-refugees-christian-or -muslim-the-faith-your-parents-instilled-in-you-will-help-you-move-o.

4. "Interview: Pope Francis." *Croix*, May 17, 2016. http://www.la-croix.com/ Religion/Pape/INTERVIEW-Pope-Francis-2016-05-17-1200760633.

5. "Pope Blasts Christian, Muslim Fundamentalists while Leaving Turkey." Reuters, December 2, 2014. http://www.jpost.com/Christian-News/Pope -blasts-Christian-Muslim-fundamentalists-while-leaving-Turkey-383405.

6. Sandro Magister. "There's a War of Religion, but the Pope Keeps Quiet or Stammers." *Chiesa*, November 21, 2014. http://chiesa.espresso.repubblica .it/articolo/1350927?eng=y.

7. "Judge Jeanine: 'Time for Papacy to Get out in Front of Christian Massacre.'" Fox News Insider, July 27, 2014. http://insider.foxnews.com/ 2014/07/27/judge-jeanine-%e2%80%98it-time-papacy-get-out-front -christian-massacre%e2%80%99.

8. Abby Ohlheiser. "Pope Francis on Charlie Hebdo: 'You Cannot Insult the Faith of Others.'" *Washington Post*, January 15, 2015. https://www.washington post.com/news/world/wp/2015/01/15/pope-francis-on-charlie-hebdo -you-cannot-insult-the-faith-of-others.

9. Andrew Bieszad. "What Did the Saints Say about Islam?" 1P5, April 30, 2015. http://www.onepeterfive.com/what-did-the-saints-say-about-islam.

10. Ines San Martin. "Pope Francis Denies That Islam Is Violent." Crux, July 31, 2016. https://cruxnow.com/world-youth-day-krakow/2016/07/31/ pope-francis-denies-islam-violent.

11. Rosie Scammell. "Vatican Blasts Muhammad Cartoons as Pouring 'Gasoline on the Fire.'" Religion News Service, May 6, 2015. http://www.sltrib.com/lifestyle /faith/2484903-155/vatican-blasts-muhammad-cartoons-as-pouring.

12. Maike Hickson. "Cardinal Marx under Fire for Removing Pectoral Cross at Temple Mount." 1P5, November 16, 2016. http://www.onepeterfive.com/cardinal-marx-under-fire-for-removing-pectoral-cross-at-temple-mount.

13. William Kilpatrick. "Needed: A New Church Policy toward Islam." *Crisis*, January 28, 2015. http://www.crisismagazine.com/2015/needed-new-church-policy-toward-islam-pt-1.

14. "Pope Francis on Atheism." Richard Dawkins Foundation, May 17, 2013. https://richarddawkins.net/2013/05/pope-francis-on-atheism.

15. Matthew Deluca. "Pope Francis Digs at Vatican's Narcisstic Nature, Calls for Change." NBC News, October 1, 2013. http://www.nbcnews.com/news/other/pope-francis-digs-vaticans-narcissistic-nature-calls-change-f8C11305361.

16. "The Pope: How the Church Will Change." *La Repubblica*, October 1, 2013.

17. "Pope at Mass: Culture of Encounter Is the Foundation of Peace." Vatican Radio, May 22, 2013. http://en.radiovaticana.va/storico/2013/05/22/pope_at_mass_culture_of_encounter_is_the_foundation_of_peace/en1-694445.

18. Jeff Poor. "Bill Maher: I Think the Pope Might Be an Atheist like I Think Obama Is." *Daily Caller*, June 1, 2013. http://dailycaller.com/2013/06/01/bill-maher-i-think-the-pope-might-be-an-atheist-like-i-think-obama-is.

19. Father X. "Did Pope Francis Just Deny the Existence of Hell?" *Remnant*, March 22, 2015. http://remnantnewspaper.com/web/index.php/fetzen-fliegen/item/1611-did-pope-francis-just-deny-the-existence-of-hell.

20. David Martin. "Did Francis Just Defend Judas?" *Remnant*, April 14, 2016. http://remnantnewspaper.com/web/index.php/fetzen-fliegen/item/2450-did-francis-just-defend-judas.

21. Luke Coppen. "The Pope's Great Evangelical Gamble." *Catholic Herald*, July 23, 2015. http://www.catholicherald.co.uk/issues/july-24th-2015/the-popes-great-evangelical-gamble.

22. "Pope Francis 'Dismissed Anglican Branch as Quite Unnecessary.'" *Telegraph*, March 15, 2013. http://www.telegraph.co.uk/news/worldnews/the-pope/9933614/Pope-Francis-dismissed-Anglican-branch-as-quite-unnecessary.html.

23. Sandro Magister. "Francis's Secret Friend in Caserta." *Chiesa*, July 23, 2014. http://chiesa.espresso.repubblica.it/articolo/1350849?eng=y.

24. Jamie Weinstein. "Coulter on Pope Francis: Maybe Better Suited to Be a CNN Host." *Daily Caller*, December 17, 2013. http://dailycaller.com/2013/12/17/coulter-on-pope-francis-maybe-better-suited-to-be-a-cnn-host.

25. Gerard O'Connell. "Pope Francis Says the Church Should Apologize to Gays." *America*, June 26, 2016. http://americamagazine.org/content/dispatches/pope-francis-says-church-should-apologize-gays.

26. Rosie Scammell. "Vatican Backs Plan to Name Rome Square for Martin Luther." Religion News Service, August 26, 2015. https://www.ncronline .org/news/spirituality/vatican-backs-plan-name-rome-square-martin-luther.

27. "Fr. Cantalamessa 3rd Advent Sermon: Mary in the Mystery of Christ." Vatican Radio, December 18, 2015. http://en.radiovaticana.va/news/2015/ 12/18/fr_cantalamessa_advent_sermon_mary_in_the_mystery_of_christ/ 1195223.

28. Jonathan Luxmoore. "Martin Luther Was a 'Teacher of the Faith.'" *Catholic Herald*, August 12, 2016. http://www.catholicherald.co.uk/news/2016/ 08/12/martin-luther-was-a-teacher-of-the-faith-say-german-bishops.

29. Christopher Ferrara. "Francis and 'Saint' Martin Luther: Perfect Together." The Remnant, October 17, 2016. http://remnantnewspaper.com/web/ index.php/fetzen-fliegen/item/2817-francis-and-saint-martin-luther -perfect-together.

30. Jan Bentz. "Pope Again Criticizes 'Proselytism': 'It Is Not Licit That You Convince Them of Your Faith." *LifeSiteNews*, October 19, 2016. https:// www.lifesitenews.com/opinion/pope-to-teen-girl-proselytism-is-the -strongest-poison-against-the-ecumenica.

31. Fr. Dwight Longenecker. "Clarity, Not Just Charity, Key on Martin Luther." *Crux*, June 29, 2016. https://cruxnow.com/commentary/2016/06/29/ clarity-not-just-charity-key-martin-luther.

32. Iacopo Scaramuzzi. "Junge: Just a Few Years Ago Commemorating Luther Together Was Impossible." La Stampa, October 26, 2016. http:// www.lastampa.it/2016/10/26/vaticaninsider/eng/the-vatican/junge -just-a-few-years-ago-commemorating-luther-together-was-impossible -6gIWFaIKlE1BHn7mxz6FOP/pagina.html.

33. Francis Rocca. "Pope's Beatitudes Highlight Care for Environment and Outsiders." *Wall Street Journal*, November 1, 2016. http://www.wsj.com/ articles/popes-beatitudes-highlight-care-for-environment-and-outsiders -1477998680.

34. Claire Chretien. "Bishop Schneider: Church Has Already Answered 'Errors of Luther.'" *LifeSiteNews*, October 31, 2016. https://www.lifesitenews.com/ news/bishop-schneider-church-has-already-addressed-errors-of-luther.

35. "Reformation Is Nothing to Celebrate, Says Cardinal Müller." *Catholic Herald*, March 31, 2016. http://www.catholicherald.co.uk/news/2016 /03/31/reformation-is-nothing-to-celebrate-says-cardinal-muller.

36. Ines San Martin. "Traditionalists Spurn Deal with Rome, Charging 'Painful Confusion.'" Crux, June 29, 2016. https://cruxnow.com/vatican/2016/06 /29/traditionalists-spurn-deal-rome-charging-painful-confusion.

37. "A Few Thoughts from the Requiem Mass Celebrating the Life of Rt Rev Anthony Palmer." Michael Daly CJ Blog, August 4, 2014. https:// michaeldalycj.wordpress.com/2014/08/08/a-few-thoughts-from-the

-requiem-mass-celebrating-the-life-of-rt-rev-anthony-palmer-4th-feb-1966
-20th-july-2014.

38. Joshua McElwee. "Francis Suggests Lutherans Might Discern Taking Catholic Communion Individually." *National Catholic Reporter*, November 16, 2015. https://www.ncronline.org/news/vatican/francis-suggests-lutherans-can -discern-taking-catholic-communion-individually.

39. Sandro Magister. "Communion for All, Even for Protestants." *Chiesa*, July 1, 2006. http://chiesa.espresso.repubblica.it/articolo/1351332?eng=y.

40. "Francis Bows His Head to Receive Justin's Blessing." *Cranmer*, June 20, 2014. http://archbishop-cranmer.blogspot.com/2014/06/francis-bows-his -head-to-receive.html.

41. Ibid.

42. Philip Pullella. "Vatican Says Catholics Should Not Try to Convert Jews, Should Fight Anti-Semitism." Reuters, December 10, 2015. http://www .reuters.com/article/us-pope-jews-idUSKBN0TT1BK20151210.

43. Rachel Zoll. "A Rabbi Whose Good Friend Became the Pope." Associated Press, November 21, 2013. http://www.usnews.com/news/us/articles/ 2013/11/21/a-rabbi-whose-good-friend-became-the-pope.

44. "Proselytism and Conversion." Unam Sanctam Catholicam, http:// unamsanctamcatholicam.com/theology/81-theology/469-proselytism -and-conversion.html.

45. Andrea Tornielli. "Now May Trump Use the Influence of the US to Bring Peace to the World." *La Stampa*, November 10, 2016. http://www.la stampa.it/2016/11/10/vaticaninsider/eng/inquiries-and-interviews/now -may-trump-use-the-influence-of-the-us-to-bring-peace-to-the-world -nVuTZhdKFYu72ndEkbqSvK/amphtml/pagina.amp.html.

46. "Pope: Those Who Say 'This or Nothing' Are Heretics Not Catholics." Vatican Radio, September 6, 2016. http://en.radiovaticana.va/news/2016 /06/09/pope_those_who_say_%E2%80%9Cthis_or_nothing%E2%80%9D _are_heretics_/1235939.

47. John Allen. "Let's Face It: Americans Just Aren't This Pope's Favorites." *Crux*, May 20, 2016. https://cruxnow.com/church/2016/05/20/lets-face -it-americans-just-arent-this-popes-favorites.

48. "Pope to Latin American Religious." *Rorate Caeli*, June 11, 2013. http:// rorate-caeli.blogspot.com/2013/06/pope-to-latin-american-religious-full .html.

## Chapter Ten: The Permissive Pope

1. Carol Glatz. "In Latest Interview, Pope Francis Reveals Top 10 Secrets to Happiness." Catholic News Service, July 29, 2014. http://www.catholicnews

.com/services/englishnews/2014/in-latest-interview-pope-francis-reveals-top-10-secrets-to-happiness.cfm.

2. Gabriella Paiella. "Cool Pope Francis Is Here for Your Beauty Vlog." *New York*, May 31, 2016. http://nymag.com/thecut/2016/05/cool-pope-francis-is-here-for-your-beauty-vlog.html.

3. Terence McCoy. "Did Pope Francis Just Call and Say Divorced Catholics Can Take Communion?" *Washington Post*, April 24, 2014. https://www.washingtonpost.com/news/morning-mix/wp/2014/04/24/did-pope-francis-just-call-and-say-divorced-catholics-can-take-communion.

4. Alvaro Real. "Francis' Annullment Reform Born of Personal Knowledge." Aleteia, September 9, 2015 http://aleteia.org/2015/09/09/francis-annulment-reform-born-of-personal-knowledge.

5. Matt Roper. "Pope Wants to Scrap Centuries-Old Ban on Priests Marrying and Told Divorced Woman 'Living in Sin' That She COULD Receive Holy Communion, Claims Confidante." *Daily Mail*, March 12, 2015. http://www.dailymail.co.uk/news/article-2972258/Pope-wants-scrap-centuries-old-ban-priests-marrying-told-divorced-woman-living-sin-receive-Holy-Communion-claims-confidante.html.

6. Abby Ohlheiser, Michelle Boorstein, and Sarah Pulliam Bailey. "Pope Francis Announces Biggest Changes to Annulment Process in Centuries." *Washington Post*, September 8, 2015. https://www.washingtonpost.com/news/acts-of-faith/wp/2015/09/08/pope-francis-is-reforming-the-catholic-churchs-marriage-annulment-process.

7. Martin Barillas. "Catholic Dioceses Bend Church Law for Marriage Annulments." Spero News, September 12, 2015. http://www.speroforum.com/a/HXAGQDTAMJ45/76417-Catholic-dioceses-bend-church-law-for-marriage-annulments#.V8HvTI-cFmA.

8. Cindy Wooden. "Pope Francis Says a 'Large Majority' of Marriages Are Invalid." *Catholic Herald*, June 17, 2016. http://www.catholicherald.co.uk/news/2016/06/17/pope-francis-says-a-large-majority-of-marriages-are-invalid.

9. John Jalsevac. "Vatican Transcript Alters Pope's Bombshell Remark on Validity of Catholic Marriages." *LifeSiteNews*, June 17, 2016. https://www.lifesitenews.com/news/vatican-transcript-alters-popes-bombshell-remark-on-validity-of-catholic-ma.

10. Matthew Boudway and Grant Gallicho. "An Interview with Cardinal Walter Kasper." *Commonweal*, May 7, 2014. https://www.commonwealmagazine.org/interview-cardinal-walter-kasper.

11. Monsignor Charles Pope. "One Priest's Concern about Recent Remarks by the Pope." *National Catholic Register*, June 24, 2016. http://www.ncregister.com/blog/msgr-pope/one-priests-concern-about-recent-remarks-by-the-pope.

12. Michelle Boorstein. "Church Must Show More Compassion, Respect for Same-Sex Couples, Vatican Document Says." *Washington Post*, October 13, 2014. https://www.washingtonpost.com/news/local/wp/2014/10/13/vatican-meeting-see-the-positive-even-in-irregular-families.

13. "Catholic Bishops Make a 'Seismic Shift' in Attitude toward Gays." CBS News, October 13, 2014. http://www.cbsnews.com/news/catholic-bishops-make-a-seismic-shift-in-attitude-towards-gays.

14. John Thavis. "A Pastoral Earthquake at the Synod." John Thavis blog, October 13, 2014. http://www.johnthavis.com/a-pastoral-earthquake-at-the-synod#.V8HxVY-cFmA.

15. Francis X. Rocca. "Bishops Hand Pope a Defeat on His Outreach to Divorced Catholics." *Wall Street Journal*, October 24, 2015. http://www.wsj.com/articles/bishops-hand-pope-a-defeat-on-outreach-to-divorced-catholics-1445715350.

16. Francis X. Rocca. "Cardinal Pell: Synod Says No to 'Secular Agenda.'" Catholic News Service, October 16, 2014. http://www.catholicnews.com/services/englishnews/2014/cardinal-pell-synod-says-no-to-secular-agenda.cfm.

17. Conor Gaffey. "Journalist Publishes Recording of Cardinal's Controversial Interview." *Catholic Herald*, October 17, 2014. http://www.catholicherald.co.uk/news/2014/10/17/journalist-publishes-recording-of-cardinal-kaspers-comments-on-african-bishops.

18. Jan Bentz. "Famed Catholic Philosopher: How Can Christ and Our Lady Read Amoris Laetitia without Weeping?" *LifeSiteNews*, June 9, 2016. https://www.lifesitenews.com/news/famed-catholic-philosopher-how-can-christ-and-our-lady-read-amoris-laetitia.

19. Ibid.

20. "Official English Translation of Bishop Schneider's Reflection on Amoris Laetitia." *LifeSiteNews*, April 26, 2016. https://www.lifesitenews.com/news/official-english-translation-of-bishop-schneiders-reflection-on-amoris-laet.

21. John-Henry Westen and Matthew Cullinan Hoffman. "Pope: 'No Other Interpretation' of Amoris Laetitia Than Allowing Communion for Divorced/Remarried in Some Cases." *LifeSiteNews*, September 9, 2016. https://www.lifesitenews.com/news/pope-no-other-interpretation-of-amoris-laetitia-than-allowing-communion-for.

22. John-Henry Westen. "Pope Calls Italy's Foremost Abortion Promoter One of Nation's 'Forgotten Greats.'" *LifeSiteNews*, February 25, 2016. https://www.lifesitenews.com/news/pope-calls-italys-foremost-abortion-promoter-one-of-nations-forgotten-great.

23. Alan Keyes. "Has the Pope Fallen Off the Pro-Life Wagon?" Barbwire, March 2, 2016. http://barbwire.com/2016/03/02/pope-fallen-off-pro-life-wagon.

24. "'March for Life' Embarrasses Pope Francis—Abortion Is Only a Question of Economic Systems?" Eponymous Flower, May 11, 2016. http://epony mousflower.blogspot.com/2016/05/march-for-life-embarrasses-pope -francis.html.

25. Christopher Lamb. "Italy's Historic Same-Sex Legislation Begs the Question: Is the Church's Position Changing?" *Tablet*, February 26, 2016. http:// www.thetablet.co.uk/blogs/1/906/0/italy-s-historic-same-sex-legis lation-begs-the-question-is-the-church-s-position-changing-.

26. Kieran Corcoran. "Now the Pope Wades into Brexit Row: Francis Wants Britain to Stay in EU." *Express*, January 20, 2016. http://www.express.co.uk/news/ uk/636585/POPE-against-Brexit-Francis-wants-Britain-to-STAY-in-EU.

27. Alessandro Speciale. "Benedict and Francis: How Much Difference Is There?" Religion News Service, June 19, 2013. http://www.huffingtonpost .com/2013/06/19/benedict-and-francis-difference_n_3467987.html.

28. Carey Lodge. "Ireland Gay Marriage Referendum: Meet the Priests Who Are Voting Yes." Christian Today, May 21, 2015. http://www.christiantoday .com/article/ireland.gay.marriage.referendum.meet.the.priests.who.are .voting.yes/54392.htm.

29. Antonia Blumberg. "Irish Bishop on Gay Marriage: 'I Would Hate for People to Vote No for Bigoted Reasons.'" *Huffington Post*, June 10, 2015. http://www.huffingtonpost.com/2015/05/22/bishop-of-derry-gay -marriage_n_7421894.html.

30. Mark Binelli. "Pope Francis: The Times They Are A-Changin'." *Rolling Stone*, January 28, 2014. http://www.rollingstone.com/culture/news/pope -francis-the-times-they-are-a-changin-20140128.

31. "U2's The Edge Rocks the Vatican's Sistine Chapel." Catholic News Service, May 3, 2016. https://cruxnow.com/church/2016/05/03/u2s -the-edge-rocks-the-vaticans-sistine-chapel.

32. "Patti Smith Responds to Christian Groups." *Express*, November 19, 2014. http://www.express.co.uk/celebrity-news/537368/Patti-Smith-responds -to-Christian-groups.

33. Uki Goni. "Pope Francis Rejects Donation from Argentinian President with 666 in Sum." *Guardian*, June 14, 2016. https://www.theguardian.com /world/2016/jun/14/pope-francis-mauricio-macri-argentina-charity -donation-666.

34. Fr. George Rutler. "A Misplaced Grief: The Vatican and David Bowie." *Crisis*, January 13, 2016 http://www.crisismagazine.com/2016/a-misplaced-grief-the -vatican-and-david-bowie.

35. Ginger Adams Otis. "Vatican Criticized after Sexy Blond Featured in #LifeofWomen Campaign." *New York Daily News*, February 2, 2015. http://www.nydailynews.com/news/world/vatican-criticized-sexy-blond -lifeofwomen-promo-article-1.2100707.

36. Cindy Wooden. "Pope Discusses Women in the Church, Divorce, His Own Spirituality." Catholic News Service, July 29, 2013. http://www.catholic news.com/services/englishnews/2013/pope-discusses-women-in-the -church-divorce-his-own-spirituality.cfm.

37. Christopher Lamb. "New Vatican Magazine Criticizes Church for 'Ignoring Role of Women.'" *Tablet*, May 3, 2016. http://www.thetablet.co.uk/news/ 5509/0/new-vatican-magazine-criticises-church-for-ignoring-role-of-women-.

38. Joshua McElwee. "Francis to Create Commission to Study Female Deacons in Catholic Church." *National Catholic Reporter*, May 12, 2016. https://www.ncronline.org/news/vatican/francis-create-commission -study-female-deacons-catholic-church.

39. Claire Chretien. "Pope's Deaconess Commission Includes Women's Priesthood Supporter." *LifeSiteNews*, August 2, 2016. https://www.lifesitenews.com/ news/popes-deaconess-commission-includes-womens-priesthood-supporter.

40. David Gibson. "Are Married Priests Next on Pope Francis' Reform Agenda." Religion News Service, May 2, 2014. https://www.ncronline.org/news/ theology/are-married-priests-next-pope-francis-reform-agenda.

41. Austen Ivereigh. "Next Synod Likely to Focus on Ordaining Married Men." *Crux*, August 12, 2016. https://cruxnow.com/analysis/2016/08 /12/next-synod-likely-focus-ordaining-married-men.

42. Edward Pentin. "Next Synod Will Be on 'Young People, the Faith, and Discernment of Vocation.'" *National Catholic Register*, October 6, 2016. http://www.ncregister.com/blog/edward-pentin/next-synod-will-be-on -youth-faith-and-vocational-discernment.

43. Thomas Fox. "Report: Pope Meets with, Hugs Transgender Man." *National Catholic Reporter*, January 30, 2015. https://www.ncronline.org/blogs/ncr -today/report-pope-francis-meets-hugs-transgender-man.

44. Joshua McElwee. "Francis: Sexual Morality Determined Case by Case, Even for Transgender." *National Catholic Reporter*, October 2, 2016. https://www.ncronline.org/news/vatican/francis-sexual-morality -determined-case-case-even-transgender.

45. Stephanie Kirchgaessner. "Vatican: Pope Did Not Show Support for Kim Davis." *Guardian*, October 2, 2015. https://www.theguardian.com/ world/2015/oct/02/vatican-pope-kim-davis-same-sex-marriage.

46. Tommy Christopher. "You Can Like the Pope Again! Vatican Distances Pope from Kim Davis." The Daily Banter, October 2, 2015. http:// thedailybanter.com/2015/10/you-can-like-the-pope-again-vatican -distances-pope-from-kim-davis.

47. Dan Zak. "Meet Yayo Grassi, the Gay Man Who Is Friends with Pope Francis." *Washington Post*, October 2, 2015. https://www.washingtonpost .com/news/acts-of-faith/wp/2015/10/02/meet-yayo-grassi-the-gay-man -who-is-friends-with-pope-francis.

48. Paul Vallely. "The Crisis That Changed Pope Francis." *Newsweek*, October 23, 2014. http://europe.newsweek.com/crisis-changed-pope-francis-279303.

49. "The Pope: How The Church Will Change." *La Repubblica*, October 1, 2013.

50. "Transcription of Pope's Press Conference on Return from Armenia." Zenit, June 28, 2016. https://zenit.org/articles/transcription-of-popes-press-con ference-on-return-from-armenia.

## Chapter Eleven: How Francis Is Undoing the Legacy of Pope John Paul II and Pope Benedict XVI

1. "The Pope: How the Church Will Change." *La Repubblica*, October 1, 2013. http://www.repubblica.it/cultura/2013/10/01/news/pope_s_conver sation_with_scalfari_english-67643118.

2. Maike Hickson. "Kasper: Pope Intends 'Not to Preserve Everything as It Has Been.'" 1P5, April 23, 2016. http://www.onepeterfive.com/kasper-pope -intends-not-to-preserve-everything-as-it-has-been.

3. John-Henry Westen and Maike Hickson. "One of Pope's Closest Advisors: How Pope Francis Is Changing the Church." *LifeSiteNews*, June 4, 2015. https://www.lifesitenews.com/news/one-of-popes-closest-advisors -how-pope-francis-is-changing-the-church.

4. Francis Rocca. "Pope Francis and the New Rome." *Wall Street Journal*, April 3, 2015. http://www.wsj.com/articles/pope-francis-and-the-new-rome -1428075101.

5. Ibid.

6. Ibid.

7. Gregory Tomlin. "Pope Decries Fundamentalist Catholics Who Believe in Absolute Truth while Four Jihadists Arrested for Radical Threats against Him." The Christian Examiner, December 2, 2015. http://www .christianexaminer.com/article/pope-decries-fundamentalist-catholics -who-believe-they-hold-to-the-absolute-truth-while-four-jihadists-arrested -for-radical-threats-against-him/49867.htm.

8. Fr. Antonio Spadaro. "A Big Heart Open to God." *America*, September 30, 2013. http://americamagazine.org/pope-interview.

9. Ibid.

10. Michael Sean Winters. "First Impressions of Francis." *National Catholic Reporter*, March 15, 2013. https://www.ncronline.org/blogs/distinctly -catholic/first-impressions-francis.

11. Sandro Magister. "For the First Time, Francis Contradicts Benedict." *Chiesa*, July 29, 2013. http://chiesa.espresso.repubblica.it/articolo/1350567?eng=y.

12. Sandro Magister. "The Francis Transformation." *Chiesa*, October 3, 2013. http://chiesa.espresso.repubblica.it/articolo/1350615?eng=y.

13. Salvatore Cernuzio. "Pope Holds Two Hour Meeting with Roman Clergy." Zenit, February 19, 2015. https://zenit.org/articles/pope-holds -two-hour-meeting-with-roman-clergy.

14. Carol Glatz. "Pope Francis: Mass in Vernacular Helps People Understand God, Live the Faith." Catholic News Service, March 9, 2015. https://www .ncronline.org/blogs/francis-chronicles/pope-francis-mass-vernacular -helps-people-understand-god-live-faith.

15. "Old Mass? Just a Kind of Fashion!" *Rorate Caeli*, February 15, 2015. http://rorate-caeli.blogspot.com/2014/02/important-pope-francis-on -feb-14-young.html.

16. Ines San Martin. "Francis Warns of 'Rigid' Liturgy, Confesses Soft Spot for Old Ladies." *Crux*, November 11, 2016. https://cruxnow.com/vatican/2016/11 /11/francis-warns-rigid-liturgy-confesses-soft-spot-old-ladies.

17. Ines San Martin. "Vatican Squelches Rumors of New Rules on Mass Facing East." *Crux*, July 11, 2016. https://cruxnow.com/vatican/2016/07/11/vatican -says-no-new-rules-coming-mass-facing-east.

18. Christopher Lamb. "Cardinal Sarah's Very Public Slap-Down Shows Pope Is Willing to Use His Authority." *Tablet*, July 13, 2016. http://www.thetablet .co.uk/blogs/1/930/0/cardinal-sarah-s-very-public-slap-down-shows -pope-is-willing-to-use-his-authority-.

19. Fr. Brian Harrison. "Francis Purges Conservatives from Divine Worship Congregation." *Catholic Family News*, October 29, 2016. http://www .cfnews.org/page88/files/22a89f85bceeed07846bd8db23a92171-647 .html.

20. Maike Hickson. "Famed German Philosopher Makes Waves for Criticizing Pope Francis' 'Autocratic' Style." *LifeSiteNews*, April 27, 2015. https:// www.lifesitenews.com/news/famed-german-catholic-philosopher-makes- waves-for-criticizing-pope-francis.

21. "Pope Francis Issues Marching Orders for New Pro-Life Leaders." *Crux*, August 18, 2016. https://cruxnow.com/vatican/2016/08/18/pope-issues -marching-orders-new-pro-life-leader.

22. Tom Roberts. "Pope Francis Appoints Archbishop Cupich to Congregation for Bishops." *National Catholic Reporter*, July 7, 2016. https://www.ncr online.org/news/vatican/pope-francis-appoints-archbishop-cupich -congregation-bishops.

23. Michael O'Loughlin. "Controversial Preacher, Writer Timothy Radcliffe Given Vatican Role." Crux, May 16, 2015. https://cruxnow.com/church/ 2015/05/16/controversial-preacher-timothy-radcliffe-given-vatican-role.

24. Christine Niles. "Pope Appoints Fr. Timothy Radcliffe Consultor for Pontifical Council for Justice and Peace." *Church Militant*, May 16, 2015. http://www.churchmilitant.com/news/article/breaking-pope-appoints-fr .-timothy-radcliffe-consultor-for-pontifical-counc.

25. John-Henry Westen. "Top Adviser to Pope John Paul II Warns of a Cabal Undermining Church with Backing from Within." *LifeSiteNews*, July 11, 2016. https://www.lifesitenews.com/news/top-adviser-to-pope-jpii-warns -of-a-cabal-undermining-church-with-backing-f.

26. Sarah MacDonald. "Documentary Considers Francis' Past and Future." CatholicIreland.net, March 18, 2015. http://www.catholicireland.net/rte -documentary-pope-francis.

27. David Gibson. "Belgian Bishop Says Catholic Church Should Bless Same-Sex Couples." Religion News Service, January 8, 2015. https://www.washington post.com/national/religion/belgian-bishop-says-catholic-church-should -bless-same-sex-couples/2015/01/08/a72ec292-976b-11e4-8385 -866293322c2f_story.html.

28. Maike Hickson. "Kasperite Bishop Appointed Head of Pontifical Academy for Life." 1P5, August 17, 2016. http://www.onepeterfive.com/kasperite -bishop-appointed-head-pontifical-academy-life.

29. Pete Baklinski. "Vatican Sex Ed 'Surrenders' to Sexual Revolution: Life and Family Leaders React." *LifeSiteNews*, July 29, 2016. https://www.lifesite news.com/news/vatican-surrenders-to-sexual-revolution-with-release -of-sex-ed-program-life.

30. Pete Baklinski. "Petition Urges Pope Francis to Withdraw 'Nightmare' Vatican Sex-Ed Program." *LifeSiteNews*, August 22, 2016. https://www.life sitenews.com/pulse/catholic-pro-life-org-launches-petition-asking-pope -francis-to-withdraw-nig.

31. Pete Baklinski. "Amoris Laetitia Is 'Objectively Unclear' since Even Bishops Have Conflicting Interpretations: Cardinal Caffarra." *LifeSiteNews*, May 30, 2016. https://www.lifesitenews.com/news/amoris-laetitia-is-objectively-un clear-since-even-bishops-have-conflicting.

32. Jude Dougherty. "Deliberate Ambiguity." *Wanderer*, June 1, 2016. http://thewandererpress.com/catholic/news/featured-today/deliberate -ambiguity.

33. "Cardinal Kasper Disses Cardinal Ratzinger." RomanCatholicBlog, April 17, 2005. http://romancatholicblog.typepad.com/roman_catholic_blog/2005/ 04/cardinal_walter.html.

34. Sandro Magister. "The German Option of the Argentine Pope." *Chiesa*, April 28, 2016. http://chiesa.espresso.repubblica.it/articolo/1351283? eng=y.

35. Sandro Magister. "Martini Pope: The Dream Come True." *Chiesa*, October 15, 2013. http://chiesa.espresso.repubblica.it/articolo/1350623?eng=y.

36. Laurie Goodstein. "Vatican Ends Battle with U.S. Catholic Nuns' Group." *New York Times*, April 16, 2015. http://www.nytimes.com/2015/04/17/ us/catholic-church-ends-takeover-of-leadership-conference-of-women -religious.html.

37. John Allen. "Vatican Probe Ends with an Olive Branch for American Nuns." *Crux*, December 16, 2014. https://cruxnow.com/church/2014/12/16/vatican-probe-ends-with-an-olive-branch-for-american-nuns.

38. John Allen. "With Pope's Cardinal Picks, Bernardin's 'Seamless Garment' Is Back." *Crux*, October 9, 2016. https://cruxnow.com/analysis/2016/10/09/popes-cardinal-picks-bernardins-seamless-garment-back.

39. Christopher Ferrara. "Francis Attacks the Cloistered Convents." Fatima Network, July 25, 2016. http://fatimaperspectives.com/fe/perspective876.asp.

40. Joshua McElwee. "Cardinal to Religious: Those Who Abandon Vatican II Are 'Killing Themselves.'" *National Catholic Reporter*, April 9, 2015. https://www.ncronline.org/news/global/cardinal-religious-those-who-abandon-vatican-ii-are-killing-themselves.

41. Geoge Weigel. "Has the Vatican Already Forgotten the Lessons of John Paul II?" National Review Online, July 13, 2015. http://www.nationalreview.com/article/421079.

42. Anian Christoph Wimmer. "Interview with Robert Spaemann on Amoris Laetitia." Catholic News Agency, April 29, 2016. http://www.catholicnewsagency.com/news/full-text-interview-with-robert-spaemann-on-amoris-laetitia-10088.

43. Fr. Raymond de Souza. "Francis Has an Excellent Chance to Heal His Rift with Followers of St. John Paul II." *Catholic Herald*, July 21, 2016. http://www.catholicherald.co.uk/issues/july-22nd-2016/poland-is-pope-franciss-last-chance-to-heal-a-rift-over-st-john-paul-ii.

44. Davor Trbusic. "Croatians Eager to See Cardinal Stepinac Declared a Saint." *Crux*, May 11, 2016. https://cruxnow.com/church/2016/05/11/croatians-eager-to-see-cardinal-stepinac-declared-a-saint.

45. John Allen. "Not Everyone in El Salvador Is Celebrating the Romero Beatification." *Crux*, May 23, 2015. https://cruxnow.com/church/2015/05/23/not-everyone-in-el-salvador-is-celebrating-the-romero-beatification.

46. John Allen. "Thoughts on the Rise of 'God's Consultants.'" *National Catholic Reporter*, December 20, 2013. https://www.ncronline.org/blogs/ncr-today/thoughts-rise-gods-consultants.

47. Peter Popham. "Sex and Blackmail Allegations at Heart of Vatican Leaks Scandal." *Independent*, December 5, 2015. http://www.independent.co.uk/news/world/europe/sex-and-blackmail-allegations-at-heart-of-vatican-leaks-scandal-a6762031.html.

48. Carol Glatz. "Vatican Signs New Contract with External Financial Auditor." Catholic News Service, June 10, 2016. http://www.catholicregister.org/faith/item/22483-vatican-signs-new-contract-with-external-financial-auditor.

49. Ines San Martin. "When Pope Backs Workers, Vatican Laity Wonder, 'What about Us?'" *Crux*, May 21, 2016. https://cruxnow.com/church/2016/05/21/when-pope-backs-workers-vatican-laity-wonder-what-about-us.

50. Maike Hickson. "Cardinal Schönborn: Francis Wants to Win Over Opposition in Loving Ways." 1P5, August 11, 2016. http://www.onepeterfive.com/cardinal -schonborn-francis-wants-win-opposition-loving-ways.

## Chapter Twelve: Will Paul Correct Peter?

1. Sandro Magister. "Thirteen Cardinals Have Written to the Pope. Here's the Letter." *Chiesa*, October 12, 2015. http://chiesa.espresso.repubblica.it/ articolo/1351154?eng=y.
2. Madeleine Teahan. "Nearly 500 Priests in Britain Urge Synod to Stand Firm on Communion for the Remarried." *Catholic Herald*, March 24, 2015. http://www.catholicherald.co.uk/news/2015/03/24/nearly-500-priests-in -england-and-wales-urge-synod-to-stand-firm-on-communion-for-the -remarried.
3. Gerard O'Connell. "Pope to Synod Fathers: Don't Give in to the Conspiracy Theory." *America*, October 7, 2015. http://americamagazine.org/content/ dispatches/pope-synod-fathers-dont-give-conspiracy-theory.
4. John-Henry Westen. "Explosive Video: Pope 'Will Show Whose Side He Is on During Synod, Says Archbishop." *LifeSiteNews*, September 10, 2015. https://www.lifesitenews.com/news/explosive-video-pope-will-show -whose-side-hes-on-during-synod-says-archbish.
5. Philip Pullela and Tom Heneghan. "Three Years on, Pope Leaves Catholic Conservatives Feeling Marginalized." Reuters, March 11, 2016. http:// www.reuters.com/article/us-pope-anniversary-conservatives-idUSKCN0 WD0TF.
6. Michelle Boorstein and Elizabeth Tenety. "Conservative Catholics Question Pope Francis's Approach." *Washington Post*, October 14, 2013. https:// www.washingtonpost.com/national/on-faith/2013/10/12/21d7f484 -2cf4-11e3-8ade-a1f23cda135e_story.html.
7. Anthony Faiola. "Conservative Dissent Is Brewing Inside the Vatican." *Washington Post*, September 7, 2015. https://www.washingtonpost.com/ world/europe/a-conservative-revolt-is-brewing-inside-the-vatican/ 2015/09/07/1d8e02ba-4b3d-11e5-80c2-106ea7fb80d4_story.html.
8. Edward Pentin. "Cardinal Burke on Amoris Laetitia Dubia: 'Tremendous Division' Warrants Action." *National Catholic Register*, November 15, 2016. http://www.ncregister.com/daily-news/cardinal-burke-on-amoris-laetitia -dubia-tremendous-division-warrants-action.
9. Michelle Boorstein. "Pope Francis Urged Mercy toward Divorced Catholics. Now Bishops Are Deciding What That Really Means." *Washington Post*, July 8, 2016. https://www.washingtonpost.com/news/acts-of-faith/wp/2016/07 /08/pope-francis-urged-mercy-towards-divorced-catholics-now-bishops -are-deciding-what-that-really-means.

10. Jeanne Smits. "Belgian Archbishop: 'Time Has Come' for Pope Francis to Defend Church's Tradition." *LifeSiteNews*, January 8, 2016. https://www.lifesitenews.com/news/belgian-archbishop-time-has-come-for-pope-francis-to-defend-churchs-traditi.

11. Claire Chretien. "Bishop: Amoris Laetitia's 'Intentional Ambiguity' Means People Will Do 'Whatever They Want.' " *LifeSiteNews*, July 8, 2016. https://www.lifesitenews.com/news/bishop-amoris-laetitias-intentional-ambiguity-means-people-will-do-whatever.

12. Maike Hickson. "Kasper: Pope Intends 'Not to Preserve Everything as It Has Been.' " 1P5, April 23, 2016. http://www.onepeterfive.com/kasper-pope-intends-not-to-preserve-everything-as-it-has-been.

13. Jan Bentz. "Cardinal to German Bishops: Push for Change While We Have Francis as Pope." *LifeSiteNews*, November 14, 2016. https://www.lifesitenews.com/news/german-cardinal-push-for-change-while-francis-is-leading-church.

14. Francix X. Rocca. "Pope's Teaching on Divorce Divides Bishops." *Wall Street Journal*, July 10, 2016. http://www.wsj.com/articles/popes-teaching-on-divorce-divides-bishops-1468166653.

15. Edward Pentin. "Cardinal May Resist Pope's Attempts to Change Teaching." Newsmax, February 10, 2015. http://www.newsmax.com/EdwardPentin/Cardinal-Burke-Catholic-Church-German-Catholic-Church-Pope-Francis/2015/02/10/id/623988.

16. Maike Hickson. "Cardinal Caffarra on Marriage, Family, Amoris Laetitia, and Confusion in the Church." 1P5, July 11, 2016. http://www.onepeterfive.com/cardinal-caffarra-on-marriage-family-amoris-laetitia-confusion-in-the-church.

17. "Malcolm Muggeridge and Vatican II." Musings of a Pertinacious Papist, June 22, 2013. http://pblosser.blogspot.com/2013/06/malcolm-muggeridge-and-vatican-ii.html.

18. Ross Douthat. "In Search of the Francis Effect." *New York Times*, September 23, 2015. http://douthat.blogs.nytimes.com/2015/09/23/in-search-of-the-francis-effect.

19. "How Is It That No One Saw It Coming?" Deus Ex Machina Blog, June 23, 2016. https://sarmaticusblog.wordpress.com/2016/06/23/epic-francisfail-how-is-it-that-no-one-seen-it-coming.

20. Ibid.

21. "The Popular Pontificate of Pope Francis: Two Views." Fr. Z's Blog, August 27, 2014. http://wdtprs.com/blog/2014/08/the-popular-pontificate-of-pope-francis-two-views.

22. Walter Mayr. "Where Is Pope Francis Steering the Church?" *Der Spiegel*, May 29, 2015. http://www.spiegel.de/international/world/how-pope-francis-became-a-rebel-in-the-vatican-a-1035629.html.

23. "Full Text of Benedict XVI's Recent, Rare, and Lengthy Interview." Catholic News Agency, March 17, 2016. http://www.catholicnewsagency.com/news/full-text-of-benedict-xvis-recent-rare-and-lengthy-interview-26142/.

24. Walter Mayr. "Where Is Pope Francis Steering the Church?" *Der Spiegel*, May 29, 2015. http://www.spiegel.de/international/world/how-pope -francis-became-a-rebel-in-the-vatican-a-1035629.html.

25. Jacopo Barigazzi. "Pope Alienates Base, See Numbers Drop." *Politico*, January 12, 2016. http://www.politico.eu/article/a-pope-flop.

26. Walter Mayr. "Where Is Pope Francis Steering the Church?" *Der Spiegel*, May 29, 2015. http://www.spiegel.de/international/world/how-pope-francis -became-a-rebel-in-the-vatican-a-1035629.html.

27. Walter Mayr. "Where Is Pope Francis Steering the Church?" *Der Spiegel*, May 29, 2015. http://www.spiegel.de/international/world/how-pope-francis -became-a-rebel-in-the-vatican-a-1035629.html.

28. John Allen. "Chicago's Exiting Cardinal: 'The Church Is about True/False, Not Left/Right.'" *Crux*, November 17, 2014. https://cruxnow.com/church/2014/11/17/chicagos-exiting-cardinal-the-church-is-about -truefalse-not-leftright.

29. Cindy Wooden. "Pope Francis Undaunted by Critics." Catholic News Service, July 5, 2016. http://americamagazine.org/issue/pope-francis-undaunted -critics.

30. Rod Dreher. "I Am Still Not Going Back to the Catholic Church." *Time*, September 29, 2013. http://ideas.time.com/2013/09/29/im-still-not-going -back-to-the-catholic-church.

31. John-Henry Westen. "U.S. Evangelical Leaders Warn Catholics That Pope Francis Is Moving Church to the Left." *LifeSiteNews*, September 28, 2015. https://www.lifesitenews.com/news/u.s.-evangelical-leaders-warn -catholics-that-pope-francis-is-moving-church.

32. Sandro Magister. " 'Seeking Clarity': The Appeal of Four Cardinals to the Pope." Chiesa, November 14, 2016. http://chiesa.espresso.repubblica.it/articolo/1351414?eng=y.

33. David Gibson. "Pope Francis Dismisses Critics of His Teachings." Religion News Service, November 18, 2016. https://www.ncronline.org/news/vatican/pope-francis-dismisses-critics-his-teachings.

34. Claire Chretien. "Vatican Expert: Sources Say Pope Francis 'Boiling with Rage' over Amoris Criticism." *LifeSiteNews*, November 18, 2016. https://www.lifesitenews.com/news/vaticanist-pope-francis-boiling-with-rage -over-amoris-criticism.

35. Laurie Goodstein, Adam Pearce, and Sergio Pecanha. "Pope Francis' Race against Time to Reshape the Church." *New York Times*, November 18, 2016. http://www.nytimes.com/interactive/2016/11/18/world/europe/pope-francis-cardinals-shape-church.html?_r=0.

# Index